T0330354

AVOIDING THE NEWS

REUTERS INSTITUTE GLOBAL JOURNALISM SERIES

REUTERS INSTITUTE GLOBAL JOURNALISM SERIES

BENJAMIN TOFF,
RUTH PALMER, AND
RASMUS KLEIS NIELSEN

AVOIDING THE NEWS

Reluctant Audiences for Journalism

Columbia University Press / *New York*

Columbia University Press
Publishers Since 1893
New York   Chichester, West Sussex
cup.columbia.edu

Library of Congress Cataloging-in-Publication Data
Names: Toff, Benjamin, author. | Palmer, Ruth, 1979 January 16– author. |
Nielsen, Rasmus Kleis, 1980– author.
Title: Avoiding the news : reluctant audiences for journalism / Benjamin Toff,
Ruth Palmer, Rasmus Kleis Nielsen.
Description: New York : Columbia University Press, 2023. | Series: Reuters
Institute global journalism series | Includes bibliographical references and index.
Identifiers: LCCN 2023027784 (print) | LCCN 2023027785 (ebook) |
ISBN 9780231205184 (hardback) | ISBN 9780231205191 (trade paperback) |
ISBN 9780231555883 (ebook)
Subjects: LCSH: News avoidance (Psychology) | News audiences. |
Journalism. | Mass media.
Classification: LCC PN4784.N485 N54 2023 (print) | LCC PN4784.N485
(ebook) | DDC 302.23—dc23/eng/20230726
LC record available at https://lccn.loc.gov/2023027784
LC ebook record available at https://lccn.loc.gov/2023027785

Printed and bound by CPI Group (UK) Ltd, Croydon, CR0 4YY

Cover design: Chang Jae Lee
Cover image: © Shutterstock

CONTENTS

CONTENTS

ACKNOWLEDGMENTS

A ll authors accumulate debts of gratitude. Ours are many and varied and have only grown since we started this project in 2015. Ben and Ruth did more than a 160 interviews and led on developing and expanding both the empirical work and intellectual scope of the project well beyond anything Rasmus had dared to imagine when he first suggested a closer qualitative look at news avoidance.

Among our colleagues, we build on the work of many academics interested in people's relationships with media and news. Special thanks go to Irene Costera Meijer, Kim Christian Schrøder, Richard Fletcher, and Stephen Coleman, all of whom joined us in an early workshop as we developed ideas that became central to the work that underlies this book. Multiple configurations of research teams at the Reuters Institute for the Study of Journalism were also instrumental in helping us think through how to approach this subject and make sense of what we were finding along the way. Antonis Kalogeropoulos, Kim Andersen, Morten Skovsgaard, Stephanie Edgerly, Kathy Cramer, Matt Carlson, and Talia Stroud gave invaluable feedback at various stages as our project developed, and over the years an entire scholarly community specifically focused on news avoidance has also formed, to whom we are very grateful, but whose numbers have grown too high to name.

We are also particularly indebted to the anonymous reviewers who took the time to carefully read, reflect on, and engage with our work amid a global pandemic and invariably stressful circumstances in their own lives. Their insights pushed us to clarify our own thinking and were enormously helpful in that regard.

Many thanks to Kantar and Essman Research/SPPG for their help in recruiting study participants and arranging interviews as well as to the team at YouGov for their assistance with our survey data collection. We also thank Rebecca Edwards, Nick Mathews, and Gretel Kahn, who provided critical assistance on myriad practical and logistical matters involved in conducting this study across three countries and finishing this manuscript. Thanks to Philip Leventhal and Columbia University Press for their support in seeing this project through to publication.

At the more practical level, we also thank the Google News Initiative for supporting the ongoing Digital News Project at the Reuters Institute, which, in addition to producing the *Digital News Report* survey that we draw on, also made it possible to invest significant time and effort in the extensive qualitative research that much of the book is based on. We are likewise appreciative of the support provided by the University of Minnesota, whose Grant-in-Aid funds made our U.S. interviews possible, as well as by the Hubbard School of Journalism and Mass Communication, whose funding we drew on to conduct our survey of U.S. news consumers.

As part of a team of collaborators, each of us has individual thanks to express. Ben is particularly thankful for his partner and his parents, whose encouragement, thoughtfulness, and patience over the years made this book possible. He also thanks his colleagues at Minnesota for their camaraderie and support, especially their willingness to allow him to leave for three years to return to the Reuters Institute to continue researching news audiences. He also thanks Rasmus for hiring him as a postdoc to lead what was then an inchoate version of this project and both him and Ruthie for being fantastic collaborators and coauthors from whom he has learned immeasurably. Ruth is grateful to Rasmus and Ben for inviting her to be a part of this adventure and for ensuring it was not just intellectually fulfilling but also fun. Many thanks to her friends and family for their unfailing encouragement and to IE University staff and faculty for unflagging support. Rasmus thanks his whole family for their continued support for his decision to spend so much of his life working on journalism and Ben and Ruthie for being such an inspiration to work with.

And, finally, we thank our interviewees for changing the way we see consistent news avoidance, how we see the news, and, indeed, how we see ourselves through the lens of their experiences. The analysis contained in these pages is possible only because of their willingness to talk with openness, at length, and in such nuanced ways about their choices and their lives, and we hope the book will be as thought-provoking for readers as the process of working on it has been for us.

AVOIDING THE NEWS

1

IS IGNORANCE BLISS?

News can feel overwhelming these days because it seems inescapable—on our phones, on our TVs, on the bus, at the doctor's office—everywhere. And since news covers real-world events, often with a focus on problems ("We don't cover the planes that land," as some journalists say), it can seem both terrifying and cruel. The opposite of escapism, news can plunge us into issues we are already fighting to manage in daily life—or, worse, events that feel both painful and beyond our control. Little wonder, then, that global surveys show that growing numbers of people feel fatigued by news and avoid it at least sometimes. Many people say that they don't trust it, that it negatively affects their mood, that it doesn't seem relevant, or that at the end of the day they just don't feel there is anything they can do about any of it anyway.[1]

If you're reading this book, there is a good chance you, too, deliberately avoid news from time to time. We do, too, and we study news for a living. Maybe you have a routine where you check news only at certain times each day—say, for a half hour in the morning and never right before bed. Or you disconnect during vacation. Maybe there were times you took a complete break—perhaps at the height of a contentious election or the COVID-19 pandemic.[2]

Such occasional or situational news avoidance is probably healthy. Mounting evidence shows that people who take periodic breaks or selectively implement strategies to curtail their news exposure report feeling better than people who don't[3] and that the break does not necessarily translate into significantly less news use overall.[4] As long as people remain at least minimally informed (although just *how* informed remains a long-standing debate), it is perfectly reasonable to devise strategies to manage the constant flow of news and information many of us feel bombarded by.[5]

Avoiding news *altogether*, though? Now that might be a problem, but with news seemingly ever present, is it even possible?

It is.

This book is about people who avoid news not from time to time but all the time. Many of their reasons—such as the feeling that all news is bad news—will resonate more widely, and our findings have implications for more selective forms of news avoidance as well. But we focus especially on people who are *consistent* news avoiders: people who say they consume news less often than once a month or never.[6] This group is a minority of the public, to be sure, averaging 3 percent across the forty-six markets covered in one international study.[7] But the figure is as high as 10 percent in some countries, and it's on the rise in many.[8] We are talking about millions of people and in many countries more than the number that pays to subscribe to digital news.[9] If you are an American who reads *The Atlantic*, *The Guardian*, or *The New Yorker* online (let alone all of them!), you are part of a smaller group than those who consistently avoid the news.[10]

Our central question is what it means to avoid the news consistently in a world of abundant news supply and ease of access. Drawing on a combination of interviews with more than a hundred consistent news avoiders in the United Kingdom, Spain, and the United States, interviews with a smaller contrasting group of highly engaged "news lovers" in the United States, and extensive survey data, we explore how people who consume little to no news understand, explain, feel about, and largely manage without it.

Our central finding is that only some of the reasons that consistent news avoiders feel alienated from news are directly related to the news.[11] As we show throughout the book, news avoidance—like other forms of media use—is not just a response to the content on offer. It is also fundamentally shaped by who we are, what we believe, and the tools we rely on to find, access, and navigate content. This conclusion may seem counterintuitive and, frankly, disappointing for those who may be looking for easy ways to address news avoidance and counter waning public engagement. Surely, one might (understandably) think that the main reason people avoid news must be news itself, so the solution must be to fix the news or maybe to offer people more of it. Surely then they'll come around. Unfortunately, it's not and it isn't and they won't.

The heart of the matter is best illustrated through a metaphor that, inspired by our own experiences, we came to think of as "the oyster problem." The oyster problem goes something like this. In many parts of the world, if you ask people if they like raw oysters, they may well tell you—adamantly—that they do not.[12] If surveyed about oysters, they will say they don't like the taste or texture. They "strongly disagree" that oysters have any redeeming features at all. However, upon further questioning in, say, an interview, respondents reveal that they have never tried oysters. Or they did once or twice, but only at a single restaurant (possibly one that you, the interviewer, believe serves terrible oysters). Yet they believe—nay, they *know*—that they do not enjoy oysters. They will not seek out oysters. They will not opt for oysters at a free buffet, much less pay for them at a fancy restaurant.

You see where we're going here. People develop tastes and preferences and opinions about things such as oysters—and, yes, news—for many reasons besides direct personal experiences. Maybe they didn't grow up with oysters, so they find them unfamiliar, unappetizing, incomprehensible, and expensive. These preferences are rarely purely individual but rather are social and relational: people are influenced by what they have heard about oysters and by the habits and opinions of their social circles. Maybe influential people have told them many reasons why oysters are bad. Maybe those people tweet about it. A lot. People who really like oysters may have strong views on oyster refuseniks and maybe a prejudice or two about what their (unreasonable) distaste says about them—and vice versa. Indeed, *you* might like oysters, yet "I don't like oysters" is their opinion. They certainly have no intention of spending their hard-earned cash trying to learn to like them. There is, after all, so much else to consume and enjoy. As you can see, efforts to get them to appreciate oysters that focus only on improving standards of oyster quality (let alone serving up more oysters) probably won't change their minds.

When we began this study, we thought we would find that most consistent news avoiders reject news because they have specific grievances with news: the way information is presented, what topics it focuses on, who features in it, and so on. That was, indeed, part of what we found. But we also ran into the oyster problem constantly. We discovered that consistent news avoidance is not only in part a product of what people believe about news content and the information it contains—whether those beliefs are based on firsthand experience with news or not—but also in part a product of factors well beyond the form and content of news, including people's social identities, the ideologies they embrace, and their relationships with the media platforms and infrastructures that undergird the way they encounter and engage with information.

This complex interweaving of factors means that addressing growing news avoidance is not as simple as making news more trustworthy and less bleak (although that could help, and we have some suggestions). Nor is publishing more news the answer. Addressing news avoidance requires understanding the challenges people face in their daily lives; how they perceive different media as compounding or alleviating those challenges; the ways they go about accessing and selecting sources; and how those sources fit into their understandings of who they are and what they believe in. It may involve accepting—however unwelcome to people deeply invested in existing forms of journalism—that news isn't always as essential for everyone or every purpose as many journalists and journalism scholars may like to think. Taking consistent news avoiders seriously brings all these elements into focus. Beyond that, it offers an opportunity to reflect on behaviors that may feel more familiar—say, those of the news lovers we also interviewed

4

for this project or even our own media habits—and to see them through an entirely different lens. Doing so requires meeting people where they are. In this book, that is what we try to do.

WHY NEWS AVOIDANCE IS A PROBLEM

News avoidance has been a topic of growing interest among scholars and journalists in recent years for a number of reasons. As our lives become more mediated, strategies to manage the onslaught of information have become more widespread and more meaningful. Opting out of media means little when there are few media to be had, but it can require a deliberate choice and conscious effort when media are everywhere and tuning out requires real trade-offs.[13] Regarding journalism specifically, understanding news audiences' interests in general and their disengagement with news in particular has become increasingly urgent as the news industry in many parts of the world continues to struggle with digital transitions that have seen audiences and advertisers trading traditional offline media for online offerings and big platforms.[14] In an offline environment, news was a small but relatively significant part of most people's daily media routines. In an online environment, news use is in many cases more intermittent, accounting for just a fraction of most people's time spent with media.[15] This means that many people are consuming less news than their peers did in the past and that the number of people who say they are interested in the news is also in decline.[16] Less than half of internet users in many countries say they have even visited a news website or app in the past week, and all news media combined draw only about 3 percent of people's attention online.[17]

In this already challenging environment, recent reports that increasing numbers of people say they sometimes or often avoid news are concerning to journalists.[18] A recent survey of news industry leaders in fifty-three countries found that 72 percent were worried about the issue.[19] They should be. Journalism exists in the context of its audience. Its social significance, political importance, and, indeed, its sustainability—from a commercial point

5

of view and in terms of legitimacy (especially for public-service media)—are premised on its connection with the public. That connection is weakened when millions of people consistently avoid the news. News avoidance is particularly troubling for those who believe journalism should serve the whole public, not just those most highly engaged in (or willing to pay for) it. As we discuss further later in this chapter, those who consistently avoid news disproportionately come from already disadvantaged groups, challenging the idea that journalism is as inclusive and egalitarian as journalists might like to think.

But is news avoidance a problem for the public? For many people, at least occasionally avoiding news feels not only justified but also healthy and righteous. The failings of news media are recurrent themes in popular culture, including cartoons, movies, song lyrics, television shows, and graffiti, which suggests they resonate widely. Those critiques often imply that we would be better off without news or should at least give ourselves a break—that, in the words of singer-songwriter Lukas Nelson, we all should "turn off the news and build a garden."[20] Those who value journalism may look to movies such as *Spotlight* and *All the President's Men* for popular cultural representations of the profession, but how many more will come up with more negative, fictional examples when they think of journalism, such as Zoe Barnes in *House of Cards*, Scott Templeton in *The Wire*, and even Rita Skeeter in the Harry Potter universe?

Books with titles such as *Slow News* and *Resisting the News* spell out some of the arguments in favor of limiting exposure to news or opting out of it altogether.[21] Some of the most common include: it is too relentlessly negative and therefore bad for mental health; it is untrustworthy and biased; it misrepresents minority issues or communities if it represents them at all; the commercial logic behind much news media leads to sensationalism, clickbait, and overall low quality; and news is inefficient and poorly tailored to individual information needs, especially compared to digital alternatives.

We see merit in all of these critiques of news media, as do self-critical journalists. News is maddeningly imperfect, perhaps most frustratingly so in the ways it is shot through with many forms of structural inequality in terms of class, race and ethnicity, gender, sexual orientation, religion, and more, which can powerfully influence how and how much different communities are represented, reflected, and respected.[22] That issue, along with the other arguments enumerated earlier, presents a strong case for limiting one's exposure to news at least sometimes and certainly for supplementing mainstream news with alternatives.

But all these arguments in favor of news avoidance assume that people stay at least minimally informed about news; they work for people who are already at least somewhat engaged in current events and politics. *Consistent* news avoidance represents a different situation, however. We argue that it *is* a problem both for the individuals who engage in it and for society as a whole. The main reason is that news consumption and political engagement are indelibly intertwined. Studies have shown that a "virtuous circle" exists between news use and political engagement.[23] Because people who consume more news tend to engage more in politics, politicians also cater to them more.[24] A similar dynamic exists between the people who engage with news and the people whom news media serve. In a competitive marketplace for attention and an unforgiving business environment, publishers allocate newsgathering resources at least in part in response to demand.[25] To those who have, more will be given. Thus, it is the case not just that news avoiders are less well served by news media *today* but also that news media are also less likely to try to serve them well in the future because they do not represent an "institutionally effective audience"—a population likely to bring profit to commercial news outlets or to sustain nonprofit news media.

As we show, consistent news avoiders tend to be found especially among segments of society that are already socially and politically disadvantaged, such as women, younger people, and those from lower socioeconomic classes (although not necessarily among people of color, however much conventional news sources have historically been harmful to such communities). This greater avoidance leaves those groups less informed and less equipped to advocate for themselves in the political realm than already dominant groups. They are less likely to be served by news media in the future and less likely to receive the attention of the politically powerful. It also leaves them less capable of holding the news media to account when the media fail to meet the needs of their communities. After all, it is vital to have at least some firsthand knowledge of the institutions one is trying to change.

News avoidance is a problem not only when it comes to exacerbating divides between the haves and have-nots in political and civic life but also because it may further polarize the public along ideological lines in that news avoidance does not occur equally among all people along the political spectrum. In some countries, it is more common among those holding particular political viewpoints. That makes political debate between people of different perspectives even more challenging because groups that avoid news are less likely to draw on the same set of facts. Some research has found that news users see a greater range of ideological views online than offline, throwing into question the popular idea that digital echo chambers are making us more polarized.[26] However, if more people on the political right avoid news (as is the case in the United States) or more people on the left avoid news (as is more common elsewhere in the world),[27] and if some members of the public avoid news in part because they feel alienated from or indifferent toward conventional left–right party political debate (as is the case in many countries), these trends raise serious concerns about the erosion of a shared basis of factual information about public affairs.

This would be a problem if news avoiders simply got no current events information, but it is magnified because many do—they just do not get it from news media. Many are heavily dependent on other people in their lives to keep them updated about current affairs, or they turn to the internet for answers.[28] There they may follow alternative sources such as YouTube personalities who share their own interpretations of news stories—sometimes conspiracy theories. As we discuss in chapter 5, many consistent news avoiders reject traditional watchdog journalism and prefer these alternative sources. Many of these sources have much to offer, but some are problematic. Politicians in the Donald Trump mold may try to take advantage of suspicions about legacy institutions and use digital platforms and alternative channels to communicate with these potential followers.

Crucially, the alternative sources on which news avoiders often rely—many kinds, including talk radio, satirical sources, and other forms of influential commentary—rarely do actual information gathering in the field. Rush Limbaugh was not on the ground in Syria. Nor was Trevor Noah or John Oliver. Nor are various online influencers, whatever other qualities they have to offer. They riff on information they get from news media. Or they just riff. So many of the most adamant news avoiders are not really avoiding news; they are just consuming a version of it that has skipped the "seek truth and report it" aspiration at the heart of professional journalism. Although some do avoid all mediated forms of news—many news avoiders rely entirely on their partners or parents to inform them about current events and politics—this practice can still leave them hobbled in the civic arena, overly reliant on secondhand sources to filter news for them in a kind of high-stakes telephone game. Moreover, news literacy and political knowledge are cumulative. When people are reliant on others to digest news on their behalf, they do not develop the skills to find, filter, and verify current events information or accumulate their own stores of political knowledge.[29] Journalism and news media are not perfect. Far from it. But decades of research have found that news, despite its imperfections, demonstrably helps people better understand the world beyond their personal experience.[30]

In sum, consistent news avoidance can perpetuate long-standing inequalities as individuals and groups who are already disadvantaged socially and politically miss out on information and an opportunity to build essential skills to battle for change and as news media lose sight of their needs, values, and interests, over time coming to serve them even less well. News is not the only source of information needed for engaging in political life, and certainly not all forms of journalism as practiced are beneficial for all communities. In some places and in some forms, they most certainly are not. Taking breaks is fine. Supplementing mainstream news with alternative sources can be informative. Critiquing news when it comes up short is essential. But we do think that independent, professionally produced news, despite its many flaws, plays a crucial role in democracy that no other institution or profession can.[31] News can feel disempowering, but tuning it out completely only ensures that societal problems continue to fester—problems that news media at their best can help citizens to address.

FOLK THEORIES OF JOURNALISM AND MEDIA CHOICE NARRATIVES

The first step toward addressing the problem of news avoidance is to understand it better. In this book, we use two key concepts to help us do that: *folk theories of journalism* and *media choice narratives*. These concepts are useful for explaining not just news avoidance but also news consumption and other forms of media use as well.

When we ask people to explain why they do or do not use certain forms of media, they give explanations that draw on available vocabularies and cultural scripts that they have learned over time are socially acceptable explanations for certain behaviors. Sociologists have long been interested in such phenomena. C. Wright Mills called them "vocabularies of motive." Michele Lamont and Laurent Thévenot call them "repertoires of justification," and they are part of Ann Swidler's "tool kit" of culture.[32] Because many people have been exposed to the cultural norm that they *should* consume news, it is unlikely that news avoiders will offer completely idiosyncratic explanations when asked to explain why they do not do so. They will draw on vocabularies of motive that they know are at least somewhat socially acceptable justifications for not consuming news.

These justifications include *folk theories of journalism:* lay beliefs about what journalism is, how it works, what it means, and how people should relate to it.[33] Social scientists use the term *folk theories* to refer to implicit parts of everyday life that provide ways of thinking about and guides for acting upon the world around us. Folk theories provide generalized views of how the world works and conceptions of what it contains that are distinct from fact and practice and purport to capture patterns in what is happening. They can be more or less explicit. They can be shared or contentious. In some cases, they are purely speculative, but in most cases they integrate facts with personal experience or secondhand sources. Like scientific theories, they are often durable enough that one individual experience or piece of evidence will not decisively falsify them, but we may begin to reconsider them when they repeatedly fail to explain what we encounter to our satisfaction. They sometimes draw on academic jargon but are different from scientific theories in that they are *folk* theories and thus not subject to the institutionalized forms of contention and communal evaluation that scientific theories are subject to and in that they tend more toward enabling action than toward the accumulation of knowledge.

For the most part, folk theories are social phenomena. Although it is possible to embrace one's own unique folk theory, such theories are almost always learned from others and shared by many. Despite the many cultural and contextual differences between the three countries we studied—the United Kingdom, Spain, and the United States—everywhere we went, we heard news avoiders continually draw on similar folk theories of journalism to explain their news avoidance. Some of the most common ones include those we have already mentioned in this chapter: news is too negative, news is biased, news is untrustworthy. These beliefs are plausible. But as with scientific theories, some folk theories are, for lack of a better word, wrong. It can be difficult to judge in some cases, but not in others. Maybe we think the earth is flat. This is not true if by "earth" and "flat" we mean what is generally meant by those terms. Maybe we think that journalists are simply told by the government what to do. This is demonstrably not so in the countries we cover here. But irrespective of whether a given folk theory is true in any verifiable sense, because folk theories are widely believed and can influence people's actions, it is important to try to understand them rather than to simply debunk or dismiss them, let alone ignore them.

On the one hand, a single origin for a folk theory is often impossible to pin down because such theories circulate so widely and are informed not just by personal experience but also by many influences, including media and political discourse. This is the oyster problem: people draw on a variety of sociocultural influences to explain their aversion to something when they may have only minimal direct experience to draw on. On the other hand, sometimes the origins of folk theories are pretty clear. The most prominent example today is probably the idea that mainstream news is "fake news," a folk theory propagated gleefully by Donald Trump and other populists and authoritarian leaders as a reason the public should not trust it. This theory now sits in many citizens' cultural tool kits throughout the world, a ready-made explanation for why they don't trust mainstream news.[34]

When news avoiders explain why they avoid news, they rarely offer just one folk theory or reason to explain themselves. They string together multiple overlapping explanations, interweaving their folk theories of journalism with other vocabularies of motive (often related to the circumstances of their daily lives or their own personalities) in coherent narratives to explain their media-related behaviors. We refer to stories that people use to explain why they choose or reject particular media fare as *media choice narratives*. We all tell our own versions of them to explain our media preferences when asked (and sometimes to justify them to ourselves). For example, a news avoider might say that they are too anxiety-prone to handle negative news, that they have too little time to sit down and digest complex political news, or that it is all fake or biased anyway, so it is not worth their time.

Some of our choices about media are based on very conscious decisions with underlying reasonings that we can articulate easily. Fans and antifans illustrate this well: people who worship Beyoncé or hate *Keeping Up with the Kardashians* have no problem telling you why.[35] For news enthusiasts, political hobbyists, and people with strong partisan views (most likely many of those reading this book), expounding on the virtues and failings of different news sources can be gratifying and even fun. That goes for some consistent news avoiders as well: they have made a conscious, active choice to stop consuming news, and they explain the rationale behind that decision with relish. Others struggle more to explain their reasons for consuming so little news because their news avoidance is habitual or they simply never developed a habit of consuming news. Indeed, habitual behaviors are often hard for us to explain because they may have begun intentionally, but as they become routine over time, we engage in them with little reflection.[36]

In the end, when we are asked to explain more sustained behaviors, such as why we tend to binge-watch shows or use Spotify rather than Apple Music or, indeed, consume or avoid news, our media choice narratives are a mix of justifications for actions that are probably habitual (and therefore not done with a particular motive in mind) and explanations for actions that are more conscious and deliberate. It is often difficult or impossible for the speaker (or indeed the listener) to distinguish between which aspects of these media choice narratives are justifications for behaviors that are unreflectively engaged in and those that are more conscientiously undertaken. The narrative that emerges simply feels right. Like folk theories, media choice narratives are not unique to news avoiders but rather tools we all use to account for ourselves by reconciling choices made, experiences lived, and aspirations longed for.

STUDYING NEWS AVOIDERS

The bulk of the story we tell in this book comes from in-depth interviews we conducted in the United Kingdom, Spain, and the United States between 2016 and 2020, supplemented with survey data. We briefly explain here some of the key choices we made in designing our study, but we encourage interested readers to consult the appendixes for a detailed description of our qualitative methods, including more information about the choice of countries (appendix A). We also provide thumbnail sketches of each study participant (appendix B) and sample interview guides (appendix C). For those interested, in online supplementary appendixes (https://osf.io/ru5a4/) we also provide methodological details and the complete questionnaire for an original survey we conducted of U.S. news audiences (more on that survey later in this chapter). The online appendixes also include additional analyses we conducted concerning how we define news avoidance; statistical models we performed related to the findings in our empirical chapters; and the original Spanish versions of quotes from the participants in Spain, which Ruth translated into English.

There are many ways to study how people consume news and other forms of media. You can observe people, ask them, collect digital traces. But studying *nonuse* of media is harder, especially if the goal is to understand the "why" behind people's behaviors and how they experience them. Deciphering what it means *not* to engage in something requires qualitative investigation, as Nina Eliasoph argues in her classic work on how people avoid politics.[37] So we knew from the beginning that to understand consistent news avoidance, we had to talk to people—to rely on their own self-reports about their behavior. There are downsides to this methodology, of course, because people tend to misreport their news consumption (although they often inflate it, suggesting that news avoidance is more common than surveys suggest).[38]

As we explained earlier, one of the main reasons news avoidance is a problem for society is that it can reproduce existing inequalities if it leads to already-disadvantaged groups becoming even less informed. For that reason, we knew we wanted to focus on people who avoid news not selectively or occasionally but consistently over time. That behavior is more common among people in lower socioeconomic strata, so we wanted to talk mainly to them. We therefore recruited working- to middle-class people ages eighteen to forty-five in the United Kingdom, Spain, and the United States using a simple "screener" question drawn from the *Digital News Report* (*DNR*), a large multicountry survey of news audiences conducted annually by the Reuters Institute for the Study of Journalism at Oxford. That question asked respondents, "Typically, how often do you access news? By news we mean national, international, regional/local news and other topical events accessed via any platform (radio, TV, newspaper or online)."[39] We designated people who answered "never" or "less often than once a month" as consistent news avoiders. Our final sample of interviewees consisted primarily of consistent news avoiders in the United Kingdom ($N = 43$), Spain

(N = 40), and the United States (N = 25), with a subset interviewed twice in the United Kingdom and the United States. We also interviewed a smaller sample of "news lovers" in the United States (N = 25)—people who said they accessed news "more than ten times a day"—to compare their experiences with those of the news avoiders. Because it is very uncommon for people consuming news so often to fall into lower socioeconomic brackets (or to be young), we did not require that news lovers be working to middle class or younger than forty-five to participate in our study. And, indeed, the news lovers we interviewed tended to be older and more socioeconomically advantaged than the news avoiders.

A few things are important to notice about what this approach means for how we define news avoidance in this book. First, although the screener question did include a basic definition of "news," once the interviews began, we allowed interviewees to define news in whatever way came naturally to them. That is, we did not interrupt them to say, "No, no, no—what you are talking about here is not really news." Defining news has become more difficult with the proliferation of different kinds of sources online, but even before our lives were so heavily digital, studies found that audiences' ideas about what constituted news were all over the map.[40] For that reason, we wanted to let participants define news in their own way because we were interested in what news meant to them.[41] That said, if anything, many people we interviewed seemed to define news more narrowly than the screener question allowed, almost always referring to fairly conventional mainstream news sources such as newspapers (online or offline) or broadcast and cable news. Essentially, for many, "news" meant content produced by professional journalists and published by news media. That said, the types of news most accessible in people's minds—what they seemed to consider prototypical news—did vary a great deal depending on the country and the political ideologies they embraced, as we explain in the chapters that follow.

Second, we did not require that interviewees say that they intentionally or actively tried to avoid news, only that they did not consume it (or did so less than once a month). This is a point of contention among news avoidance scholars. Some argue that the word *avoid* implies intentionality and so should be used only for people who deliberately go out of their way not to consume news.[42] Others advocate for two separate categories for intentional and unintentional news avoidance.[43] As soon as we began interviewing people, it became clear to us that the distinction between intentional and unintentional news avoidance, so clear in theory, turns out to be impossibly blurry in practice. Consistent news avoidance is a habitual behavior, so it does not fall easily into intentional or unintentional categories. For some, it begins intentionally and over time becomes simply routine. Consistent news avoiders also give multiple reasons for their behaviors, some of which seem intentional, others unintentional, and many in between. And today, algorithms that categorize people as interested or uninterested in news further blur the distinction between intentional and unintentional news avoidance by increasing or decreasing the likelihood that they will be "incidentally" exposed to it on social media.[44] For all these reasons, we do not believe it is best to define news avoiders as such based on their motivations but rather based on the amount of news they consume.[45] Consistently not engaging with any news—in a context of unprecedented abundance and easy access and in light of journalism's stated aspiration to serve the whole public—requires effort; hence, we use the term *avoidance* even though not every individual act involved is intentional in the moment it is carried out.

Although the people we interviewed for this book consistently avoided news at the time we interviewed them, that does not mean their avoidance was permanent.[46] Some had consumed more news in the past but gave it up either on purpose or without even realizing it was happening, usually because of a change in life circumstances, such as a move to a new home or the birth of a child.[47] Others said they hoped to consume more news in the future. In other words, although for efficiency's sake we refer to our interviewees throughout the book as "consistent news avoiders" or just "news avoiders," for most people news avoidance is not an identity—one is not either a news avoider or a news user for life—but rather a category we use to capture behavior that can and sometimes does change over time.

We chose to make this study a comparative one because comparing media use behaviors across countries can be very revealing about how different contextual factors can shape behavior. Comparative qualitative studies are rare because they are methodologically challenging, and we detail our approach further in appendix A. Briefly: we decided to do interviews in the United Kingdom, Spain, and the United States in an effort to strike a balance between similarities and differences in terms of political information environments; all three are large, wealthy Western democracies, but each has distinct cultural, political, and, importantly, media system traditions, which we discuss further when relevant in the pages to come. We conducted the U.K. interviews in 2016–2017, in the wake of the Brexit vote in the summer of 2016. In Spain, we conducted interviews in 2017–2018, right after the controversial referendum on Catalan secession took place. In the United States, we conducted interviews in 2019–2020, during the presidential primary campaign season. These events dominated the news at the time, and interviewees referred to them often.

One of the challenges of presenting interview-based data is how to convey the texture and depth of individual experiences when they fit into a broader pattern but no single story is representative. We try to meet that challenge by including many short quotes and some longer ones that illustrate the patterns we found. When possible, we also include more thick descriptions of individual cases, and for readability we translated all the Spanish quotes into English. All the names are pseudonyms.

In addition to interviews, we rely on survey data, primarily international comparative quantitative data from the Reuters Institute *DNR*s of the past few years, as well as on an original survey we fielded with YouGov in August 2020 ($N=1,200$), cited as U.S. News Audiences Survey 2020 in the figures, with a representative sample of Americans covering topics specifically related to this study. We draw on these data to show how news avoiders compare to other types of news consumers, often breaking down our survey results into five different types of news users (figure 1.1). Two of these types have already been introduced: consistent news avoiders at the low end of the spectrum and news lovers at the high end. The remaining segments we slice into three additional groups of news users on the basis of responses to the same screener question taken from the *DNR*.

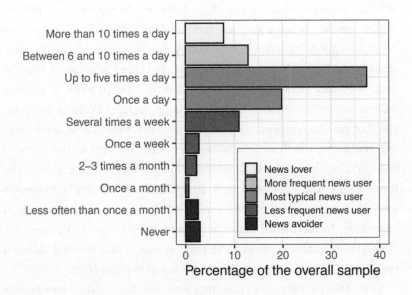

FIGURE 1.1. Types of News Use in the United States. Five-point classification of U.S. news users based on their self-reported frequency of accessing news.

Source: U.S. News Audiences Survey 2020.

WHAT WE FOUND: THE ROLE OF IDENTITIES, IDEOLOGIES, AND INFRASTRUCTURES IN NEWS AVOIDANCE

So why *do* people consistently avoid news? As we explained from the outset of this chapter, it is true that they are often critical of news content and the information in it. There is no question that news content contributes to news avoidance. But our central argument in this book is that who people are, what they believe, and how they access news—all that they bring with them before even considering a particular news article or media source on its own merits—often shape news avoidance just as much as or even more than news content. This is the oyster problem. A good illustration is one to which we all can relate. We completed the final interviews for this book in February 2020, right before the gravity of the COVID-19 pandemic hit. Studies since then have found that many people who normally consume news felt the need to take a break or limit their news intake in order to protect their mental health after the initial tide of news about COVID-19 began to recede.[48] News just felt too draining for many people as they tried to manage health worries, financial precarity, and increased caretaking responsibilities, all under a cloud of generalized anxiety.

We found that many consistent news avoiders feel like this *all the time.* In their media choice narratives, they tended to characterize themselves as more anxious or sensitive than the average person. Many said they struggled financially or were working multiple jobs or trying to find work, caring for ill family members, struggling with their own health concerns, or dealing with all these situations. Many felt that they did not have time for news or were so exhausted they preferred to spend their limited free time on less draining, more rewarding activities. Some argued that news was hard to follow because they did not have the education, background, or previous exposure to news to decipher it. In other words, they felt that consuming news was so personally costly, it just was not worth doing—and the cost was not about money.

There were differences between countries, but fewer than one might imagine. What British, Spanish, and American news avoiders thought of as prototypical news certainly differed in key ways that corresponded largely to each country's media system or the most prominent forms of news available in each country. In the United Kingdom, sensationalistic tabloid papers such as the *Sun* seemed to be the most accessible examples of news in many participants' minds. That was not the case in Spain, where British-style tabloids do not exist; there, interviewees primarily thought of all news as overtly, even shamelessly partisan. In the United States, news avoiders mentioned a range of news products, but one of their biggest complaints was that news blended opinion too much with fact, and cable news was the perpetrator that came most quickly to mind. But these differences in the specific critiques that news avoiders made about the content of news masked striking commonalities across the three countries.

Avoiding news is sometimes and even often experienced as a choice; however, not all media choice narratives frame it this way. It became very clear to us when collecting and comparing news avoiders' narratives and even more when we supplemented those findings with survey data that consistent news avoidance is not just a product of individual choices but of broader contextual and structural forces that shape people's relationships with news. We divide these forces into three main themes, which overlap and intersect with one another and which we analyze throughout the book: *identities*, *ideologies*, and *infrastructures*.

IDENTITIES

People's identities—by which we mean who they are and the social groups they are born into, socialized in, and identify with as adults—play a particularly important role in increasing or decreasing the likelihood that they will consume a lot of news or none at all and in shaping what those practices mean to them.[49] As the communication scholars Jacob Nelson and Seth Lewis have argued, "People's approach to and trust in news is as dependent on what they bring to the news as it is on what news brings to them."[50]

For example, consistent with past studies, we find that some types of people—namely young people, women, and people of lower socioeconomic status—tend to avoid news more than their counterparts.[51] Simply put, the perceived costs of consuming news are higher for people in these groups. Interviewees of lower socioeconomic status and working mothers with heavy caretaking responsibilities at home often said they had no time or energy for emotionally and intellectually demanding news. Many women had been socialized from early on to think of news and politics as primarily a male domain, and in adulthood they continued to see signs that this was true: their female friends did not consume news or talk about politics, just as their mothers and grandmothers had not.[52] Meanwhile, less educated and less wealthy news avoiders had often been exposed to less news and, especially, less *discussion* of news and politics while they were growing up than news lovers had.[53] As adults, they felt they had little foundational knowledge on which to build. Understanding political and economic news in particular felt like a strain.

Other social identities such as race and religion can also shape how people experience news avoidance. Given the many ways mainstream news fails communities of color, one might assume they would be more likely to avoid it, but we did not see evidence of that in our survey or qualitative data (although in both cases sample sizes limit our ability to zero in on these subgroups). We did, however, find evidence in our interviews that race is an important lens through which people of color understand their relationship to news, whether they are avid news lovers or news avoiders. Similarly, devoutly religious news avoiders and news lovers said their faith shaped everything they did, from the general media choices they made to the role news played in their daily lives.

While we saw signs that early socialization to news can influence news avoidance, we found that ongoing socialization in adulthood is an even greater determinant of news avoidance. Some news avoiders we interviewed had been exposed to news as children, but almost none belonged to what we call "news communities" in adulthood: social circles that not only kept up with news but also exerted strong pressure on group members to do so. In sharp contrast, news lovers usually belonged to multiple, overlapping configurations of such groups. These news communities play a key role in helping people to sustain a news habit because they help reinforce the belief—often in the face of much evidence to the contrary—that their news consumption is important and could potentially make a difference somehow.

IDEOLOGIES

Beliefs about citizens' roles and responsibilities can also be thought of as part of a person's ideology. In this book, we use the term *ideology* to refer to general beliefs about politics, not strictly a right–left political orientation or partisanship.[54] Although in some cases in some countries (the United States in particular) news avoidance tends to be more concentrated on one side of the ideological divide (the right) than the other, we found, consistent with past research, that it was not a distinct political viewpoint so much as a general lack of interest in politics altogether that better predicted consistent news avoidance.[55] Few of our interviewees aligned themselves with any political party. Many declared that they were either completely apolitical or staunchly antipolitical—that no party represented them. Some said they did not know what the parties stood for or what *right wing* and *left wing* meant. What most united them ideologically was that they felt uninterested, turned off, and alienated by politics.[56]

In practical terms, having no clear ideological leaning makes news consumption more difficult because a strong political identity can serve as an important heuristic that helps people decipher the vast array of information they may encounter about the prevailing debates of the day.[57] Nearly all the news lovers we interviewed had a strong sense of where they stood politically, and that understanding helped them navigate the news landscape. By contrast, without any partisan identity to guide them, many news avoiders felt they had no signposts; all news was equally biased and untrustworthy. Rejecting news—or any medium for that matter—can also have a performative quality: it can be a way of expressing beliefs and values.[58] For some of our more adamantly and vocally antipolitics interviewees, news avoidance appeared to play that role: avoiding news was a way to express disapproval of a political and media system they saw as failing them. That was also the case for some American news avoiders who self-identified as right wing. They said mainstream media was fake and skewed to the left and that it deliberately muffled or distorted conservative views. Their folk theories of news echoed the anti-news-media political rhetoric raining down from the top echelons of the Republican Party and perpetuated by right-wing media.

Importantly, though, right-wing news avoiders in the United States were not the only news avoiders who espoused folk theories that had been perpetuated by populist leaders. Many news avoiders, including those who identified as apolitical or left leaning, spoke of fake news or of not being able to trust any news at all—especially not knowing *what* to trust. Folk theories about news, in particular those that are well suited to work as vocabularies of motive to justify news avoidance, may originate in centers of political power or on one side of the political spectrum, but when set free in the wild, they spread. They can erode trust in news even among people who do not identify with the ideological position of those who spread these folk theories in the first place—and who most benefit from their widespread adoption.

INFRASTRUCTURES

Like so many things in life, the media that people use (and don't use) often comprise a combination of their individual choices and external factors that define those choices. Contemporary news avoidance can be understood only by grappling with people's identities and ideologies as well as with the relationship they have with particular media platforms that shape how they find, access, and engage with information. We use the term *infrastructures* for this relationship with platforms in a nod toward media scholarship on *structuration*, which focuses on the role played by media structures in shaping audience behaviors.[59] Whereas some structural factors are social, such as gender and class, others are more material, pertaining to the array of media available, accessible, and familiar to people in the particular contexts of their daily lives.

In today's high-choice environment, where social media platforms and other digital intermediaries play an increasingly central role in shaping encounters with news,[60] media habits look markedly different from what they were just a few years ago. Those less interested in news have many more options in the menu of media fare available to them.[61] Nearly everyone we spoke to had some kind of internet access at home or on their phones, and only a few said they did not have a television. Technically, they all could easily access many types of news. But because they were uninterested in news, they were unlikely to seek it out, and few did. Decisions made around broader media, whether specific to digital platforms or to other offline pathways to information—decisions typically made for reasons unrelated to news—play a particularly powerful role in shaping what news people are exposed to even before they have an opportunity to actively avoid it or not.[62]

When it comes to digital infrastructures, many audiences have grown accustomed to the ease with which they are able to feel informed about major stories in the news by encountering headlines and alerts and conversations about news incidentally as they go about their lives. We found that many news avoiders believed news would *find* them, making it less important for them to carve out time for it. They believed whatever relevant information did not find them could easily be discovered by turning to a second digital tool: powerful internet search engines. These dual ideas, "news finds me" and "the information is out there," in combination led many news avoiders to feel they could manage just fine without making the news a deliberate part of their daily routines.

But the infrastructures of contemporary media, although appealing in theory, did not always make life easier in practice. Many news avoiders repeatedly expressed a third folk theory, "I don't know what to believe," which captured a range of frustrations many felt about how to make sense of the conflicting perspectives and commentary they encountered when they did attempt to engage with news. That stood in contrast to news lovers, who tended to know the sources they trusted, which in turn made it easier for them to parse the information they encountered efficiently and effectively. By developing habits around the specific forms and modes of news they accessed, which they had personally curated to fit the rhythms and routines of their daily lives, news lovers often found considerable enjoyment from paying attention to news, even as they echoed many of the same critiques that news avoiders made about its content.

* * *

We use the terms *identities*, *ideologies*, and *infrastructures* as a kind of shorthand for the major factors underlying news avoidance that we found over the course of our research. Each helps to explain the phenomenon of news avoidance, but in truth they are deeply enmeshed with one another and not easy to tease apart. They act as a kind of filter through which people experience and assess news content. Together, these interconnected factors provide what we hope is a more complete portrait of the individual lived experiences of news avoiders and help to provide an answer to the central question we began with: What does it mean to avoid the news consistently in a world of abundant supply and ease of access? To the extent that identities, ideologies, and infrastructures shape people's relationships with news, they also have the potential to exacerbate inequalities, the fourth *i* in figure 1.2, which illustrates the key aspects of consistent news avoidance in our empirical analysis.

We have tried to capture faithfully news avoiders' perspectives so that readers can better understand how they avoid the news and why, but in so doing we hope this book illuminates broader truths about what it means to be an audience for news in the contemporary media environment. Those who are most enthusiastic about news and journalism—we count ourselves in that group—may be surprised to find in the coming pages that news avoiders' news habits may not seem so unreasonable in light of the specific

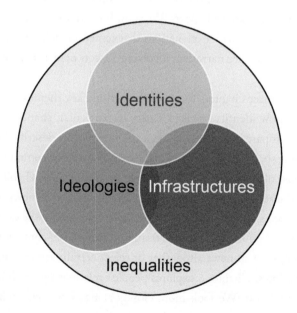

FIGURE 1.2. Factors That Shape News Avoidance. Summary figure illustrating the interconnected factors that shape news avoidance.

circumstances in their lives, the challenges they are contending with, and their particular vantage point on the world and their place in it. On multiple occasions, immersing ourselves in these perspectives has certainly led us to reflect on our own relationship to news and what continually convinces us that paying attention to news is a valuable use of time. We hope this book serves as an invitation to readers to do the same.

CHAPTER OVERVIEW

We begin in chapter 2 by explaining what kinds of people are more likely to avoid news consistently, setting up some of the reasons behind those patterns, and introducing readers to a few of the individuals we interviewed for this study. In chapter 3, we dive deeper into our interviewees' media choice narratives. We explore the most common arguments news avoiders provided for why they avoid news. We show how they interweave arguments about news together with explanations that center on their own lives to form coherent media choice narratives involving aspects of identity, ideology, and infrastructure.

The next three chapters focus on those three key themes. In chapter 4, we look at how identity, social identity in particular, shapes news avoidance. We compare how news avoiders and news lovers described their early and ongoing socialization to news and explore how news communities and a shared sense of civic duty can help people to sustain a news habit—but also how their absence may be key for explaining consistent news avoidance. Chapter 5 looks at how ideology shapes news avoidance. We examine how news avoiders' political views, partisan and otherwise, contribute to their choice to opt out of news altogether or reject certain kinds of news along ideological lines. Chapter 6 explores people's relationships with infrastructures they rely on. We look more closely at news avoiders' folk theories about digital platforms and the alternative information pathways they use to find, access, and navigate the contemporary information environment without news.

Finally, in chapter 7 we recap our main findings and draw out the implications for both scholars and journalists. We cautiously proffer some recommendations for how consistent news avoidance might be addressed based on our findings, including efforts to reach avoidant audiences through forms of journalism that make more explicit why stories matter and fit better into their busy lives. We also advocate for initiatives that amplify the social benefits of news consumption and for media literacy interventions to counteract widely held misconceptions about journalism. Our most ambitious recommendations require real change in the practice of journalism, including industry-wide public-relations efforts designed to defend the unique value proposition of independent, professional journalism. Changing habits may ultimately require first changing minds about what news is (and is not) and how it seeks to serve the greater good.

* * *

It would be easy to write off consistent news avoiders as a small segment of the public—a lost cause. Sometimes it feels as if the news media already have. It is probably easier to get people already consuming news to consume more and even to pay for it than it is to address the many overlapping structural, circumstantial, and individual factors—the identity-, ideology-, and infrastructure-related causes—that can lead them to turn away from news altogether or simply never to turn to it in the first place. If anything, our findings confirm how complex this phenomenon really is and how difficult countering it will be.

But consistent news avoidance falls along existing lines of inequality and helps perpetuate those inequalities, and there are signs that such avoidance is growing. News avoiders' media choice narratives differ in some respects from those of the average news user, but the folk theories of journalism and other vocabularies of motive that they use to justify turning away from news are widespread, are key to understanding media use, and can cast a new light on our own habits and preferences as well. That is why we need to listen to them.

2

WHO *ARE* CONSISTENT
NEWS AVOIDERS?

When we tell friends and colleagues that we research people who consume basically no news at all, one of the most common questions they ask is some version of "Who *are* these people?" To committed news consumers, especially those who *love* news, avoiding news consistently and habitually seems mysterious, possible only for the most radical or reclusive of characters. In fact, consistent news avoiders are in many ways (and perhaps, to some, surprisingly) quite normal, but they do tend to have some common traits. That is, some kinds of people are more likely than others to avoid news in a sustained way over time.

Some of these patterns are quite similar around the world. In general, consistent news avoidance tends to be more common among young people, women, and lower socioeconomic classes. There are also some important political divides regarding who avoids news. In the United States especially, it is much more common among people on the right ideologically. In most other parts of the world, it is more common on the left. But a bigger and more persistent gap lies along what the political scientists Yanna Krupnikov and John Barry Ryan call "the other divide": the divide between people who are deeply involved in politics and rarely, if ever, avoid news consistently and those who are largely indifferent toward politics and avoid news far more often.[1] To be clear, we are not suggesting that all or even most young people, women, or people of lower socioeconomic classes avoid news consistently. That is verifiably not the case. But if you do meet someone who consumes practically no news at all, there is a good chance they will fall into one or more of these categories.

Most of this book grapples with *why* and *how* news avoidance happens, using brief quotes from a wide range of interviewees to answer those questions, but we begin in this chapter by introducing three consistent news avoiders in greater depth: Sofía, a twenty-year-old student in Spain; Andrea, a thirty-eight-year-old working mother in the United Kingdom; and William, a twenty-eight-year-old construction worker in the United States. We want readers to get a sense not only of *who* we are describing when we talk about news avoiders—to understand that there are complex individuals behind each quote—but also how they fit into broader patterns of who avoids news. These examples also illustrate how the larger argument in this book plays out in the lives of individuals—that who we are (*identities*), what we believe (*ideologies*), and the media pathways we use (*infrastructures*) have a profound influence over how we relate to news. These factors are difficult to pull apart, intersecting in different ways in the three cases we describe, but cumulatively they also mirror and reproduce deep-rooted social *inequalities*—a point we return to at the end of this chapter.

NEWS AVOIDANCE AMONG DIGITAL NATIVES

[Watching news] is something I've never done because it doesn't interest me. . . . When it comes to politics, I don't talk about it or understand it. . . . I'd like to be up-to-date because people say, "Oh, it's general culture," but I don't know if it's how they present them or the topics they're covering, but I'm like, "God, here they go talking again," and really, if my mom is watching the TV, and they come on, I say turn it off or I get on my phone or I leave or I go do something else.

—Sofía (Spain)

Sofía lives with her mother in a working-class neighborhood in northern Madrid. At the time of our interview, she was twenty years old and taking a part-time course in international commerce, but her main problem, as she saw it, was that she was still struggling to decide what to do with her life. Her priorities in the meantime were spending time with friends and trying to manage her anxiety, which had led to a trip to the emergency room when she was studying for her college entrance exams. She described herself as addicted to her phone, which she used mostly for WhatsApp, Instagram, and YouTube. She explained that news only seemed to cover politics (which she was adamantly bored by), accidents, weather, and sports, whereas "I like topics like music, makeup, fashion. Topics that interest a ton of people, really; . . . [news outlets] don't have those things." In the end, she felt that the main reason to be informed was to be able to participate in social or professional conversations about current events, which she did not need to do at this point in her life. She explained, "I imagine that now since I'm studying, it's not necessary, but I imagine that when the day comes that I have to work, depending on the job, obviously, it will be a good idea to be informed."

Most news avoiders we interviewed were Sofía's age or slightly older: young adults in their twenties or thirties. Research has long shown that age is intertwined with rates of news consumption: simply put, people tend to consume more news as they get older.[2] In our U.S. survey data, the average age of news lovers was nearly two age brackets higher than news avoiders, almost a twenty-year difference. We find a similar dynamic internationally. In all but one of the markets covered in the *DNR 2022*, rates of consistent news avoidance were higher among younger groups, including the three countries that are the focus of this study (figure 2.1).[3]

So why are young people more likely to avoid news consistently than older people? The example of Sofía illustrates a few key points. For one, she had trouble relating to the topics that she saw in the news (way too much

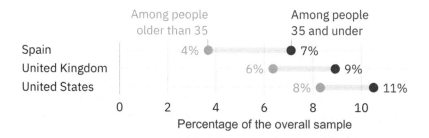

FIGURE 2.1. Rates of Consistent News Avoidance by Age. Percentages of consistent news avoiders for Spain, the United Kingdom, and the United States for older and younger respondents in 2022.

Source: *Digital News Report 2022*, https://reutersinstitute.politics.ox.ac.uk/digital -news-report/2022.

politics, for instance, which we elaborate on later), and she thinks that inability to relate may have to do with her stage of life. She conceded that she had plenty of free time, but right now following news was just not a top priority. Indeed, some research finds that even when young people see news use modeled by their parents at home, there is often a lag before they adopt news consumption habits in later adulthood.[4] Among the news avoiders we interviewed who were just a bit older than Sofia, we saw evidence that interests and preferences related to news can indeed grow and change as people get older. Take Bruce (United States), a thirty-something parent of young kids. Bruce explained that he had recently begun to pay closer attention to news and politics, which he largely attributed to getting older. As he put it, once he "started paying taxes," he began to think, "Hey, this stuff really affects me."

And yet, as was the case for Bruce, just as priorities start to shift, young adults may find they have less time than ever to consume news. Their interest grows right when their free time evaporates. Many young parents like Bruce feel that the daily demands of caretaking responsibilities and full-time work leave little time available for news, even as they start to see the appeal and value of it in ways that Sofia clearly did not—at least not yet.

Indeed, on the other end of the spectrum, we have retirees, who tend to be more interested in news and have more time for it. This was especially clear to us when interviewing news lovers in Iowa, many of whom were in their fifties or sixties or older. Many were no longer working full-time, and their children were grown. They spent a significant number of hours each day consuming news, and it was clear they not only had time for it but also used it to structure their days. They described the television programs they watched at specific times and the repertoires of websites or apps they visited habitually. Indeed, when we asked news avoiders why they thought some people devoted so much more time and attention to news, many thought it ultimately came down to time: news lovers just had way more of it, in part due to their age and stage of life. Avoiders saw time spent with news as a luxury; some people just had "nothing better to do," as Joyce (United States) put it. Of course, this phenomenon is also heavily shaped by socioeconomic class, as we discuss further later.

As we also see in Sofía's case, some reasons young people are more likely to consistently avoid news are less related to news content and more tied to the digital environment in which they encounter news. These kinds of factors are closely related to what we refer to in this book as "infrastructures" and what earlier research called the "texto-materialistic" reasons why some people avoid news—that is, characteristics related to the material form and delivery of news that some people find off-putting.[5] Whereas older people, like many of the news lovers we interviewed, may have great affection for traditional forms of news, such as newsprint and broadcast news with their authoritative anchors intoning the events of the day, younger people who have grown up consuming most of their information digitally, much of it via mobile phones and social media, often feel no such attachments. Sofía at one point recalled a time when, encouraged by her parents, she tried to pay closer attention to news by reading it on her phone. (Newsprint was messy and impractical, so she did not even consider it.) But the experiment had been short-lived because even on her phone she found the format—small print, long stories—so awkward. Meanwhile, the television news that her mother watched seemed old-fashioned, slow, and tedious. She wondered how the TV news anchors did not die of boredom.

We found that the digital natives we interviewed, perhaps even more than being actively turned off by the form or content of news, felt they did not *need* to dedicate time specifically to consuming news from a news source because they would see it on social media anyway. Academics who study digital communication have taken to calling this phenomenon the "news finds me" perception: the assumption that one need not seek news out because all the news that is really worth knowing will simply land on one's digital doorstep.[6] Although this assumption is not unique to young people, they spend more time on social media, and more of them report social media as their main source of news,[7] so they are more likely to have this belief continually reaffirmed.

Young news avoiders like Sofía are also highly aware of a diverse array of other forms of media that are competing for their attention. These media include streaming services, social media, and messaging apps, which many interviewees, including Sofía, described as important parts of their media diets. Scholars have argued for years that as media options expand, people who were never particularly interested in news will consume less of it because they now simply have more access to more appealing fare.[8] Although this expansion of media choices applies to people of all ages, young people tend to have greater facility with and exposure to the contemporary media landscape and all of its wide-ranging, attention-grabbing offerings. In combination with the various other reasons young people may be less attracted to traditional forms of news, described earlier, the vast array of alternatives may be especially likely to lead them away from news (or to keep them from forming an interest in it in the first place).

Moreover, algorithms may compound the likelihood that young people will not develop a news habit even as they age. If young users never like, follow, or otherwise engage with anything related to news topics online, thereby training algorithms to screen out such content, they may not get enough initial exposure to ignite an interest that could develop later on.[9] For news lovers, the ease of access afforded by digital media makes it possible to consume larger and larger quantities of news—to convert a personal preference into something akin to an addiction. But, for avoiders, especially young ones, these same infrastructures may well be integral to why and how some turn away from news altogether.

NEWS AVOIDANCE, GENDER, AND CLASS

> There's nothing I can do whatsoever to change anything, so reading it is only going to make me feel, like, scared, and there's nothing I can do to change that. Then once I've read it, that's how I feel: it's just doom and gloom.
>
> —Andrea (United Kingdom)

Andrea's story shares some similarities with Sofía's, but her relationship with news highlights other factors that we also saw replicated across a wide range of interviewees. At thirty-eight, Andrea was older than Sofía. She was also a mother raising three young kids and a full-time housecleaner in the United Kingdom, so she had little free time. She said she had dreams of becoming an astrophysicist when she was younger, but many things had gotten in the way of that plan. She explained that she has "a very busy household; I don't really sit down and have time to watch news." The way news made her feel was another reason she gave for avoiding it, noting, "I think sometimes when you read it, it can make you feel worse in yourself, so I've kind of switched off from wanting to know about all the negative things in the world because there's so much nastiness." Like Sofía, she actively disliked news and did not see its relevance to her life, but her reasons could be traced less to age and more to other aspects of her identity—namely, those related to her gender and socioeconomic class.

News avoidance of all forms is more common among women. In our U.S. survey data, about three out of five news avoiders were women—a dynamic replicated across most countries worldwide. In the *DNR 2022*, women are overrepresented among consistent news avoiders in three-quarters of the countries studied, including in Spain, the United Kingdom, and the United States. These gender gaps are not huge. They typically amount to a few percentage points. They also tend to be highest in countries where there are persistent gender gaps in other spheres, such as politics and business. However, they persist even in more egalitarian societies such as Germany, the Netherlands, and Denmark. This is especially the case when examining gender differences that intersect with socioeconomic class, which we return to later.

There are many reasons why these differences in news avoidance by gender arise. As we expand on in the next chapter, which focuses on people's stated reasons for avoiding news, women tend to consume less news in part due to their heavy caretaking responsibilities and persistent divisions of labor in the home that often afford men more time to keep up with news (at least in heterosexual relationships). Of course, such gender divides are also learned; they don't simply happen all by themselves. Socialization processes around news reinforce the notion that news, especially political news, is produced largely *for* male audiences.[10]

To be sure, patterns evident in survey data are not easily reduced to distinct or discrete causes in individual cases. Andrea did not attribute her consistent news avoidance to being a woman, but she and many other news avoiders did talk at length about how news made them feel—how negative they found it and how the idea of consuming it so often filled them with dread and anxiety. Those attitudes are by no means limited to women, but they may be felt more acutely by those with heavy caretaking responsibilities, which do disproportionately fall on women.[11] In our interviews, mothers often said they avoided news in part because it felt like an endless cycle of "doom and gloom from every corner of the globe," as Andrea put it. She explained, "It's things like that that scare me as a parent for my children." Many news avoiders in fact talked of wanting their homes to be a refuge from so much negativity in the world. Although this sentiment was more often expressed by women in our interviews, some men said the same thing, especially those who had heavy childcare responsibilities. For example, stay-at-home father Ryan (United Kingdom) decided to make his home free from news altogether because "I don't want my kids listening to bombs going off and how many people died or some gun massacre somewhere."

When we asked Andrea if there had been much news in her home when she was growing up, she responded, "I come from, like, a big working family, if you know what I mean, and all the men were out working, and the mums and stuff were all at home, cooking, and nobody were really bothered about the news, no." This quote encapsulates nicely how, in addition to gender disparities in news avoidance, social class influences how people relate to news. People of lower socioeconomic status are much more likely to be consistent news avoiders than those who are more advantaged economically. For example, in our U.S. survey just 11 percent of news avoiders held a bachelor's degree compared to just less than half of those with above-average news consumption habits. Similar differences were noticeable when it came to household income (figure 2.2). News avoiders were also nearly twice as likely to be unemployed (28 percent) compared to typical news users (17 percent) and news lovers (8 percent).[12]

Although socioeconomic divides in levels of news use exist in all three countries we studied, the role of class in shaping how people related to news was most heightened and visible in the U.K. interviews. Andrea, for example, talked openly about how her class identity—her profession, her income

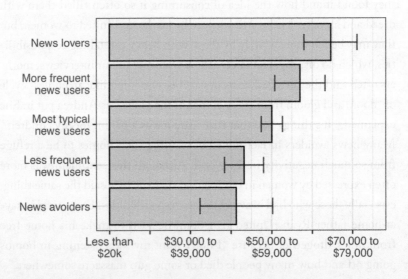

FIGURE 2.2. News Use by Annual Household Income. Differences in average household income by frequency of accessing news. Error bars reflect 95 percent confidence intervals for the subgroups.

Source: U.S. News Audiences Survey 2020.

level, her educational background—affected many aspects of her life. She described feeling increasingly like an outsider in her neighborhood in Leeds, which she had seen change over time due to gentrification.

> Everything is more expensive, everything is just becoming more expensive; I'm constantly looking out for more bargains shopping and everything. Where I live round here, because it's affluent, because I'm not necessarily really like a rich person or owt like that, I feel like a bit funny to go to, like, the local bars on the High Street and stuff because everyone's in, like, Gucci and drives the Porsches outside and stuff, and I'm just sat there with my Primark on, so I'd feel like I don't really fit in, but I feel like I belong here because I've always lived round here, but I feel like I don't fit it a bit, so I tend not to socialize up on the main street.

In what exact ways does class affect Andrea's relationship to news? A substantial academic literature suggests a variety of links connecting class, news consumption, and internet use.[13] We found on the one hand that class, like gender, shapes perceptions about whom news is for and how worthwhile it might be to pay attention to news. Higher levels of education, also associated with higher socioeconomic status, can make following the news easier, a sentiment expressed by many interviewees who felt they did not have the educational background to grasp certain kinds of news, especially political and economic news. People with more resources in general also tend to have more time and money to spend on news as well as energy (in terms of emotional and intellectual resources)—another theme that loomed large in our interviews. Consuming news—especially certain brands in certain contexts—can also be a way for people to perform their class identities.[14] Furthermore, class shapes the kind of work people do, which in turn shapes news consumption: unlike many white-collar jobs in which people sit in front of a computer all day, manual labor and service jobs often leave less opportunity for news consumption, and they rarely require employees to keep up with news to get the job done. Indeed, Andrea, who worked cleaning houses, said she thought "not being around the TV enough" was one reason she did not consume more news.

Crucially, class also affects the types of people individuals converse with regularly and how often they talk about news, as we discuss in detail in chapter 4. It can even affect a sense of connection to the rest of the world. Distant matters can feel close to home when someone knows people who live in those far-off places or has traveled there, which is often more likely for people with more resources. Indeed, whereas the news lovers we interviewed often talked about their trips abroad and their interest in global affairs, news avoiders almost never did so. Sure enough, in our U.S. survey data we found that news avoiders were especially unlikely to report having traveled outside the United States or having close friends or family who had lived or worked abroad (figure 2.3).

To be clear, class is a complex phenomenon and cannot be fully captured by simple variables such as education, income, a person's profession, and global outlook. Nor is gender reducible to a strict binary. But consistent news avoidance does fall disproportionately and unequally among those who hail from less advantaged backgrounds and women. As Andrea's story helps to underscore, both factors shape not only encounters with news but also views about the world, one's place in it, and how news fits into all of that.

NEWS AVOIDANCE AND IDEOLOGICAL BELIEFS ABOUT POLITICS

If [news] was more middle of the road and open, more truthful, then I would probably start watching mainstream news again, but I don't see that happening anytime soon.

—William (United States)

Finally, consider our third news avoider: William, a twenty-eight-year-old construction worker. William lived in a mobile-home park with his wife and three kids younger than ten. He consumed a great deal of political information from Facebook, where he followed a lot of what he described

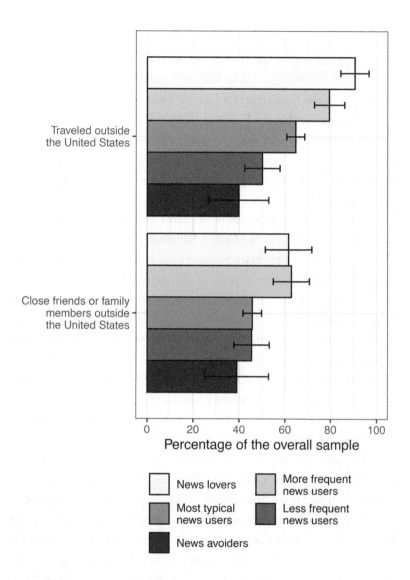

FIGURE 2.3. Experiences Abroad. Differences between news avoiders and others by how likely they were to have traveled outside the United States or reported having close friends or family members who had lived abroad. Error bars reflect 95 percent confidence intervals for the subgroups.

Source: U.S. News Audiences Survey 2020.

as "independent newspeople." They included sources such as InfoWars and Ben Shapiro, known for conservative commentary. William was also increasingly active politically. When we interviewed him following the Iowa caucus in 2020, William said he had even gone so far as to caucus for the first time to show his support for Donald Trump, even though it was not a competitive race within the Republican Party. But William's growing interest in politics had not led him to pay more attention to conventional news sources. Instead, he rejected conventional news as deeply ideologically biased, so he deliberately sought out alternative sources of information elsewhere on the internet.

Of course, there are elements of William's story that overlap with Sofía's in Spain and Andrea's in the United Kingdom: his relative youth, his use of social media as an important pathway for information, his socioeconomic status. But there are other aspects of William's relationship to news that are also clearly about *ideology*, which seemed to matter as much as if not more than other aspects of his identity or the infrastructures he depended on day to day to find information. Among the news avoiders we interviewed, ideologically based rejection of conventional (or "mainstream") news was especially common among news avoiders in the United States. More often than not, when U.S. news avoiders had a partisan leaning, they typically placed themselves squarely on the right. This is especially apparent in our U.S. survey data, where we found news avoiders disproportionately tended to be Republican and to identify as conservative. News lovers in contrast leaned more toward the Democratic Party and were more liberal.

One challenge in interpreting these data, however, is that it can be difficult to tell whether conservatives in the United States actually consume less news or are simply using the question to voice their disapproval of the news media. Such "expressive responding" is not surprising given widespread tropes around "liberal bias" in the news media in the United States and leading political figures' vocal antagonism toward news. Some U.S. news avoiders may well consume quantities of information comparable to that of more typical news consumers—sometimes even more—but may do so largely from alternative sources. William is a good example of this phenomenon. He specifically told us he avoided news because of "one-sided narratives and the lying," but he kept up with political affairs online via a number of political commentators. It even turned out that he occasionally did tune in to local news channels, which he said he found to be less politically biased than national news sources.

As is so often the case, patterns in the United States are not necessarily replicated elsewhere in the world.[15] Differences in rates of news consumption along ideological lines tend to be relatively small in most countries. What's more, they also are quite small in comparison to the much larger divide between those who are unsure about where to place themselves ideologically at all versus those who identify themselves on the right or the left.[16] In the *DNR 2022*, rates of consistent news avoidance are higher on the ideological right in only about a third of all markets, but they are disproportionately highest practically everywhere among those who say they "don't know" where they stand on the political spectrum (figure 2.4). In most countries, the latter segment also tends to be a larger share of the public compared to the number of people who place themselves on either the left or the right.[17]

This raises a separate issue around ideology that is also evident in William's story. Up until recent changes in the political climate, William had not necessarily considered himself particularly interested in politics. He didn't grow up in a family that talked much about it. "Politics is one of those things where it's not super important to a lot of people," he said. "It's low on the totem pole of things that have happened to our family in the last decade or so." This aspect of William's orientation to political life is especially typical of consistent news avoiders. Indeed, both Andrea and Sofía said they were uninterested or actively turned off by politics. In our U.S. survey, when we asked how interested respondents were in "information about what's going on in government and politics,"[18] news lovers and more typical news users were vastly more likely than news avoiders to say they were interested (figure 2.5).

In fact, across most countries no single variable is more predictive of whether someone consistently avoids news than their level of interest in politics and civic affairs.[19] In every market in the *DNR 2021*, news avoidance is more concentrated among those who say they are *not* interested in

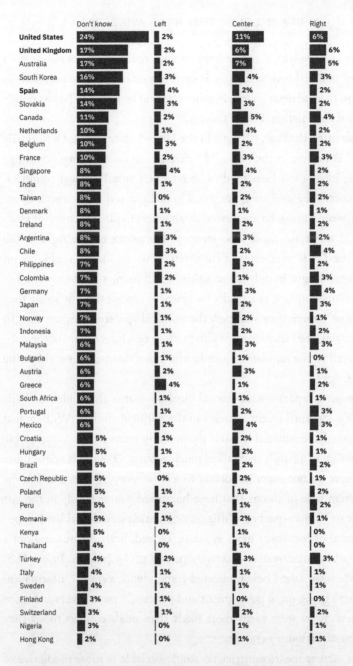

	Don't know	Left	Center	Right
United States	24%	2%	11%	6%
United Kingdom	17%	2%	6%	6%
Australia	17%	2%	7%	5%
South Korea	16%	3%	4%	3%
Spain	14%	4%	2%	2%
Slovakia	14%	3%	3%	2%
Canada	11%	2%	5%	4%
Netherlands	10%	1%	4%	2%
Belgium	10%	3%	2%	2%
France	10%	2%	3%	3%
Singapore	8%	4%	4%	2%
India	8%	1%	2%	2%
Taiwan	8%	0%	2%	2%
Denmark	8%	1%	1%	1%
Ireland	8%	1%	2%	2%
Argentina	8%	3%	3%	2%
Chile	8%	3%	2%	4%
Philippines	7%	2%	3%	2%
Colombia	7%	2%	1%	3%
Germany	7%	1%	3%	4%
Japan	7%	1%	2%	3%
Norway	7%	1%	2%	1%
Indonesia	7%	1%	2%	2%
Malaysia	6%	1%	3%	3%
Bulgaria	6%	1%	1%	0%
Austria	6%	2%	3%	1%
Greece	6%	4%	1%	2%
South Africa	6%	1%	1%	1%
Portugal	6%	1%	2%	3%
Mexico	6%	2%	4%	3%
Croatia	5%	1%	2%	1%
Hungary	5%	1%	2%	1%
Brazil	5%	2%	2%	2%
Czech Republic	5%	0%	2%	1%
Poland	5%	1%	1%	2%
Peru	5%	2%	1%	2%
Romania	5%	1%	2%	1%
Kenya	5%	0%	1%	0%
Thailand	4%	0%	1%	0%
Turkey	4%	2%	3%	3%
Italy	4%	1%	1%	1%
Sweden	4%	1%	1%	1%
Finland	3%	1%	0%	0%
Switzerland	3%	1%	2%	2%
Nigeria	3%	0%	1%	1%
Hong Kong	2%	0%	1%	1%

FIGURE 2.4. Consistent News Avoidance by Ideological Leaning. Percentages of consistent news avoidance by whether people place themselves in the center or on the left or right ideologically in different global media markets.

Source: Digital News Report 2022, https://reutersinstitute.politics.ox.ac.uk/digital-news-report/2022.

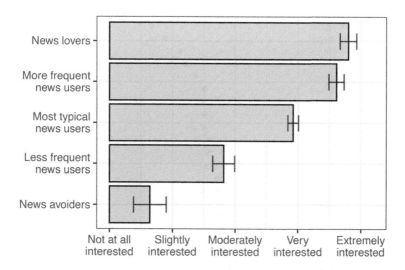

FIGURE 2.5. "How Interested Are You in Information About What's Going on in Government and Politics?." The relationship between news use and political interest. The correlation between these variables is among the strongest by far. Error bars reflect 95 percent confidence intervals for the subgroups.

Source: U.S. News Audiences Survey 2020.

politics and nearly nonexistent among those who say they are (figure 2.6). (We refer to data from 2021 because this question about political interest was not included in the *DNR 2022*.)

Research has long documented that news use and political interest feed on each other. It is difficult to say one *causes* the other, but they reinforce each other in a feedback loop sometimes called a "virtuous circle." That is, just as many people pay attention to news because they are interested in politics, the reverse is also true: many become interested in politics *because* they pay closer attention to news.[20] As the political communication scholars Judith Moeller and Claes de Vreese note in their study of political learning among adolescents, "The more people know about politics, the more they are inclined to take on an active role in a democracy," and the more people

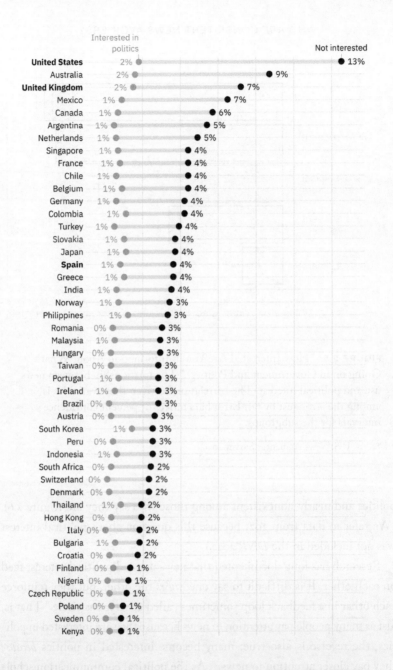

Interested in politics | Not interested

Country	Interested in politics	Not interested
United States	2%	13%
Australia	2%	9%
United Kingdom	2%	7%
Mexico	1%	7%
Canada	1%	6%
Argentina	1%	5%
Netherlands	1%	5%
Singapore	1%	4%
France	1%	4%
Chile	1%	4%
Belgium	1%	4%
Germany	1%	4%
Colombia	1%	4%
Turkey	1%	4%
Slovakia	1%	4%
Japan	1%	4%
Spain	1%	4%
Greece	1%	4%
India	1%	4%
Norway	1%	3%
Philippines	1%	3%
Romania	0%	3%
Malaysia	1%	3%
Hungary	0%	3%
Taiwan	0%	3%
Portugal	1%	3%
Ireland	1%	3%
Brazil	0%	3%
Austria	0%	3%
South Korea	1%	3%
Peru	0%	3%
Indonesia	1%	3%
South Africa	0%	2%
Switzerland	0%	2%
Denmark	0%	2%
Thailand	1%	2%
Hong Kong	0%	2%
Italy	0%	2%
Bulgaria	1%	2%
Croatia	0%	2%
Finland	0%	1%
Nigeria	0%	1%
Czech Republic	0%	1%
Poland	0%	1%
Sweden	0%	1%
Kenya	0%	1%

FIGURE 2.6. Consistent News Avoidance by Levels of Interest in Politics. Percentages of consistent news avoidance among those interested and not interested in politics for different global media markets in 2021. Respondents who said they were "extremely," "very," or "somewhat interested" in politics have been combined in a single category as "interested" in the figure; those who responded "not very" or "not at all interested" have been combined and labeled as "not interested."

Source: Digital News Report 2021, https://reutersinstitute.politics.ox.ac.uk/digital-news-report/2021.

follow the news, the more likely they are to be knowledgeable about the public agenda and the political issues and affairs that are the substance of public life.[21] Some researchers now suggest that as media infrastructures have fragmented and become more varied, political interest has become more important as a deciding factor in how much news individuals consume.[22]

We think this divide around political interest deserves some additional attention because the issue is not just that news avoiders are less interested in politics but also that they tend to view themselves as less equipped to engage in political life—to effect change or make a difference in their political system. Political scientists call this attitude "political efficacy," or the "feeling that political and social change is possible, and that the individual citizen can play a part in bringing about this change."[23] In our U.S. survey data, we see a small though significant difference in the strength of these attitudes among news lovers compared to news avoiders (figure 2.7), who tend to view themselves as not only less interested in politics but somewhat less empowered as well.[24]

These differences may seem minor, but there is more to them than meets the eye. We have more to say about political efficacy and its relevance to the phenomenon of news avoidance in chapters 3 and 5. In particular, it is important to differentiate between what political scientists refer to as political efficacy's internal and external dimensions.[25] That is, for some people, a lack of political efficacy comes down to feeling internally as if they have little power or agency to create political change, whereas others see the source of the problem as external to themselves, viewing the political system as largely unresponsive to the public.[26] Divides along lines of political efficacy tend to be much larger in its internal dimensions. That said, in practice, just like age, gender, and class, the two dimensions of political efficacy are not easily reducible to distinct independent variables in surveys. Such variables are in fact interdependent and intertwined, at least in people's lived experiences.

* * *

This chapter has sought to set the stage for those that follow by answering a basic yet elusive question: "Who *are* consistent news avoiders?" Survey

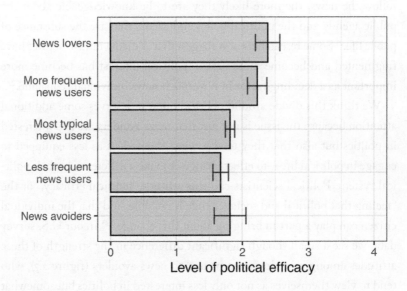

FIGURE 2.7. Political Efficacy. News lovers in the United States had somewhat higher levels of political efficacy compared to news avoiders and those who consumed news less frequently. Political efficacy is measured by averaging agreement or disagreement with three statements: "Sometimes politics and government seem so complicated that a person like me can't really understand what's going on"; "People like me don't have any say about what the government does"; and "Public officials don't care much what people like me think." Error bars reflect 95 percent confidence intervals for the subgroups.

Source: U.S. News Audiences Survey 2020.

data shows clear patterns around age, gender, socioeconomic class, and political interest, but only by looking more closely at individual lives—as we have tried to do with Sofía in Spain, Andrea in the United Kingdom, and William in the United States—do we get a sense of how and why these patterns occur. Importantly, the key point is not that all or even most young adults, women, or people from lower socioeconomic classes avoid news consistently but rather that consistent news avoidance is more common in these groups than among older adults, men, and the wealthy and more educated. The examples of Sofía, Andrea, and William further illustrate how news avoidance is a product of individuals' *identities, ideologies,* and *infrastructures* as well as how news avoidance contributes to *inequalities* on a macrolevel. News avoidance would be less worrisome if it were simply a matter of personal taste, but information is deeply linked to power and privilege. How well we are able to navigate the systems that shape our lives depends to a large extent on how much we know about how those systems are organized and how empowered we feel to change them. Paying attention to news can provide people with the keys to unlock those systems, but, as we have seen, groups more likely to avoid news consistently also tend to be those that are already relatively disadvantaged.

Of course, there are other aspects of inequality that we have not highlighted in this chapter, mostly because they did not come up as often in our interviews. Race and ethnicity, for example, so central a factor in American politics, does not appear to be a major driver of news avoidance. That was also the case in our survey data. That is, Black and Hispanic respondents were just as likely to be news avoiders or news lovers as white respondents. However, the fact that race and ethnicity are not important for differentiating between news avoiders and other types of news consumers does not mean that racial and ethnic identities do not matter for people's relationships to news. Indeed, as we show in later chapters, social identities rooted in race can be important lenses through which people make sense of their own media choices. The same can be said for many other aspects of identity, including religion, sexuality, culture, and place.

In many instances throughout this chapter, we have highlighted general tendencies—averages—to make some broad points about what types of people tend to avoid news and why those patterns persist. But it is worth underscoring that each of the individuals we interviewed cannot be easily reduced to a set of quantifiable variables. The best way to understand them and the way they think and feel about news is to listen closely to how they explain their news avoidance in their own words—to their media choice narratives, as we seek to capture in the next chapter.

3

WHY NEWS AVOIDERS SAY THEY DON'T USE NEWS

Paloma works a high-stress job at a Spanish high school and has a two-year-old at home. By evening, she said, "I have so little time that maybe I need those moments I can find, a few minutes to disconnect, . . . so for those ten minutes maybe I put on a video, so we can laugh a bit before bed." News, by contrast, felt like "taking on another worry"— often government corruption—and so, she asked, why worry about what you can't control? "I feel so incapable of changing anything and so frustrated about it," she said. "It's all a big cycle, isn't it? Have politicians stolen from us again? Ah! They've stolen from us again. . . . It's always the same. The situation doesn't change. The names change, but the news is the same." News was both mentally and emotionally draining and relentlessly tedious. The costs were clear, and the benefits imperceptible. On balance, she concluded, "I can't dedicate time to that now."

As we showed in the previous chapter, when it comes to *who* avoids news, some types of people avoid news more than others, which raises concerns about how news avoidance may exacerbate inequalities. We also introduced the idea that people's relationship to news is shaped by who they are (their identities), their beliefs (their ideologies), and how they access media and information (infrastructures). In chapters 4–6, we focus on those three factors one by one, but in this chapter we examine what news avoiders said when asked to explain in their own words why they consume so little news. In most cases, there was no single explanation for each person; they offered up a series of intersecting reasons. But the stories they told about why they opted for or against different types of media—their media choice narratives—illustrate how identities, ideologies, and infrastructures combine in different ways yet often lead people to similar conclusions about the value of news in their lives.

The reasons why people end up consuming certain kinds of media and not others can rarely be explained as a simple weighing of pros and cons. Habits and contextual factors come into play—such as what the people who live with us want to watch or listen to—that we do not necessarily think of easily when we are asked to explain our media diets. And yet, as the example of Paloma illustrates, when news avoiders explain in their own words the main reasons they avoid news, their explanations often *do* come out as cost–benefit analyses. They interweave folk theories about what they believe news is like and what it can offer them with commentary about the demands of their daily lives and details about their personalities, values, and preferences. As is true with all stories people tell about why they do things, the news avoiders undoubtedly smooth some edges and highlight certain facets while omitting others altogether. In other words, these narratives can't be accepted entirely at face value. And yet it is important to take seriously how people explain their own avoidance of news because their subjective understanding guides their behavior toward news, shapes their discussions about it, and likely affects choices made in the future.

In this chapter, we break down news avoiders' media choice narratives into their core components. Much of the chapter focuses on two kinds of costs that interviewees associated with consuming news: first, critiques involving the form and content of news, which we call "it's not me, it's news" explanations for avoiding news, and, second, the ways news avoiders felt their own circumstances or personalities made consuming news particularly difficult or unpleasant, which we call "it's not news, it's me" explanations. We then show how these two types of costs combine in news avoiders' assessments of whether news is relevant and worthwhile. After all, the determination of whether news stories really matter in a person's life—whether they are pertinent enough to be worthwhile—is really an evaluation of news content seen through the lens of individual wants, needs, and limitations.

In the final part of the chapter, we contrast news avoiders' narratives with those of the news lovers we interviewed in Iowa. We found that news lovers actually agreed with some of news avoiders' criticisms about news content but saw consuming it as less costly and more beneficial; they found it empowering despite its costs. News avoiders, by contrast, often felt the benefits of news were scarce or nonexistent. News, they argued, even if you could trust it, was mostly sad and scary, about distant matters that did not affect them and that they could not influence. How could that be worthwhile?

IT'S NOT ME, IT'S NEWS

Media observers and journalism professionals often assume that if people avoid news, it must be because they don't like news, and most research on news avoidance focuses on the characteristics of news that turn people off. As we show later in this chapter, that is only half the story (if that), but many news avoiders do have complaints about the form and content of news, and in this section we dissect the most common ones—namely, that news is unpleasant, untrustworthy, and impenetrable and that it inadequately represents certain groups. Although these critiques were sometimes related to news coverage of specific events, more often they were sweeping indictments of what news avoiders believed to be broad tendencies in news coverage. Their complaints were sometimes based on firsthand experience but were more often heavily reliant on secondhand information and impressions from passing exposure. They were, in short, folk theories. Insofar as folk theories of journalism capture beliefs, they are most obviously related to ideology, but when looked at closely, they are also expressions of what people believe about themselves and their perceptions of what kinds of information are accessible to them—their identities and infrastructures.

NEWS IS DOOM AND GLOOM

> I just don't want to be faced with the misery and the doom and gloom of constant negative news. There's no, like, inspirational stories.
>
> —Andrea (United Kingdom)

> For me, watching news is a synonym for misfortunes, for sorrows, and that's why I'm not interested in seeing it or knowing about it.
>
> —Celeste (Spain)

The folk theory that news is just "doom and gloom" (the Spanish equivalent is "penas y penurias," or sorrows and hardships), with few or no positive stories covered at all, was one of the most common complaints interviewees leveled against news in all three countries. Indeed, although the idea that news is too negative is widespread even among news consumers, surveys, including our own (figure 3.1), show that news avoiders are especially likely to say that news tends to depress or upset them.[1]

We found that news avoiders anticipated that news would drain them emotionally and cause them anxiety. They took preventative measures to avoid it, preferring entertaining or upbeat media that would help them recharge in the limited time they had. Some interviewees said gloomy news was not just sad but also manipulative—that news producers were "scaremongering" or "fearmongering," deliberately drumming up the terror, crime, and misery to attract larger audiences. For example, Carly (United States) explained that she preferred more hopeful stories, such as "we're cleaning up the oceans," but they seemed rare. The absence of more positive stories made her wonder, "Is it because things are more dismal right now, or is it because the media preys on the fearmongering, and when you're worried about how the outcome is going to go, you pay more close attention?"

Across all three countries, news avoiders seemed to feel *all* news was too doomy and gloomy, citing violent crime, suffering refugees, incessant

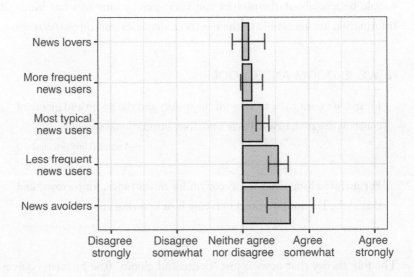

FIGURE 3.1. "News Tends to Upset or Depress Me." Rates at which different types of news users in the United States said they agreed with the statement that "news tends to upset or depress" them. Error bars reflect 95 percent confidence intervals for the subgroups.

Source: U.S. News Audiences Survey 2020.

political infighting, war, and natural catastrophes as examples. (No doubt COVID-19 would have topped this list had we continued interviews beyond February 2020.) That said, we did notice some country-specific trends. In the United Kingdom, where terrorist attacks had recently occurred in London and Manchester, terrorism was often mentioned as exhibit A of depressing news, while Spaniards spoke more about corruption. The coverage of such events seemed relentless, repetitive, and devoid of solutions or hope. For many Americans, cable news was the number-one culprit in disseminating such depressing news. Charlie (United States), a conservative interviewee who said in the screener interview that he consumed almost no news at all, actually consumed a great deal of alternative sources online. He recalled that he used to watch cable news all afternoon but stopped at one point, explaining, "I just realized it just made me unhappy; . . . there's only so much negativity you can have in your life before it just beats you down. At some point, you just got to be, like, 'I'm just going to remove that.'"

NEWS IS UNTRUSTWORTHY

"You can't trust it" was another common reason interviewees gave for avoiding news. This, too, is consistent with survey research: distrust of news content is one of the most common reasons given for news avoidance worldwide and the top reason in some countries.[2] Our own U.S. survey results (figure 3.2) showed that the people who consume the least news were the most skeptical and distrusting of it, even news they typically used or encountered on social media.

Interviewees saw "you can't always trust news" as something all reasonable people just know to be true. In that regard, it is a classic folk theory, a belief not necessarily based on firsthand or any other kind of evidence but thought of as commonsense. Most interviewees had never met a reporter or been in a news story, but for those who had, the experience did not shake and in some cases just confirmed their sense that journalists are not to be trusted—a finding that is consistent with prior research on ordinary people's interactions with reporters.[3] Alaina (United Kingdom), for example, had agreed to speak to a British tabloid about her sex life in exchange for money. She recalled that "when it was published, it was stuff you hadn't even said. Like they said my boyfriend owned an electrical company. I said, 'I wish he did because I wouldn't be living here.' I never once said he owned an electrical—he's a delivery driver. That's a big difference." Alaina said that appearing in an inaccurate news story just confirmed what she already knew: "I think there's always been that stigma of 'don't always believe what you read in the paper.'"

Some interviewees struggled to articulate the reasons why they distrusted news, but their intuition told them something was off. As Nicole (United Kingdom) put it, when she read newspapers, she just felt "distrust, deep in my gut." When interviewees across the three countries could articulate their

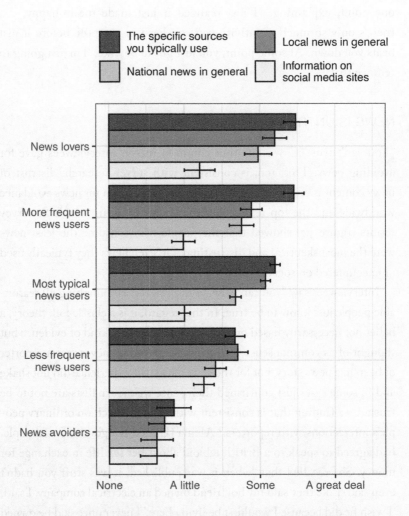

FIGURE 3.2. "When It Comes to Reporting the News, How Much Do You Trust the Following?." Rates at which different types of news users in the United States said they trusted sources of news and information. Error bars reflect 95 percent confidence intervals for the subgroups.

Source: U.S. News Audiences Survey 2020.

reasoning, they said the main evidence that news outlets could not be trusted was that they reported the same stories differently. Our U.S. survey findings indicate that this sentiment is not unique to news avoiders, but it is much less common among heavy consumers of news (figure 3.3).

As Nico (Spain) explained, "Each [news outlet] is always going to lean one way—*El Mundo* will go to one side, *El País* will lean to the other side; . . . each one is going to say what's in their interest." Note that Nico sees the difference in reporting by two of Spain's national newspapers as evidence of bias "in their own interest." We heard similar sentiments consistently in all three countries: interviewees did not see the differences between news outlets' ways of reporting the same story as justifiable— say, as evidence of different approaches, human error, or even legitimate

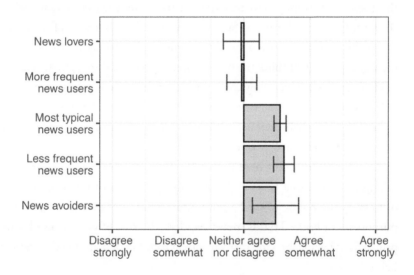

FIGURE 3.3. "When Different Sources of News Give Different Accounts of What's Going On, It Makes Me Less Likely to Trust All News Sources." News avoiders and more typical news users said they saw disagreement between sources as a sign that all news is untrustworthy, whereas news lovers did not. Error bars reflect 95 percent confidence intervals for the subgroups.

Source: U.S. News Audiences Survey 2020.

disagreements on ideological grounds. No, they saw different versions of the same story as evidence that news is *intentionally* distorted to manipulate people to serve narrow and sometimes shady agendas. That said, we did find some differences between countries regarding trust. In some cases, especially in the United Kingdom, where many news avoiders had tabloid papers in mind when they talked about news, interviewees said that commercial interests were the main cause of distortion and bias in the news. More often, however, in all three countries interviewees said news was distorted by political interests, which we discuss in depth in chapter 5.

In the most extreme expression of the folk theory that news is untrustworthy, interviewees spoke of "cover-ups." Caitlin, a former cop in the United Kingdom, said her years on the police force had exposed her to a great deal of corruption in general and taught her that much news was "what the government want you to hear, the way they want you to think, and what they want you to believe." In Spain, many described intentional efforts to divert the public's attention away from potentially damaging stories. José (Spain) explained, "I think the media covers up a lot of things, that, because of ideology or whatever, they cover up a lot of things so maybe you only get half the information, you never get all the information. I think they keep some things for their own benefit because the government doesn't want it known or different people don't want it known."

The important point here is that "everyone knows" that distortion is taking place and that news is slanted *on purpose*, either to increase profits or to sway the public toward a false interpretation of events for political purposes—or both. That is, news avoiders' distrust of news is not borne primarily of having seen too many incorrect facts but of doubting the *motives* behind news.

NEWS TAKES TOO MUCH MENTAL EFFORT: IT'S DIFFICULT, BORING, TEDIOUS, AND TRIVIAL

Many news avoiders also felt that the way news is presented made it difficult to understand. Some said they were not educated or clever enough to understand news (as we discuss later), but other interviewees put the blame squarely on news itself, in particular what they felt was the cryptic way political and economic news is presented. For example, Aria, a Spanish college student, said, "I look at the news, and it seems like they're explaining to an economist or a politician, . . . and there are things I don't understand, so I say, 'Why am I going to watch the news if they explain it so you don't understand?'" Other interviewees said they felt traditional news assumed too much prior knowledge. As Gracie (United Kingdom) put it, "You're expected to know about all of these people, and it [the news] doesn't explain who they are, so, again, it's not accessible."

Many of these same interviewees also said they found news boring and monotonous. Here complaints about news content merged with complaints about the format, which they said was too long, repetitive, and impenetrable. They argued that news always covered the same types of stories— mostly depressing rehashes of politics or crime—and repeated the biggest stories ad nauseum. For example, recall from chapter 2 that twenty-year-old Sofía (Spain) wondered how TV anchors do not die of boredom. She explained, "In Spain it's always the same: when it rains, they bring up the same tiny villages that aren't prepared for rain that have flooded, and then, yes, the politicians, which is also monotonous. If I watch and really listen to it, it seems so boring, so boring." Nicole (United Kingdom) said she had gotten sick of hearing constant news about the Manchester terror attacks on the radio and ended up turning it off. It upset her, and "it was on every single day, and it was on every news bulletin on the radio."

Like Nicole, interviewees often named the biggest news stories of the day as prime examples of news that seemed depressing, incessant, and constantly the same and therefore rarely worth following closely. In the United Kingdom, Brexit seemed like a broken record. Spaniards saw the Catalan independence issue and political corruption as never-ending. In the United States, both liberal and conservative news avoiders were sick of political fighting over Trump. So although this explanation took somewhat different forms in different countries, news avoiders consistently found news just plain tedious *as well as* depressing and mentally taxing. Why put all that effort into understanding what was going on if you already knew how it would (never) end? Gonzalo (Spain) made that point, comparing news to the fictional TV series he preferred: "I mean, a thriller creates suspense; you say, 'Damn, how might this turn out? How might that turn out?' The news, in the end, you know how it's probably going to end . . . with those people who are robbing or those who are killing. . . . If you've watched two hundred episodes of a series, and they don't tell you anything, if they're still showing the same plot and they don't tell you anything different, and they don't go anywhere with it, I turn it off."

NEWS POORLY REPRESENTS "PEOPLE LIKE ME"

A growing body of journalism research shows that minority groups are often underrepresented in newsrooms and news content and that minority communities often feel misunderstood and misrepresented by mainstream journalists.[4] We found some evidence consistent with these patterns. Some interviewees said they were turned off by news because it poorly represents certain people, often people like themselves. Depending on the interviewee, they said people of color, young people, "locals," conservatives, or people suffering abroad are not portrayed fairly or are not portrayed at all. Jane, for example, a Black news avoider in the United Kingdom, cited the "denial of racism" as the most important problem facing her country. She specifically blamed the news media and "the way that things are portrayed and the way that people are portrayed" as a major source of the problem. Some interviewees had strong spiritual identities and felt that basically all news is a distraction from that vastly more important spiritual path. As Bruce, an Evangelical Christian in Iowa, put it, "The world is slowly falling apart and crumbling due to sin," so news seemed both depressing and trivial by comparison.

However, critiques of how news portrayed specific groups were rarely the core of news avoiders' media choice narratives, and these critiques came up just as often in our interviews with news lovers. This result may have been due in part to the fact that most people in our sample of interviewees were not from marginalized or historically underrepresented communities. As we explain in more detail in the next chapter, some of these identities—being a Black American, for example—absolutely shaped how interviewees experienced and interpreted news. However, they were less often stated reasons for why interviewees said they consumed more or less of it.

* * *

As noted from the outset of this section, each of the critiques about the form and content of news, like the ones we have discussed here—that news is too depressing, untrustworthy, unintelligible, and misrepresentative—is usually interwoven in coherent media choice narratives rather than singled out as *the* reason someone avoids news. Irene (Spain) illustrates well how a range of complaints about news content can tumble out in a coherent litany:

> I think [the news] is always the same. In my view, it's all super negative, and each of us has enough negative stuff already with the things that can affect us more directly. Maybe my mindset is selfish; I don't know. But it's always war, always politicians doing whatever they want, always stealing, always murders that you don't understand. I also don't love sports, and, well, the weather could save it. The weather, yes, is important—to know what to wear, if you're going to get wet or you're not going to get wet, to see the condition the highways are in. But as for the general information, as I was telling you, I think the media is always very focused on the same thing, very repetitive, and it's also my personal issue that I think they are doctored in some way.

IT'S NOT NEWS, IT'S ME

The critiques about news described in the previous section integrate various folk theories about what news is like, theories that are expressions of who people are, what they believe about the world, and their perceptions about the availability of different forms of information—that is, their identities, ideologies, and infrastructures. In some cases, however, interviewees' media choice narratives focused squarely on themselves and how aspects of who they were and how they lived their lives made news unappealing relative to other media available to them. In that regard, their stories were explicitly about identities and infrastructures. They said they avoided news more because of their own personalities and life circumstances than because of anything about the news itself.

Take an exchange with Paco, a Spanish father of two little girls and news avoider who had been struggling to find work for more than a year. His wife worked full-time, and he managed their home:

RP: Well, do you think the news pays enough attention to people like you?

Paco: I think so, the news does. The problem in this case, I think, is the individual himself—the opposite.

RP: [laughs] Then it's not the content. You don't have a problem with the content or anything.

Paco: No, no . . .

RP: Then if you had to say what are the main reasons you don't consume more news, what would you say?

Paco: Well, evidently, my family. The attention to my family. Fundamentally. That is, the day has twenty-four hours. If it maybe had two or three more, I'm not saying I wouldn't [consume more news].

Paco did not have a single bad thing to say about the news. He felt he should probably be more informed but had trouble finding the time. As he summed up the problem, it wasn't news—it was him. We refer to explanations like this as "it's not news, it's me" reasons for avoiding news. They are rarely discussed in studies of news avoidance, which tend to focus much more on which aspects of news content people dislike. Surveys rarely give news avoiders the option to choose, say, "I am an anxious person" as their reason for skipping news. But we found that people blamed themselves for avoiding news *at least* as often as they blamed news. In the following subsections, we dissect the "it's not news, it's me" explanations that came up most often in our interviews, beginning with personality factors and followed by news avoiders' life circumstances.

PERSONALITY FACTORS

Many news avoiders described themselves and their aversion to news as in part a product of their own deep-seated proclivities and personal characteristics. Interviewees often said they had just never been interested in news, that they had always found it deadly dull. It is hard to say what "interest in news" really means or where it comes from. As we discuss further in the next chapter, preferences are constructed over time through a combination of nature and nurture. But interviewees often saw "interest in news" as baked in from birth. In the most striking cases, they contrasted themselves and their own lack of interest in news with siblings and other family members—even twins—who had "always" been drawn to current events. For example, Daniel (United States) recalled that for as long as he could remember, his twin brother and his mother had shared an interest in discussing news and politics, while he "kept [his] nose out of it." In that regard, he and his brother were "completely opposite." He explained that, "personality-wise, I'm the type that just, again, I don't draw myself into it. . . . I'm not lazy, but I'm pretty laid-back, and stuff like that just doesn't draw my interest."

Some interviewees felt that people who enjoyed news were smarter or more intellectually curious than they were. Brian (United States), for example, contrasted his own abilities with his wife's intellectual capacity and curiosity: "My wife, she's smart; . . . she's definitely more of the news person, and she retained—she can read something and actually remember what it says. Me—I'll read it and try to regurgitate it. And I'm, like, I only get about probably 5 percent of it." When we asked him why he thought his wife was more interested in news than he was, he offered, "She just likes to learn. She's a learner; she likes to learn. She likes to pick up new information." By contrast, he felt exhausted after work and preferred not to have to "decipher" news.

News avoiders like Brian felt it was clear that for some other people "deciphering" news was not the mentally draining chore that it was for them, but they were not always sure whether the problem was them or the news itself. Some did see clearly that the problem was cumulative: not following news in the past made it harder for them to understand it now. Recall Gracie (United Kingdom) from earlier in the chapter, who said she felt news expected audiences to know too much already. She later acknowledged that her own lack of interest had left her ill-equipped to understand the new information being reported, concluding resignedly, "I spent thirty years not really paying much attention to the news. There's so much to catch up on that it blows my mind, that I don't understand what's going on. So I sort of gave up really."

Was it a lack of curiosity or interest in the world that prompted the news avoidance? Many weren't quite sure. When asked why she thought some people were so much more interested in news than she was, Jodie (United Kingdom) was conflicted. "It's not that I'm not interested in what goes on in the world," she said before adding, "I suppose I don't show it very much, do I?" She eventually concluded that maybe news lovers were just more interested in "everything outside your own little world, I guess." Indeed, as we explain later, news lovers expressed many of the same sentiments but in reverse: they thought of themselves as congenitally curious, with a kind of compulsion to be informed about a wide range of topics that they contrasted with the attitude of the more news avoidant people they knew.

Many news avoiders also said they avoided news because they suffered from anxiety. Based just on our interviews, we cannot prove that news avoiders are categorically more anxious than the average person or non–news avoiders, but we can say without a doubt that they *perceived* themselves to be more sensitive and anxious than most, and they often said those traits made avoiding news not just a preference but also a necessity.[5] They felt they needed to be especially careful to conserve their emotional energy, which news otherwise sapped. This claim went hand in glove with complaints that news was too negative. As Marta (Spain) explained, "I don't know if I [avoid news] partly also to protect myself, knowing how I am.

Sometimes I get anxious easily. I mean to say that I overthink things. So there are a lot of things I prefer not to know in order to be calmer."

Some news avoiders were less certain about the connection between their anxiety and their avoidance of news, but they said managing anxiety was a big part of their lives. Some were on medication for it. Others recalled specific moments when a particular news story triggered their anxiety, thus proving that they were better off avoiding news altogether. Here the intersection between negative news content and personality factors was especially clear. For example, Haylie (United Kingdom) recalled a time when she was reading the free *Metro* newspaper on a bus in Manchester: "I remember there was a story that was about this woman who'd been kept in a cellar for ten, fifteen years, and it just was making me feel so anxious. My husband said to me, 'I'm banning you from reading newspapers.' To be fair, it did help me because I stopped reading bad news."

STRESSFUL AND DEMANDING CIRCUMSTANCES

When you're trying to wind down or trying to be there for your family, that emotional burden is the last thing that I want.

—Carly (United States)

Sometimes news avoiders said it was not their personalities (or not *only* their personalities) but their current life circumstances that made consuming news difficult or unappealing. Here, too, we cannot say whether their circumstances actually *were* more stressful than the average person's circumstances—although, compared to the news lovers we interviewed, news avoiders' lives often appeared that way. The relevant point is that news avoiders in all three countries perceived themselves to be under a great deal of stress. They were often juggling multiple jobs and children, unemployed or overworked, and managing strained finances. Our interviews underscored the extent to which gender—a factor we introduced in chapter 2—played a role here: working mothers who had heavy caretaking responsibilities at home were the quintessential example of this phenomenon. Take Dion

63

(United States), who said the most important issue in her life was "keeping my kid alive." While juggling around-the-clock medical care for her special-needs daughter, she also worked as an in-home aide. "I'm poor as hell," she said. "I work when I can—when I have a nurse for my daughter. It sucks." Tellingly, she contrasted her work, which she found exhausting but fulfilling, with what she thought about news—the opposite, "not rewarding but draining."

Like Dion, many news avoiders said "no time" was one of the main reasons they avoided news. Our U.S. survey shows a strikingly similar result. News consumption was highly correlated with whether respondents felt they had "enough time to keep up with the news" (figure 3.4).

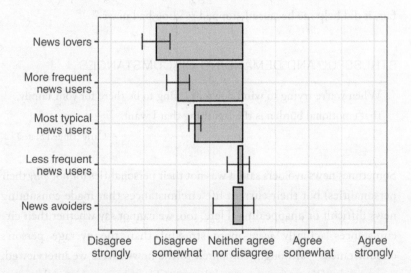

FIGURE 3.4. "I Generally Don't Have Enough Time to Keep Up with the News." Although most respondents disagreed that they generally did not have enough time to keep up with news, less frequent news users and news avoiders were the least likely to disagree. Error bars reflect 95 percent confidence intervals for the subgroups.

Source: U.S. News Audiences Survey 2020.

On its face, this pattern was clear, but the story became more complicated in interviews. Patricia (United States), when asked to sum up the main reason she didn't pay more attention to news, said simply, "Time. I think it takes time," adding, "I'd rather be doing other things. I'd rather be . . . I think you work so much and you're away from home so much, when you are home, you just want to chill. You don't want to hear anything. You just kind of want to be in your own little world. I've got other stuff I'd rather do." Like Patricia, interviewees often allowed that they did have *some* free time, but in coming home at the end of a stressful day, they preferred to use it on activities that they found relaxing or rejuvenating so they could get on with their responsibilities the next day. In other words, "no time" was often shorthand for "I would rather do something less draining and more gratifying with the limited time I have."

Although some interviewees said, like Patricia, that they preferred to tune out all media in their leisure time, in many cases interviewees said they chose to spend that time on other forms of media—say, watching a movie on Netflix or cartoons with their children or scrolling through social media. In the early days of the internet, the political scientist Markus Prior predicted that as media choices proliferated, audiences for news would become increasingly stratified. Those who preferred entertainment would turn away from news because they had access to other options, whereas those who preferred news could consume more of it than ever before.[6] Our findings are consistent with Prior's, showing how changing infrastructures may alter how some people relate to news. However, such preferences did not emerge all on their own; they were often a reaction to stressful life circumstances or could be chalked up to different personality traits.

* * *

As was the case in the previous section, the "it's not news, it's me" explanations usually occurred in tandem with one another. Whether due to an anxiety-prone personality or anxiety-producing circumstances—two explanations for news avoidance that were not easy for interviewees or us to disentangle—news avoiders said they felt overwhelmed in a way that news made worse. And they were not that interested in it anyway! Raquel (Spain) illustrates that attitude well. When we asked her to summarize the main reasons she avoided news, she said, "Well, look, for lack of time, for my way of being above all, because I worry too much about other people, and I think that the more I find out, the more I worry. So I prefer not to. That is, in the end, it's more for lack of time, really, and because I'm not interested."

DECIDING WHAT'S WORTHWHILE AND RELEVANT: IT'S BOTH NEWS *AND* ME

At the end of our interviews, we gave news avoiders the opportunity to recap what they saw as the *main* reasons they avoided news. Almost all of them gave some version of "I don't think it's worthwhile," much like what Raquel said. Indeed, as we have shown, the "no time for news" explanation is basically a claim that news is not worth the time and energy it demands compared to other available options. In this section, we explore that claim further. Ultimately, we found that the question of whether news is worthwhile is intertwined with the question of whether it is relevant, and both of these concepts lie at the intersection of the two different kinds of narratives we have outlined. Both worthwhileness and relevance are assessments of news content in relation to one's life. The reason for news avoidance is not just news or just me. It's both.[7]

Determining whether something is worthwhile involves a weighing of costs and benefits—although, as we noted at the outset of the chapter, there are often other factors, even subtle contextual factors, that influence our choices as well. As should be clear from the previous sections, news avoiders found news costly in terms of time and effort in part because the content was depressing and intellectually demanding. Low reserves of time and emotional energy (whether because the avoiders' circumstances were particularly stressful or because the avoiders were particularly anxious people or both) made the costs seem higher still. We can now add that they felt they were getting few benefits from news in exchange for its many costs. It seemed like poor value for their investment—as Dion said, it was draining but not rewarding. They did sometimes say they missed out on *social* benefits related to following news, as we discuss further in the next chapter, but rarely did news avoiders say they saw *informational* benefits that might come from consuming news more regularly.

We think interviewees dismissed the informational value of news for a few main reasons. First, they said the "big stuff"—the really big events and issues such as terrorist attacks—would come across their radar in other ways. They did not need to consume news directly from traditional sources for this information (see chapter 6 for more on this belief). Second, they believed most of the information covered in news did not directly affect them anyway, and they therefore dismissed it as irrelevant to their lives. As Melanie (United States) put it, "Not a whole ton of it affects me directly, and sometimes you just get so busy that you just can only focus on what affects you directly and how to change that."

In theory, a person could find information relevant even if it does not directly affect them—scholars have found that news can seem relevant to people if it is of interest to other people in their social circles, for example.[8] But we found that most news avoiders, given their limited time and energy, were like Melanie: they deliberately drew a fairly narrow circle of relevance around themselves. If they were going to commit the effort to seek out, decipher, and digest new information, it needed to be about issues that were directly related to their immediate needs: cancer drugs if they were cancer survivors, local schools if they were parents, policies about student debt if they were recent graduates. News, by contrast, seemed to focus on distant matters that had little if any connection to their lives. That focus included international events, which interviewees often said seemed sad—wars, refugee crises, and other catastrophes—but of little connection to them, so the news stories about these events were of little practical value to them. As Antonio (Spain) observed, "There's no reason to know what's just happened in China or wherever so you can go about your normal life." Meanwhile, national news, including some of the most widely covered subjects in each of the three countries at the time, such as Brexit, Catalan independence, and Trump's first impeachment trial, also seemed irrelevant to news avoiders—mostly political infighting that interviewees said would not affect them and therefore was not worth their already strained attention.

Moreover, interviewees almost always said they could not change those issues. As Paloma put it at the outset of this chapter, they felt "incapable of changing anything," so what was the point? Other researchers have found that some people feel that avoiding news and politics helps them conserve energy to address matters closer to home that they feel they actually can affect.[9] What we found was similar: the news avoiders we talked to preferred to put their energy toward things they felt they could influence. In fact, some were quite involved in their communities. For example, Joanna (United States), a young mother who was an active leader in her local home-schooling community, dismissed Trump's impeachment trial as "outside of the realm of my concern." Like many interviewees, Joanna cared about what she could control and potentially take meaningful action to change. She contrasted herself with her husband, who worked for an international company and followed the news more closely. She explained, "Geographically, my sphere of influence, or sphere of interest or control, is a lot smaller. That kind of stuff just is extra noise, whereas to him it's more pertinent."

Because news avoiders so frequently talked about their own anxieties and worries about the various dangers they perceived in the world, we included a question in our survey of American news audiences that asked respondents how concerned they were about "how dangerous the world is becoming." We were surprised to find that news avoiders were the *least* concerned (figure 3.5)—evidence, we think, that news avoiders' own consumption practices may have the desired impact. Here our findings add to a growing body of evidence that limiting exposure to news does appear to be associated with less worrying.[10]

Indeed, we heard repeatedly from interviewees in all three countries that "ignorance is bliss,"[11] and in their experience it appeared to ring true. News was not worthwhile because it would make them feel bad and had little relevance in their lives. They were happy in their "own little bubble" or "own little world," as multiple interviewees concluded. For example, Jennifer

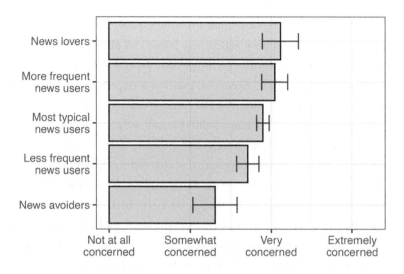

FIGURE 3.5. Concerned About . . . "How Dangerous the World Is Becoming?." News avoiders were the least likely to say they were concerned about "how dangerous the world is becoming" even as they tended to describe themselves as anxious. Error bars reflect 95 percent confidence intervals for the subgroups.

Source: U.S. News Audiences Survey 2020.

(United Kingdom), who was expecting a baby, explained that news was only ever about sickening politics or terrorism. She concluded, "I don't really want to know about how terrible this world is because, like I say, I'm about to bring a child into this world, so I quite like to live in my own little bubble and imagine that this is quite, you know, a nice place to live."

NEWS LOVERS' MEDIA CHOICE NARRATIVES

News avoiders' media choice narratives are drawn in sharp relief when juxtaposed with those of news lovers. Consider Jerry and Clint, two news lovers who live in Iowa. Both spend hours each day consuming news in various forms. Jerry is a retired small-town newspaper publisher. Clint is a working father of two, busy with a new home and plans for his upcoming wedding. Clint said he focuses on the positive aspects of even the most negative stories. He recalled, "Even 9/11, that was a tragedy, but I still liked to hear about it and liked to see how the country came together on the news." He was interested in "the story behind it and why it happened and who orchestrated those kinds of things," but, he said, "I don't want to focus on that. I'd rather focus on the people that it affected and how they're rebuilding." Jerry had a similar perspective. He contrasted himself with left-wing friends who had turned away from news after the U.S. election in 2016. Sure, the result was upsetting, but, "if anything, I probably read as much or more at that time rather than divorcing myself from it." After all, he added, "not reading the news isn't going to make it go away."

As the examples of Clint and Jerry illustrate, the news lovers we interviewed did not think news was perfect. They acknowledged some of the same critiques that news avoiders gave about news, especially that news could be overwhelmingly negative. But their response was not to avoid news. In some cases, like Jerry's, it was to consume even more. Why?

Our interviews did not provide a simple explanation, but news lovers certainly perceived news consumption as less costly than news avoiders did. On close examination, it was clear that the way they saw themselves—their identities—played a role here. Many said they were congenitally curious, and, unlike the news avoiders, very few described themselves as especially anxious people. They also had greater resources at their disposal and more formal schooling than news avoiders, and they were typically older, perhaps even retired (in line with the patterns we discuss in chapter 2). Although some had stressful jobs and demanding home lives, in general they did not seem to perceive their life circumstances as overwhelmingly stressful the way the news avoiders did. Some even made that point explicitly. For example, Frank (United States), a social studies teacher, compared his own life to that of a recently divorced colleague who was caring for a quadriplegic son. "I say, 'You know what? My stress ain't your stress.' I'm not married, I don't have kids, so I kind of just get myself up in the morning, and away I go. My biggest irritant of the day is if the cat throws up on the floor." Like many news lovers, Frank found fitting news into his daily routine quite easy.

In addition to perceiving lower costs to consuming news than news avoiders did, news lovers also perceived more benefits of various kinds, so on balance news was not just worthwhile, it was very good value. Fred, a farmer in Iowa who saw local, national, and international news as potentially relevant to his business, illustrates that point well. Note that not only does he see the news as useful for his daily life, but he also perceives the costs of getting that information as low because of his routine and his own confidence in his ability to sift through various sources of information and find the most worthwhile elements:

> I get up at five-thirty or six, and I spend a half an hour at least going through the internet looking at different news sources, farm news, what's going on in the world, the coronavirus, or whatever—all of those things because I like to be informed and know what's going on so I don't get blindsided by stuff. And I'm a fast reader, and I comprehend it quite well. Again, I'm not trying to blow my own horn, but I can. I can read fast, and so a half an hour, maybe forty-five minutes, and I've got the news that I think is going to affect me today.

As encapsulated here, news lovers like Fred felt they got informational benefits from news that made it worth the (relatively reduced) costs of consuming news. In Fred's case, even very distant events literally affected his livelihood, but news lovers often made those connections even when the effects were less obvious. In this fundamental way, news lovers' beliefs about the world and their place in it differed from those of news avoiders: they embraced an ideology of interconnectedness that news consumption both fit and fed. Unlike news avoiders, whose circle of relevance was centered on things "close to home," news lovers saw connections—or potential connections—between even very distant matters and their own lives. *Those matters, too,* felt close to home and therefore relevant. Jennifer (United States), for example, dismissed the idea that international stories might not affect her. She explained, "I want to be somewhat aware of how a choice that is happening in Alaska might affect people in Iowa. Or what's happening in the Philippines and how that can trickle into my life in one way or another. . . . I'm curious." She concluded, "I think that all the stories can affect you. I mean, we're a very global community now."

Some news lovers felt they were getting not just informational but also emotional benefits from news because it reaffirmed that feeling of connection to a wider world. Randall (United States), for example, was one of the relatively few news lovers we interviewed who described a life every bit as stressful as many news avoiders'. Unemployed, struggling with alcoholism, and panic-stricken over multiple close family members having been recently diagnosed with life-threatening cancer, Randall not only made time for news but also found it reassuring. He had multiple televisions in his house tuned in to cable news at all times. Unable to drive and stuck at home most days, he said, "I feel that I'm not part of the world, and I'm missing out on what's going on," so he found the work of journalists personally gratifying. With reverence, he said, "They open up the world for us."

In contrast to news avoiders, news lovers like Randall felt more anxious if they missed news than if they consumed it, concerned they were missing out on important events. Our survey data bore out that conclusion as well: news avoiders in the United States were far less likely than other groups to say they felt "disconnected from the world" when they did not follow news, whereas news lovers said the reverse (figure 3.6).

News lovers sometimes agreed with news avoiders that they could not *directly* influence current events very much, but they had a deep confidence that *knowing* about those events could help them take meaningful action, be it to avoid problems, educate others, or make informed political choices. They took comfort in such beliefs. Debra (United States), for example, a single mother who "wore all the hats" at work and at home, said news was an important practical tool for her. She explained, "I just don't like surprises in my life. So if I can head those off—like consuming news about a crash, so I can avoid it."

Whereas news avoiders considered news to be a lot of irrelevant but upsetting information about matters they could not control, news lovers said the information helped them take informed action and made them feel more

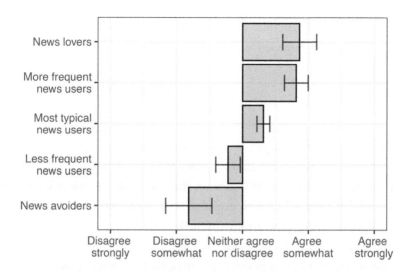

FIGURE 3.6. "I Feel Disconnected from the World When I Don't Follow the News." News avoiders were significantly less likely than other groups to say they felt "disconnected" from the world when they didn't follow the news. Error bars reflect 95 percent confidence intervals for the subgroups.

Source: U.S. News Audiences Survey 2020.

in control even when they could not. Take this final assessment from Barb (United States), one of the few news lovers we interviewed who said she suffered from anxiety. An artist who was on long-term disability because a car accident had left her with chronic pain, she took comfort in her news routine but also highly valued the information about national and world affairs that she got from it and the sense of control and connection it provided her:

RP: Have you ever thought about giving up news?
Barb: Yes. Yes. I can't. I need to know what's going on. I feel like if I don't know what's going on, then. . . . I don't know, somehow I feel like I have more control when I do know what's going on, even

though I don't. But in my brain somewhere, it makes me feel like, "Oh OK, we got this." You know what I mean? But I don't know. I think if I didn't know. . . . Ignorance is not bliss for me. I need to know.

* * *

The purpose of this chapter was to explore the main reasons news avoiders say they avoid news when they are given the opportunity to talk at length about it. The media choice narratives that emerged combine folk theories about what news is like with explanations rooted more explicitly in news avoiders' beliefs about who they are and how their circumstances make different forms of media accessible and attractive or not. These narratives exist at the intersection of their identities, their ideologies, and the infrastructures available to them. Ultimately, we found that news lovers said they felt more empowered and in control of their lives when they consumed more news. Even news of distant matters felt relevant, and consuming it felt easy, so it was worth the time and energy required. News avoiders felt the opposite: they saw news as mentally and emotionally draining and as providing little return on the investment because it was mostly about distant matters that would not affect them and that they could not affect. News took time and energy away from more pressing demands or more gratifying activities that would help them relax and recharge. All told, they felt more disempowered than empowered by it.

We have shown here how news avoiders' explanations for why they consume so little news are deeply intertwined with identity, ideology, and infrastructure. Each of the next three chapters focuses on one of these factors in greater depth, exploring some of the reasons for news avoidance that are often harder for individuals to articulate but that become clear if we look at patterns across many interviews. We begin in the next chapter by exploring how the ways we grow up and the groups we belong to as adults—our social identities—can shape our relationships to news.

4

IDENTITIES

How Our Relationships to Communities
Shape News Avoidance

Brenna (United Kingdom) is a consistent news avoider who lives with her partner and two small children. She works as an administrator for construction sites in Leeds. Her granddad watches news but rarely discusses it with the family. Since her mother never picked up the habit, Brenna was not exposed to much news as a child. As an adult, she explained, she rarely finds herself in social or professional situations where she needs to know about news: "I don't really do owt [anything] really news based to need to know. Because, like I say, none of my friends kind of keep up with [news], so it's not like I'd improve my relationships, my friendships with them, knowing more about the news because it isn't something they follow, either. And for my work I don't do anything where I need to know. I work with builders and, you know, road diggers and stuff, so I don't really need to know about, like, current affairs with them either."

As we discussed in the previous chapter, when people are asked to explain why they choose to consume or avoid news, they tell stories—what we called "media choice narratives"—about how they weigh the costs and benefits of consuming news. In those stories, they explain their news habits by interweaving folk theories of journalism with observations about their own personalities, life circumstances, beliefs, and other media options—aspects of their identities, ideologies, and infrastructures. The way people fit those pieces together leads them to different conclusions about the worth-whileness of news in their lives: dire coverage of far-off-seeming matters may not be a priority for a working mother with little time and emotional energy to burn. Meanwhile, a homebound and self-described political junkie may find news an energizing hobby that helps them feel connected to the world.

But thinking about news consumption or avoidance as an individual choice can take us only so far. In this chapter, we explore in greater depth how identity, specifically *social identity*, shapes the way we relate to news. By "social identity," we mean the aspects of who people are that are shaped by the different groups to which they belong.[1] Understanding this aspect of news consumption is key, as the example of Brenna illustrates, because the practice of following news is not simply the solitary act of watching a television program or reading a newspaper. We learn about news from people around us in childhood and in the groups we belong to throughout adulthood. In different ways and to varying degrees for different people, news is embedded in social relations as a topic of conversation, a point of connection, and a shared practice in which many of us seek to make sense of the world together.

We begin this chapter by exploring how our interviewees recalled news in their childhoods. The notion that early socialization influences political and media habits is not a new finding, and our research reaffirms that it matters.[2] News avoiders such as Brenna were more likely than news lovers to say they grew up in homes without news. When news was present, their complicated, sometimes negative memories often contrasted with the more idyllic scenes recalled by news lovers. We also explore how gender, race, religion, and social class can influence how we are socialized to news and how we understand our relationship to it. Our habits and beliefs about news can also be ways we express our identification with some groups and our distinction from others.

In the second half of the chapter, we explore how these processes continue in adulthood. We (somewhat unexpectedly) found that ongoing social pressure to consume news as an adult may play an even more important role than early socialization in determining whether someone sustains a news habit later in life. Both our interviews and our survey data highlight the importance of belonging to what we call "news communities"—professional, social, or family groups that exert strong pressure on members to be informed about news. These communities help people keep up with current events and reinforce the idea that doing so is part of their civic duty.

News communities are not the *only* factor that determines whether someone will become a regular news consumer. A news lover with a deep personal passion for news is likely to engage with it regardless of their social circles. But people who are less enthusiastic about news are unlikely to invest the time and resources necessary to stay informed about current events unless they are enmeshed in a community of other news users who expect them to do so.

EARLY SOCIALIZATION TO NEWS

Scholars have known for decades that the ways we engage with news and politics are shaped by early experiences, especially behaviors modeled for us by parents and other influential figures.[3] Studies continue to show that seeing news consumed at home and having discussions about news and current events with parents in "news rich" (often socioeconomically advantaged) homes increases the likelihood that a person will grow up to consume news.[4] Surprisingly, that is true even if parents engage with news on digital devices, where the news itself is presumably less visible to children compared to sharing a physical newspaper over breakfast or watching the evening news on TV together as a family.[5] And early socialization occurs beyond the home: exposure to news and politics at school and in conversations with peers also makes it more likely that people will consume news later in life.[6]

Consistent with past research on early socialization to news, our survey of Americans showed that the less people recalled discussing news with influential people while they were growing up, especially their parents, the less they consumed news as adults (figure 4.1).

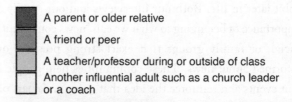

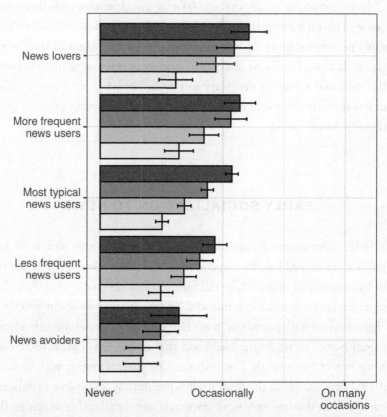

FIGURE 4.1. When You Were Growing Up . . . "Did Anyone Talk to You About Events in the News?." Rates at which different groups of U.S. news consumers recalled having discussed events in the news when growing up. Error bars reflect 95 percent confidence intervals for the subgroups.

Source: U.S. News Audiences Survey 2020.

As we explain next, the interviews we conducted add nuance to these survey findings, revealing that many news avoiders were exposed to news at home but had mixed feelings about those memories—and complex interpretations of how they had been influenced by them. We then go on to explore how different facets of social identity—namely race, religion, gender, and social class—surfaced in how interviewees recalled their early encounters with news.

CONTRASTING NARRATIVES ABOUT
NEWS IN CHILDHOOD

Recall Andrea from chapter 2, the thirty-eight-year-old full-time house cleaner in Leeds. She described several reasons why she avoids news, but among them, as she recalled, news was also barely present in her home while she was growing up. In her "big working family," where the men were "out working" and the "mums and stuff were all at home, cooking," she said, "I think we used to get a newspaper delivered when I were a kid, but I remember them just ending up piling up. Like, they never actually got read." Andrea never really saw adults reading or watching news or discussing current events. Men and women had different roles, but, as she recalled, everyone was too busy to bother about the news.

We can contrast Andrea with Ronald, a news lover from Iowa. Like Andrea, he grew up without a lot of extras, but newspapers played an important role in his home. His family delivered them for money, and reading and discussing news were communal activities:

BT: Was reading a newspaper a regular routine in the morning?
Ronald: Oh yeah.
BT: The whole family?
Ronald: Pretty much. Definitely. Because, like I said, we delivered the
   paper, and we always had them around. . . . [We] read the paper
   together. See what the coupons were. Stuff like that. Loved it. Like
   I said, I had a great childhood. I had a mom—she didn't have the
   education that most parents have—but she always instilled on us to
   get an education, and she made it our priority.

Ronald learned from his mother to see news as a source of economic and cultural capital that could improve his chances in life. He is now a self-professed news lover—a habit that he says "began with my mom and the newspaper."

Given all the evidence that early socialization makes a big difference in news consumption later in life, when we began doing interviews, we expected most news avoiders to be a lot like Andrea and news lovers to be like Ronald. We were right about the latter: many news lovers *were* like Ronald, recalling homes where news was consumed habitually and visibly and politics discussed openly. Childhood memories often played a prominent role in their media choice narratives as explanations for how they had become news devotees. They recalled seeing parents read and watch news—"religiously" as several put it—and remembered talking about news and politics as a constant, collective practice in their childhood homes. School curriculum and peer discussions played a less prominent role in their memories of news consumption, but those memories were almost never negative, and some news lovers warmly recalled specific teachers who had helped them appreciate news early on.

In some cases, their stories about their early introduction to news were almost suspiciously neat. Jerry, whose story began in Dickensian fashion with "I was brought up as a news consumer," went on to become a small-town news publisher. The only time he could remember taking a break from news for even a day was a two-week period when he followed the Grateful Dead. In retirement, his main hobby is reading and commenting on political news sites. Rachel, a young mother who was running for city council and consuming cable news almost constantly when we spoke, teared up when she said she hoped to teach her daughters to value news the way she had been taught, concluding, "I was just born into it." Whether news lovers' personal narratives about the importance of their early socialization to news were somewhat simplified or even true in any objective sense really makes no difference. The relevant point is that they recalled news in their childhoods in almost uniformly positive terms and often credited it with having instilled in them an ongoing belief that news and political engagement are important.

By contrast, news avoiders' early experiences were much more mixed—and often more negative. Some had grown up with no news at home at all and explicitly traced their lack of appreciation for news to their upbringing. For example, when we asked Ava, a British news avoider, why she thought her partner consumed so much more news than she did, she said: "I think because of the way that we've been brought up. For myself, [news] wasn't anything that was discussed. It wasn't anything that was really shown an interest in at home." She contrasted that experience with her partner's upbringing: "I think perhaps his parents, he's always grown up around the news. I think he's just more interested in what happens in the world and perhaps even understands it a little bit more than me, so he can show an interest in it. Yeah, I think that's it."

Although some news avoiders like Ava had grown up with little or no exposure to news at home, a surprising number did recall growing up with news: American news avoiders remembered a range of print and TV news in their childhood homes, while British news avoiders most often recalled older family members buying tabloids such as the *Sun* or listening to Radio 4. (As Haylie said about Radio 4, "It was on permanently.") Spanish news avoiders almost never remembered seeing newspapers at home but often recalled watching—or trying to ignore—*el parte*, the midday news broadcast, over lunch with their families.

However, unlike news lovers, who described more inclusive family scenes, most news avoiders recalled news consumption at home as an atomized, solitary activity in which some family members—almost always older and male, as we discuss later—followed news, while everyone else concentrated on other matters. In their memories, *discussion* of news was more consistently absent than news itself. Many recalled homes where politics was never discussed at all or steadfastly avoided to prevent disagreement. For example, Susana (Spain) was taught from early on that common sense dictated there are three topics one should not discuss in polite company (at least in Spain): soccer, religion, and politics.

When news avoiders did remember discussions of major news events in their childhoods, those events were almost always traumatic—lots of child kidnappings in the United Kingdom and terrorist attacks everywhere (especially those on September 11, 2001)—or at least unpleasant. For example, Haylie (United Kingdom) remembered early political discussions leaving a bitter taste. She recalled her mother talking to her about upcoming elections when she was a child and "always wanting Labour to win. I remember the next morning, saying, 'Did they get in?' And she said, 'No, it's Margaret Thatcher again.' You know, it felt like . . . not good."

In a number of cases, news avoiders said they had developed a distaste for news in part because it was pushed down their throats as children. They recalled fighting to change the channel or wanting to leave the room when it was on. In all three countries, we heard versions of what Dion (U.S. news avoider) said: "Maybe that's part of why I *don't* have any interest in [news], because it was so important growing up." Carly, an American news avoider, said that her parents' allegiance to right-wing news when she was a child "made me want to avoid it more" as a kind of "rebellion." (Carly's parents also forced her to volunteer for the phone bank at the local Republican headquarters to "earn dates" with her boyfriend, but we focus on politics in the next chapter.) Although school curriculum played a minor role in most of their memories of news exposure, some news avoiders recalled assignments in school—or, as in Maggie's case in the United States, being forced to read the newspaper as punishment for acting out in class—that had turned them off news.

HOW SOCIAL IDENTITIES SHAPE EARLY EXPERIENCES WITH NEWS

The patterns described here—mixed feelings about early news exposure, little habitual discussion of news in childhood, and news as an atomized activity practiced by only some members of the household—showed up consistently among news avoiders in all three countries. In many of the news avoiders' memories, gender and class played prominent roles in those patterns, although some—mainly in the United States—cited religion and race as important lenses through which they had learned about news from early on.

Early exposure to a gendered division of labor in the home regarding news consumption was evident in all three countries, although a bit more consistently so in Spain. News avoiders frequently described fathers and grandfathers watching the news and reading the paper, while mothers and grandmothers preferred other media and were usually too busy with household chores to sit down with news. Iris (Spain), for example, recalled, "We would be eating with the news on, or my father would be sitting on the sofa, and we had to be really quiet because he was watching the news. . . . My mother, I remember the poor thing washing the dishes." They never discussed current events at Iris's house because they were her "father's thing [cosas de mi padre]." In the United Kingdom, Ava described a similar dynamic:

> *Ava:* My dad always had a newspaper. I think dads do when we're growing up. Yes, he was always reading the newspaper. I don't really remember my mom or the three of us siblings being interested in the news or watching the news if it was on the telly. No, my dad always had a newspaper.
>
> *BT:* Did he ever talk about what was happening on the news?
>
> *Ava:* No, no, he never. He never talked politically either. He never expressed any views. I didn't up until a couple years ago just because I didn't know that much about it just because it was never discussed growing up.
>
> *BT:* Your mother didn't pay attention to the news?
>
> *Ava:* No, no, it was all the soaps. Not news.

Seeing this gendered division of labor around news consumption at home appeared to help shape some news avoiders' perception that news and politics were primarily a male domain—something that "dads do"—a perception they carried into adulthood, as we discuss in the next section.

In many cases, gender clearly intersected with class in news avoiders' childhood media narratives: working fathers came home tired, and busy mothers had little time for news. However, we found that the way class shapes one's news habits and folk theories of news can vary a great deal. Some news lovers also grew up in poorer families, but they, like Ronald, who was quoted earlier, learned while young to see news as a valuable form of education, a way to help improve their fortunes. But the news avoiders we interviewed tended to be more working class than the news lovers overall, and class emerged as a more consistent, explicit theme in the way they described news in their childhoods. Some described economic hardships that limited access to news, while others described working families with little education or time for news. Joanna, a news avoider in the United States, illustrates how class can also influence people's folk theories about whom news is for: "For a while my parents got the paper, but then it was too expensive because they had five kids and my mom stayed home. My dad was a teacher, and so they were like, 'We don't need to get the newspaper anymore.'" She added that news consumption was not "a reinforced thing" at home, "I knew my grandparents always got the paper, but I was, like, oh well, Grandpa's a lawyer, so he can get the paper. I don't know if that subconsciously was telling me that only rich people can get the news."

Class and gender were common themes in our interviews, especially among news avoiders, but other dimensions of social identity, such as religion and race, came up less often and in a more individualized way for both news avoiders and news lovers. Religion was rarely mentioned in interviews in the United Kingdom and Spain, but American news lovers and avoiders alike often mentioned their church communities (as is common in Iowa), and some said they saw everything, including news, through the lens of their religion. Mike, a news lover from Iowa, recalled that when he was a child, his family followed news and "would talk a lot about how it relates to the church," in particular the issue of abortion. But Mike emphasized that his religious identity was far more important to him than current events or politics, and we spoke to several news avoiders who expressed almost identical sentiments. Joanna, for example, recalled that her family rarely discussed issues in the news at all, except for abortion, where "religion and news would intersect." It appeared that for Mike and Joanna religious childhoods did not influence the *amount* of news they consumed so much as how they interpreted its contents and value.

We saw something similar with respect to race. For example, both Ronald, the news lover mentioned earlier, and Reggie, a news avoider who also lived in Iowa, are Black and grew up mainly with single mothers who encouraged them to watch the news. Both spoke passionately about the underrepresentation and misrepresentation of people of color in news and politics. When asked if any news stories from his youth stood out in his memory, Ronald recalled, "Black Power movement, Black Panthers, things like that. Growing up in the inner city—those were things that were pretty powerful to a young Black male." He had watched news consistently his whole life, but, he added, "being a man of color, I think it's always a lot of bias against people of color, brown people, so we aren't shown in the best light, whereas people of different races are shown in a better light." Reggie, in contrast, had little interest in news, recalling how his mother "used to pull me in to watch the news with her all the time," which led him to conclude, "I think that's probably why I don't watch it as much now." But as was the case for other news avoiders, major events could draw him in to the news when they resonated personally. He remembered stopping work to watch Obama's first inauguration: "That was pretty cool. That was pretty big for me seeing a Black guy get voted in."

* * *

In sum, both the families and social groups we are born into provide a foundation for our relationship to news early in life. Broadly speaking, people with more exposure to news and especially to *discussions* of news are more likely to be consistent news consumers later on. We found that news avoiders, unlike news lovers, who described mostly warm or at least poignant memories of their parents and teachers discussing news and politics, had memories that were far more mixed, ranging from a total absence of news and discussion about news at home to news as an isolated activity primarily for some kinds of people rather than an inclusive one to news as something pushed on them in a way that turned them off. In other words, early socialization to news may not always positively influence habits later in life. It can also teach people that news is not really *for* people like themselves, especially women and people of lower socioeconomic means. In some cases, news avoiders may even understand their early socialization to news consumption as having completely backfired.

NEWS COMMUNITIES AND ONGOING
SOCIALIZATION TO NEWS

Socialization does not stop when we reach adulthood. Many studies have shown that the habits and expectations of those around us continue to influence our media habits in general and our relationship to news in particular as we get older.[7] Within groups that value and discuss news, knowledge about current events can become a kind of currency, influencing norms that shape behavior and reinforcing the habit in a virtuous cycle.[8]

Consistent with those previous studies, our survey and interview findings indicate that belonging to what we call "news communities"—social networks in which news is a frequent topic of conversation—is important for helping people sustain their news habits. As we show in this section, belonging to a news community isn't only about knowing people who talk about news, although that helps, but also about roles within groups and social expectations that do or do not reinforce the importance of habitual news consumption. As our examples illustrate, just as childhood socialization is shaped by different dimensions of social identity, the social norms and pressures around news that adults encounter differ depending on the overlapping social groups to which they belong.

TALKING ABOUT NEWS AND BELONGING
TO A "NEWS COMMUNITY"

Not surprisingly, people who say they access news more frequently also tend to discuss the news more frequently with people around them. We found clear evidence of this in our U.S. survey data. When respondents were asked, for example, to report how often they talked to others about news in a variety of different settings and modes, including at home or over social media, news avoiders reported having significantly fewer of those interactions than people who consumed more news (figure H.1 in the supplementary online appendixes).[9]

We also found that the more people access news, the more they report having close friends and family who frequently discuss news and are interested in it (figure 4.2).[10] The differences between news lovers and news avoiders on this point were statistically significant even when we accounted for demographics such as age, race, gender, education, and income as well as for political variables such as partisanship and interest in politics (see table H.1 in the supplementary online appendixes). Even when we controlled for childhood socialization to news, news communities still remained a significant predictor for how frequently people consumed news. In other words, our survey findings suggest that *ongoing socialization may be an even more important factor than early socialization* in predicting news use by adults.

SOCIAL BENEFITS VERSUS SOCIAL PRESSURE

Our interviews gave more insight into ways that ongoing socialization can differ for news lovers and news avoiders. It was particularly evident in our interviews with news lovers that news communities help to sustain norms around the importance of following news. Many had trouble thinking of *anyone* they knew who did not keep up with the news, and some said they could not even fathom such a thing. Many described belonging to not just one but multiple overlapping groups—professional, familial, and social—that consumed lots of news and discussed it often, if not pretty much all the time. In a typical case, Frank, a high school teacher in Iowa and self-professed news fanatic (he beamed with pride about the *New York Times* subscription he got for free with his public-radio membership) could point to many different conversation partners in his news ecosystem. They included his sister, multiple groups of friends, and his colleagues in the social studies department. He said, "You go to a math department, you're probably not going to hear much in the way of talk of politics, and you get the social studies teachers together, and we talk, talk, talk, talk, talk about it. That's the coin of the realm for us!"

Discussing news was an important way news lovers connected with others, a kind of bonding agent that was valuable to their groups and held

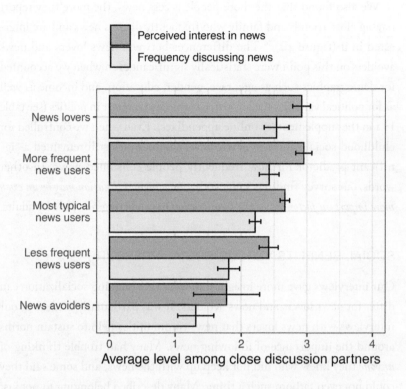

FIGURE 4.2. Differences in News Communities. Average levels of perceived interest in and discussion of news for news avoiders' close discussion partners in the United States were significantly lower compared to other news users. Interest in news was measured on a scale ranging from "not at all interested" to "extremely interested"; frequency of discussing the news was measured on a scale ranging from "never" to "always." Error bars reflect 95 percent confidence intervals for the subgroups.

Source: U.S. News Audiences Survey 2020.

them together. For some, those bonds were indelibly linked to shared routines. Fred, for example, a farmer and regular listener to Rush Limbaugh's radio program, talked about conversing about news with his family at the end of every workday. "My son and my wife, we always eat supper together at night," he explained. "He'll come home from work, and then we'll watch the news, and then we'll talk about it some."

For other news lovers, these interactions were ongoing throughout the day, with news either coming up naturally in conversations or in exchanges over text messages or group chats. Those interactions were not just exchanges of information but also ways to reaffirm shared beliefs and sources of comfort and connection. As the communication scholar James W. Carey would put it, this was news not (just) as transmission of information but as a community ritual.[11] For example, Debra, a divorced working mother in the United States, had a job managing several large associations where being informed about news was an asset. She discussed current events "everyday, all day long, via group text" with her tightknit group of friends, curated her social media accounts to keep up with news, and talked about political issues "routinely" with her family. When asked what she particularly liked about news, she replied, "Just the shared sense of community that I think things like Facebook and other apps provide. The ability to read everything in real time and then discuss it either amongst yourselves or in person or online. Just to know that you're not alone in your feelings of whatever or about whatever the news story is." She had recently gone on a date with a news avoider she met online, but she had no plans to see him again. His ignorance about current events was incomprehensible to her, evidence that they were totally incompatible.

News avoiders, by contrast, often said they perceived the possible social *benefit* to keeping up with news—it was often the only benefit many saw in consuming news at all—but experienced little social *pressure* to do so. They rarely belonged to social groups that discussed news frequently and did not have jobs where keeping up with current events was expected, much less required (which was closely tied to social class, as we discuss later). For those working in service industry professions, there often weren't even opportunities to talk about news, much less surf the web or look at news on devices. Patricia (United States) said, "We don't even really take breaks. I just sit at my desk most of the day and wait on customers, answer the phone." Colleen, a U.S. news avoider who worked at a department store, said employees were usually so separated, there was limited time to interact: "I don't want to say there's not socialization because there is, but not really. . . . It's normally like, 'Did you see what that customer just left in the fitting room?'"

Some news avoiders did describe friends or family members who sometimes discussed news or were even news lovers, but the activity of discussing news was rarely central to their relationships with these individuals, just as it had not been when they were growing up. In most cases, it was also more sporadic. When discussions of news did come up in their social circles, it was usually, as Lexi (United Kingdom) explained, "like the odd comment" rather than "an everyday topic of conversation." Members within their social groups took on different roles: news enthusiasts were mostly the exception rather than the norm, and "news avoider" was an acceptable role. As Paloma, a news avoider in Spain, noted, "You get together with a group of friends, and they start to talk about a topic, and you can't participate at all. . . . It happens to me often, very often. But, well, you use it to learn something." Like Paloma, news avoiders sometimes felt sheepish or a bit embarrassed not to be able to participate in such conversations, but they did not fear rejection from the group. They felt comfortable just listening or leaving, and many simply shrugged off such experiences. These situations did not negatively affect news avoiders' sense of their own self-worth or how they hoped others would see them.

Based on what we heard in our interviews, we developed three survey questions to try to understand the social pressures different people might feel around following the news. We first asked how strongly respondents agreed or disagreed with the statement "My friends expect me to know what's going on in the news." Not surprisingly, news lovers largely agreed with the statement, whereas news avoiders mostly disagreed (figure 4.3), reflecting stark differences in perceived social expectations among the communities to which they belonged.

We also asked how often respondents felt "left out from conversations about the news" and then the follow-up question "How much, if at all, does it bother you to be left out from conversations about the news?" Interestingly, we found no significant differences on the first question. News avoiders did not *feel* left out any more often than news lovers. But in line with our qualitative interviews, they were also less upset by such experiences than any other group—again, they did not belong to social groups in which norms dictated that they should be able to talk about news and should feel

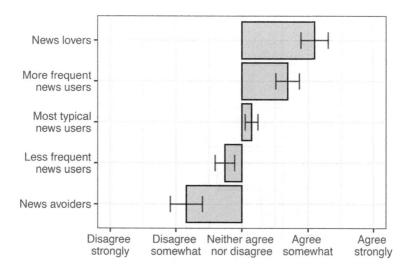

FIGURE 4.3. "My Friends Expect Me to Know What's Going On in the News." Social expectations around being knowledgeable about the news differed considerably for news avoiders and news lovers in the United States. Error bars reflect 95 percent confidence intervals for the subgroups.

Source: U.S. News Audiences Survey 2020.

ashamed if they could not. In contrast, although most news lovers professed not to be particularly troubled by the prospect, they expressed higher levels of concern than any other group about being excluded socially (figure 4.4).

To be clear, we are not suggesting that news communities are the *only* explanation for news habits later in a person's adult life. However, keeping up a news habit can feel difficult, as we explained in the previous chapter, and belonging to strong communities of other news users helps compensate for ways that circumstances or individual characteristics can make consuming news less likely for some people. Several of the news lovers we interviewed illustrated well how news communities can help an individual sustain a news habit even when the going gets tough. For example, Debra, the busy single parent in the United States mentioned earlier, was almost

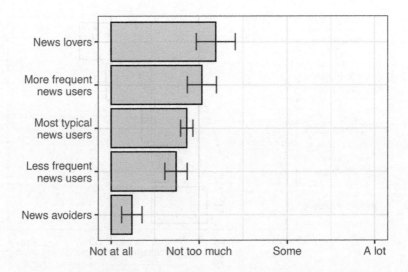

FIGURE 4.4. "How Much, If at All, Does It Bother You to Be Left Out from Conversations About the News?" Although there were no significant differences between U.S. survey respondents in how often they felt "left out from conversations about the news," news avoiders were particularly unlikely to be "bothered" by such interactions. Error bars reflect 95 percent confidence intervals for the subgroups.

Source: U.S. News Audiences Survey 2020.

apologetic at times about falling behind on current events. She explained, "It's my busy time of work, and I'm just not fully engaged because I just don't have the bandwidth." She said she could turn to her friends and her parents to "kind of fill in the knowledge gap" as needed. Staying informed was not separate from but integral to her social and professional life.

Meanwhile, in extreme cases, news avoiders struggled to name *anyone* in their lives who consumed news regularly or talked much about it, the opposite of what we saw with the news lovers. As Jodie, a news avoider in the United Kingdom, recounted, "Who would be able to give me that information? I don't [know]. . . . Everybody is pretty much as useless as I am."

NEWS COMMUNITIES AND SOCIAL IDENTITIES

Just as gender, socioeconomic class, race, and religion can affect childhood socialization to news, these social identities can also reinforce norms around the practice of following news in adulthood. These different aspects of social identity influence the types of people news avoiders and news lovers interact with, their perceptions about divisions of labor at home or among group members, and the forms of social pressure they experience (or not).

Our interviews provided only a handful of examples where race and religion appeared to affect the amount of news people said they consumed, but some interviewees did mention links between those identities, their news habits, and the communities to which they belonged. Take Mike, for example, the U.S. news lover mentioned earlier who talked about the importance of his Catholic beliefs in shaping his childhood exposure to news. His religious identity infused both his media choices and the communities of other news users with whom he interacted and engaged. When a group from his church proposed cutting out all news for ninety days leading up to Easter, he took up the challenge. "It's really in part just to block out noise in your life, focus on what's really important," he said as he described how clarifying the experience of avoiding news, however temporarily, had been.

Gender and class were more consistently evident across our interviews. Gender affected perceptions that many news avoiders expressed (often implicitly) about who news was for and what kinds of news were relevant to men and women. Time and again across all three countries, news avoiders described gendered patterns in news consumption in their adult lives that replicated the dynamics they recalled from their childhoods. Just as they remembered fathers and grandfathers being more engaged with news than mothers and grandmothers, news avoiders also often said that the news users they knew in their adult social groups—those who stood out for their particular interest in politics and news—were men. In a typical example, Chelsea, a working-class mother in Leeds (United Kingdom), described social situations where "it tends to be all the guys debate, and all the women will just go off for a gossip," insisting that she and her companions "don't talk about anything important," downplaying their discussions about relationships and kids. She elaborated on how the divide occurred "naturally," saying "the guys have a chat about whatever they chat about, and the women chat about what they're chatting about. It's not just, 'Oh right, we're talking about politics, we're going over here.' It's just we naturally divide anyway. Maybe because we live with them, and we're sick of seeing them, so when we get a chance to go out, we're, like, 'See you!'" In a kind of division of labor within their homes and social circles that replicated those in their childhoods, many women news avoiders spoke about relying on male partners to keep them informed, while they focused on other forms of work. Patricia, a U.S. news avoider, for example, said, "My husband reads constantly. He's a big-time reader. So, like, he'll read something. If he finds it really informative, he says, 'Hey, read this.' Or, 'Look at this.'" In several instances, female news avoiders described male partners who would tell them to stop following news because it made them anxious or would shame them about being uninformed. Gemma, a U.K. news avoider, recalled an instance in which she found herself engaged in a conversation about the U.S. election of 2016—"They were all talking about it, especially the husbands." When she confided to her husband that she felt "very ignorant" and "embarrassed" that she couldn't contribute, he responded, "It's your fault because you don't show an interest." Although such experiences could be construed as examples of social pressure, interviewees rarely seemed to understand them that way. They recounted these anecdotes as a way of explaining how they differed from their (male) partners, usually in ways that tended to replicate traditional gender roles.

Socioeconomic class also shaped interviewees' social groups in many ways and, in turn, the kinds and amount of pressure they felt to keep up with news. This correlation was perhaps most obvious with respect to work. At the time the news avoiders spoke to us, few of them had jobs in which they felt consuming news was an asset, much less a necessity.[12] Brenna, the U.K. news avoider quoted at the outset of this chapter, made that point explicitly, noting that keeping up with current events was unusual in all of the communities to which she belonged, including her professional community. Class also shaped news avoiders' beliefs about whom news was for and the kinds of people who kept up with it. Both news avoiders and news lovers associated news consumption generally with being well educated and white collar—it was a mark of class distinction—but, unlike news lovers, most news avoiders did not think of themselves as belonging to that group.[13] For example, Daniel, a U.S. news avoider, said he believed that by paying closer attention to news, "I'd look more intelligent probably, or I'll sound more intelligent." Likewise, multiple Spanish news avoiders said that being informed about news could be valuable, as Andrés put it, "to be an educated, cultured person [para ser una persona culta]."

Beliefs about the relationship between news and social class were also noticeable in how people divided news into high-brow and low-brow sources, particularly in the United Kingdom. Robert, a U.K. news avoider in his midtwenties, observed how his girlfriend, who was "brought up in a nicer area than me," looked down on the tabloid newspapers, the *Mirror* and the *Sun*, that he most often encountered at work. Because of her disapproval, he said he stopped reading any newspaper, noting, "I used to read it everyday, and I've pushed it right back." When another U.K. news avoider, Emily, was asked how she differentiated between sources she encountered online, she said, "I think some of the papers are like different, I want to say, 'classes' of people. You've got, like, *The Guardian* and *The Independent* that are, like, the posh ones that I wouldn't have a clue what they were saying. Then you've got the *Mirror* and the *Daily Mail*, which has got the showbiz bits."

*　*　*

As we have shown in this section, what we learn about news in childhood matters, but when it comes to sustaining a news habit in adulthood, the social groups we belong to may matter more. Even people who saw little news consumption modeled for them in childhood and even those who do not particularly enjoy news or who find it difficult will likely develop a news habit if their jobs or social circles do not just gently nudge them but push them hard to be informed about current events. The social groups to which we belong can make that more or less likely to happen and influence the ways in which it does.

BELIEVING IN A CIVIC DUTY TO STAY INFORMED

In the previous chapter, we showed how news avoiders said they rarely found news consumption enjoyable or relevant enough to compete with other responsibilities or media options. Absent these criteria, they did not see a strong overriding reason why they should engage with news. By contrast, news lovers perceived lower costs and greater benefits to news consumption. Not only did they find most news, even about distant matters, relevant to their lives, but they also got emotional satisfaction from following news.

We can now add that when news lovers found news difficult or unpleasant, they still said in interviews that they felt an overriding responsibility to consume news anyway—a civic duty to be informed.[14] Frank, the Iowa social studies teacher quoted earlier, spoke at length about the idea that consuming news was an important "obligation" he felt as a contributing member of society. He explained, "I have rights as a citizen, to be sure, but there are duties, too. One of the duties is to be informed, to be engaged in the political process in some fashion, and to care about these things. So to not be engaged in that process, to me, is an abdication of my duties as a citizen."

Based on those interview findings, we decided to include a question about civic duty on our survey, and it produced one of the most striking differences we found between news lovers and avoiders. They held radically divergent views about the statement "It's my duty to keep up with what's going on in the news" (figure 4.5). News lovers overwhelmingly agreed, whereas news avoiders almost uniformly did not.

Although we do not want to suggest that the news lovers were lying when they said they felt it was their civic duty to consume news—it seemed clear in interviews that they were sincere—it is probably fairly easy to feel that way about any activity that one finds on balance interesting and rewarding, if occasionally unpleasant or difficult. As the French sociologist Pierre Bourdieu argues, many of our tastes and interests serve as expressions of identity and class distinction.[15] So, too, do claims that consuming news is a sacred civic duty. Consuming news marks one not only as cultured and informed but also as morally dutiful—unlike other people. Meanwhile,

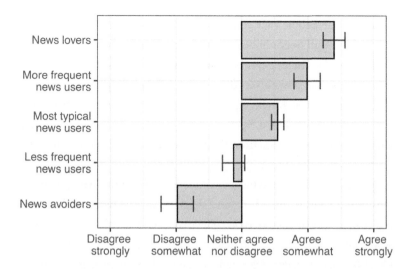

FIGURE 4.5. Civic Duty Norms: "It's My Duty to Keep Up with What's Going On in the News." Americans surveyed held divergent views about whether consuming news was an important civic "duty." Error bars reflect 95 percent confidence intervals for the subgroups.

Source: U.S. News Audiences Survey 2020.

news avoiders tended to see news lovers, unlike themselves, as people who must have a lot of extra time on their hands, which, as we pointed out in chapter 3, news avoiders did not feel applied to themselves. Some also said outright that they had grown up thinking of news as an upper-class pursuit. Although they did not say it quite so baldly, it would not seem illogical for them to view news consumption as a kind of privilege of the leisure class as opposed to a civic duty to be expected of everyone.

Indeed, the idea of news consumption as an *obligation* of citizenship was almost completely absent in interviews of news avoiders or outright rejected by news avoiders in all three countries. As David, a U.S. news avoider, put it, "Being a good citizen and consuming media, those two things are completely unrelated in my mind." He added, "I think you can be a better citizen if you stop parroting soundbites that you hear on the news and start caring for the people that you're living next to. I would much rather help my neighbor pull weeds in his lawn than spend an hour watching C-SPAN." Like David does here, news avoiders often defined good citizenship in different terms than news lovers did—as being kind to others and taking care of shared resources, for example, not as requiring engagement with news. For example, Gonzalo, a Spanish news avoider, said, "A good citizen is someone who does things from the heart and tries to do good—not because a news story makes them."

In the high-choice media environment in which we live, the belief that consuming news is something one *should* do for the health of both oneself as a citizen and the democratic collective, even if it takes extra time, willpower, emotional energy, and determination—rather like exercising, eating a healthy diet, or recycling—may be essential for helping people maintain a news habit over time. Our findings suggest that news communities in youth and adulthood help teach and sustain this belief. The news avoiders we interviewed did not belong to such communities, whereas the news lovers often explicitly traced their belief that news was a civic duty to their early training—almost like a catechism—and were often surrounded by people who helped reinforce it. For example, Frank, the news-loving social studies teacher, saw consuming news as critical to doing his job, and his colleagues frequently discussed news with him. In fact, so many different social forces helped him learn and sustain his belief that news was a civic duty that he couldn't name just one: "There's no one source. I would say it's just been something over time. . . . You know, certainly getting back to my dad, and my parents always voted, even in school board elections, all that sort of thing. So seeing that example. And then studying social studies, or I mean history, rather, and political science—sociology, too. Those are all my main courses of study as an undergraduate and graduate student. And so that's all around you; I mean, that's just sort of in the air." Very few of the news avoiders we interviewed felt these ideas were "just sort of in the air."

* * *

As we have argued in this chapter, our relationships to news—whether we consume it constantly or reject it altogether—are the product not just of choices we make as individuals but also of our social identities. The groups to which we belong, starting with our families and the categories of gender, class, race, and religion into which we are placed early on, teach us and sometimes push us to behave toward news in different ways. As we grow and find ourselves in groups more of our own choosing, pressures to consume news or not can play a defining role in helping us to sustain a news habit or see little value in doing so.

All other things being equal, people who are immersed in news communities that pressure them to be informed about current events—to the extent that they feel embarrassed when they are not—are more likely to keep up with news. But all other things are not equal. Men and people of higher socioeconomic status are more likely to find themselves in that position. Based on our data, race and religion—other important aspects of social identity—are less likely to influence how much news one consumes, but they can certainly influence how a person interprets news when they see it. In the next chapter, we explore how another important aspect of who we are and how we see the world—the political ideologies we embrace— also fundamentally shapes how we think about and relate to news.

5

IDEOLOGIES

How Beliefs About Politics Shape News Avoidance

We interviewed news avoiders and news lovers in Iowa a few months before and immediately after the media frenzy that was Iowa's presidential primary election in 2020. Iowa famously votes first in the nation, using a "caucus" system in which registered voters gather in local precincts to debate about their preferred candidates before publicly casting their votes.[1] It is an old-fashioned, in-person form of political participation that lasts for hours. Attendees give speeches to stoke enthusiasm for their preferred candidate and lure supporters away from other candidates. Depending on who is describing it, the event can seem like a thrill, a mystery, or a nightmare.

Frank, a news lover quoted in the conclusion of chapter 4, saw himself firmly in the first category. His upbringing, social circle, and job as a teacher contributed to his valuing and enjoying news—a love that was not easily separable from his love for politics. Frank had a framed picture of Franklin Delano Roosevelt, his favorite president, on the wall. He enthusiastically recounted how he had not only attended the recent caucus but also given a short speech in support of his favorite candidate, Senator Amy Klobuchar:

Yeah, it was great. I mean, not—the speech wasn't great. It was highly forgettable. You only get one minute. No, it was no Gettysburg Address. But yeah, it was great. I loved it. It was a chance to again talk about Amy Klobuchar. The thing I thought about afterward—I was so mad at myself. My cat over there, his name is FDR. And I wished I had said, "My cat's name is FDR, and even he supports Amy Klobuchar." But I never thought of it. It was after I got home, I thought, "Dang, that would have been a great line, bring my cat into this." Anyway, silly. But it was just fun . . . the Klobuchar people cheered. It wouldn't have mattered what I said. They still cheered. If I said the sky is blue, they would have cheered. . . . But it was great. Again, it was just sort of like a drug. It was so fun to be involved in this.

The contrast between how news lovers like Frank viewed political participation in general and the caucuses in particular and how news avoiders viewed them could not have been more clear-cut. News avoiders such as Daniel and Johnny illustrate that contrast well. They not only skipped participating in their local caucus in 2020 but had never attended one at all. Daniel said he knew "a little bit about it" but then continued, "I think it's— correct me if I'm wrong, I probably sound dumb again—Is it kind of like a pep rally?" Johnny visibly recoiled when we asked him if he had ever gone to a caucus. "Are you serious?" he said. "No way! That'd be horrible."

As argued in previous chapters, whether we avoid news or embrace it, the way we think and feel about news is shaped by our identities, ideologies, and the infrastructures we use to find, access, and navigate media. In chapter 4, we focused on identity. This chapter looks more closely at ideology, specifically political ideology. Readers may assume we mean liberal or conservative belief systems or ideology's close cousin, party affiliation, but that is only part of the story. As we explained in chapter 2, when it comes to consistent news avoidance, which party a person belongs to often matters less than whether a person feels a sense of belonging to any party at all. So by "political ideology" we mean a person's whole sense of where they belong in the political system, including whether they feel empowered in it and their beliefs about whether and how news can help them take meaningful political action.

Indeed, as the contrast between Frank on the one hand and Daniel and Johnny on the other highlights, news lovers and news avoiders often differ in their basic beliefs about the appeal and usefulness of politics and political engagement. We begin the chapter by looking at some of these fundamental differences. Simply put, consistent news avoiders often feel alienated from politics and public life, whereas news lovers often describe themselves as political junkies. But the two groups do share something important, which we explore in the second half of the chapter: doubts about how responsive government is to their concerns (what scholars refer to as "*external* political efficacy") and skepticism (cynicism in some cases) about how well the news media stands up for the public in the face of power. Although journalists and journalism scholars often consider holding power to account to be journalism's most important job, we found that interviewees saw journalists more as willing enablers of the powerful, in extreme cases almost as co-conspirators. As we show, folk theories about how this enabling worked differed somewhat by country, but the fundamental view of news as a poor watchdog was consistent everywhere.

Because news avoiders and news lovers alike tend to question the independence of news media from political and corporate power, we return in the last part of the chapter to the question of what, besides their basic interest in politics, differentiates these two groups. The key, we find, is that most news avoiders have little confidence in their own abilities to participate in political life or effect any kind of change if they did—what scholars call *internal* efficacy—and believe that news cannot help them do so. Many feel nothing can help. News lovers feel roughly the opposite—but why? Once more, we argue that news communities play a key role in helping news lovers sustain their belief—faith, really—that they can make a difference in politics and that news is an essential tool to help them do so. Consistent news avoiders almost always lack these news communities.

We close the chapter by examining some of the potential consequences of news avoiders' sense of alienation from politics and news in the current political climate. News avoiders justify opting out of political news by claiming that it does not empower them to make any meaningful impact in politics. But opting out virtually ensures that is true. The less they pay attention to news and politics, the less news and politicians pay attention to them.[2] Distrust and rejection of mainstream political news may also make news avoiders more receptive to appeals by powerful figures who pit themselves against it.

COMPARING NEWS LOVERS' AND NEWS AVOIDERS' IDEOLOGIES AND THEIR IMPRESSIONS OF POLITICS

As Ryan, a forty-year-old U.K. news avoider, was looking over an information sheet about this study before our interview, he volunteered, "I noticed there's some political stuff in there. I hate politics. It's probably one of the reasons I don't read the news, to be honest." That was typical of the news avoiders we interviewed in all three countries. Their views on politics ranged from "totally apolitical" to outright hatred, and they tended to try to avoid not just political *news* but also anything political at all. Most held cynical views about the nature of political institutions as out of touch and believed that engaging in political life was at best boring, distant, and confusing and at worst a complete waste of time. Indeed, our survey data from the United States showed that news avoiders compared to other groups were far less likely to say they voted regularly or participated politically (figure 5.1). Just 12 percent of news avoiders said they had attended a political rally or event, compared to 63 percent of news lovers.

News avoiders' aversion to politics did not mean they held no political views of their own. In fact, some spoke at length about policy issues they cared about. For example, Amelia (United Kingdom) said she had no interest in politics but offered a fairly detailed critique of the British criminal justice system. When asked about the seeming contradiction, she answered, "I didn't really know that's political opinions." Ryan, who said he hated politics and described himself as a "house husband," likewise recounted his

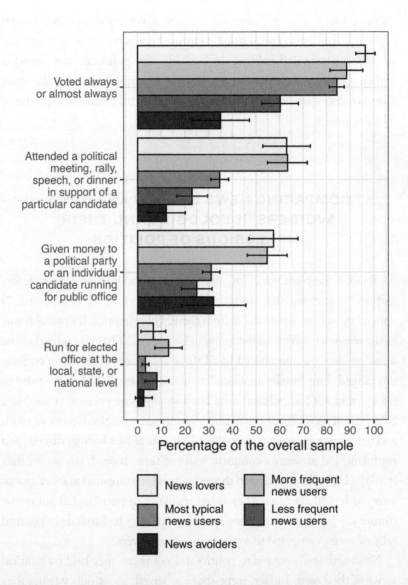

FIGURE 5.1. Political Participation. News avoiders in the United States were much less likely to say they regularly voted or had participated in politics in other ways compared to more typical news users or news lovers. Error bars reflect 95 percent confidence intervals for the subgroups.

Source: U.S. News Audiences Survey 2020.

views about transportation policy and "green" taxes. That admission led to this exchange:

BT: It's interesting that you say that because you began by saying that you have no interest in politics.

Ryan: I know. I suppose my thing is I have no interest in politicians.

After several such exchanges, it became clear to us that even when news avoiders expressed strong views on issues such as crime, climate change, or immigration or even when they were active in their local communities, they usually did not think of their own opinions or actions as "politics." They defined politics narrowly as what professional politicians do, usually at the national level and seemingly far from daily life.

News avoiders like Ryan saw news as unappealing in part because it is *about* politics—defined, again, as politicians arguing among themselves—but for many it appeared that news *is* politics. Indeed, when we asked Ryan his impressions of journalists, he responded, "I don't really know a journalist. In my head, I'm going: 'Journalist, politician.' I don't know." News avoiders tended to conflate the two realms to the point where they were indistinguishable: when we asked about news, they responded about politics, and vice versa. And because politics was so often perceived as politicians fighting among themselves about issues that have nothing to do with normal people, "like a kids' playground," as Emily (United Kingdom) put it, it is little wonder that news avoiders often felt political news was boring, tedious, and depressing. Nothing ever got resolved.

Not only did the news avoiders we interviewed tend to deeply dislike politics, but many also found political news hard to understand. Some criticized the way journalists used jargon, assuming prior knowledge about systems, terms, and personalities that most felt they did not have. But making sense of political news was also complicated because avoiders often believed that news outlets reported on political stories in divergent ways that made it difficult to discern the truth. If everyone told you something different, what distinguished fact from opinion? It all seemed like opinion. Colleen (United States), for example, explained that she was not very interested in politics and felt overwhelmed by information when it came to vote. She said, "I feel like the information, again, is so scattered that I don't get enough information about it to know who stands for what. . . . Like I said, it's too much information, and it's not clear enough. A lot of it is opinion, which is another reason I don't like a whole lot of that stuff." Many concluded it was smarter to tune out all news than to be an unsuspecting victim of political biases they were certain existed but uncertain they could identify. Overall, the costs of trying to understand political news often felt insurmountable. Given that political news already felt disconnected from daily life, it seemed like a burdensome distraction from what really mattered. In short, news about politics was the worst of everything they disliked about news in general (see also chapter 3).

The news lovers' attitudes toward politics and political news were radically different from the news avoiders' attitudes in a number of ways. Not all news lovers we interviewed were quite as upbeat about politics as Frank, whose elated description of speaking at an Iowa caucus opened this chapter. Many expressed the same complaints about news coverage of politics that we heard from news avoiders: political news could be discouraging, overwhelming, uncivil, or infused with too much partisan opinion. But news lovers believed that a good citizen *had* to follow news about politics despite its deficiencies. On the whole, they found politics interesting and were confident that they could understand and use the information being reported. Some described themselves as political junkies or "hobbyists," to borrow a term from the political scientist Eitan Hersh.[3] As the U.S. news lover and university professor Ketrick put it, "Politics is almost a pastime to me. It's like a game. It's the sport of analysis and understanding people." News lovers made it clear in our interviews that they knew as much about the game as the players, rattling off names and opinions about local, national, and international politics with ease.

Strong partisan ideologies helped them do that. Political scientists have long characterized partisan identities as beneficial for political engagement because they act as a heuristic, or mental shortcut, that helps people make sense of political information.[4] So it is important to note that we found in both our interviews and our survey that most news avoiders did not identify with any political party.[5] Some interviewees were unsure what the different political parties stood for—in Brenna's (United Kingdom) words, "I don't really understand, like, the different parties and stuff." Others were uncertain how to place themselves on a left–right ideological scale or what "left" and "right" even meant in the political context. Caleb (United Kingdom), for example, asked as he was filling out our brief survey, "Because I don't know a lot about it, could you briefly just describe left wing and right wing for me, from your own knowledge, if that's OK?" Still others, such as Manuel (Spain), more actively rejected all the parties. As he succinctly put it, "All the parties are the same shit with different names."

News avoiders' lack of party identification, whether because they actively rejected all the parties on ideological grounds or because they felt they did not understand them, meant they lacked the orienting tool that news lovers drew on to make sense of political matters. The news lovers we interviewed in Iowa embraced a wide range of political views, from libertarian to staunch progressive. But in contrast to news avoiders, they all knew where they stood on that spectrum, which meant that when they encountered political news, they were invested in the narratives and the underlying issues at stake.

News lovers mostly took for granted that political neutrality was impossible, but they were confident in their abilities to identify and opt for "news that agrees with [their] biases," as Jerry, a lifelong Democrat, put it. Others found pleasure in consuming a variety of sources so they could compare news across the political spectrum, but ideology still influenced their curation strategies. Left-leaning Gloria, for example, listened to NPR all day long and used various apps on her phone, including the *NBC News* app. She said she believed it was important to consume "a variety of sources even though I can't stomach *Fox News*—a variety to a point." On the other end of the political spectrum, Fred, a conservative farmer, paired more mainstream news sources with three hours of Rush Limbaugh daily, which he had listened to for almost thirty years. He explained that he saw Limbaugh as "the antagonist to the regular news," so he could "get both sides that way."

Clear ideological preferences also shaped news lovers' understanding of what the most critical concerns of the day were and, subsequently, why paying attention to news felt so important. Most said they were disturbed by growing partisan polarization (as were news avoiders, a similarity discussed further later), but instead of seeing it as a reason to turn away from news, they pointed it out as a reason they felt news was so important. For Trump supporters, like Fred, partisan debates mattered because the fabric of the nation, he felt, was being torn apart by liberals, who were attacking the president through impeachment. He said, "I'm just really disappointed that this has eaten up so much of our time in this country. . . . It's really divided our country more strongly than ever." Meanwhile, Trump detractors felt the fabric of the nation was being torn apart by Trump himself. "I see our personal liberties being shredded," Nancy, a liberal grandmother, told us. "I see decisions being made at the national level that are compromising the quality of life for all of us, but particularly for the next generation." She argued that, sure, one could stop following news, but doing so would solve nothing because "it's still happening, and it's happening to people. It's not happening in the abstract. It's happening to the air that you and your children are breathing." For both Fred and Nancy, a strong sense of partisan identity acted as a practical tool for helping them navigate the array of media choices available to them. In a climate where every issue felt increasingly polarized, their personal political orientation also gave them a reason to care. They felt that important aspects of their identities were implicated in those debates, even dangerously threatened by them.

In sum, news lovers felt at home with political news in part because their partisan identities helped them to navigate it and in part because they found following politics not just important but urgent. It felt close to home even when it involved subjects in faraway places. For news avoiders, in part because they did not have strong partisan identities, politics and news about politics felt distant, boring, difficult to understand, and useless—at least for them. In the next two sections, we delve further into this sentiment and the degree to which it was rooted in news avoiders' ideological beliefs about politics.

FOLK THEORIES ABOUT WHY GOVERNMENT AND NEWS FAIL TO HELP THE PUBLIC

Joyce, a U.S. news avoider, relied on government assistance programs to get medication and other services, but she described with frustration her fruitless efforts to contact policy makers about problems with those programs. She concluded resignedly, "I'm part of a society that nobody really cares about." The more socioeconomically disadvantaged news avoiders we interviewed were more likely than the news lovers to have firsthand experiences like Joyce's, but frustration with government and politics is not unique to them. Cynicism about politics is widespread, and trust in political institutions has fallen in many countries worldwide.[6] The degree to which people believe the political system is responsive to the public is what scholars call "political efficacy."[7] Political scientists often differentiate between *external* political efficacy—beliefs about the responsiveness of democratic institutions—and *internal* political efficacy—how individuals perceive their own agency and ability to effect change.[8] Both news avoiders and news lovers alike expressed low external political efficacy (the subject of this section), but low internal political efficacy was more specific to news avoiders, which we discuss in the next section.

One way scholars measure external political efficacy is by asking people whether they agree with the statement "Public officials don't care much about what people like me think," similar to what Joyce expressed. Polls show that low external political efficacy, like cynicism about politics generally, is widespread. In early 2020, a thirty-four-nation study by the Pew Research Center found that seven of every ten people in the United States and the United Kingdom and more than three-quarters of people in Spain thought elected officials generally did not care about average citizens.[9] The study also found in many places around the world steady declines in the percentage of respondents who agreed that government is run for the benefit of all people. Our U.S. survey data further underscore that news avoiders are not unique in their belief that politics is unresponsive to the public (figure 5.2).

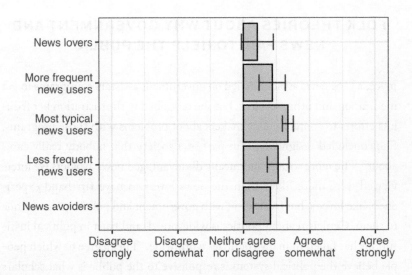

FIGURE 5.2. "Public Officials Don't Care Much About What People Like Me Think." No significant differences in external efficacy were found between news avoiders and other groups in the United States. Error bars reflect 95 percent confidence intervals for the subgroups.

Source: U.S. News Audiences Survey 2020.

In theory, in a democratic system the news media should play a vital role in ensuring that government responds to citizens' needs and in holding politicians to account when they do not serve the public well. But many people, not just news avoiders, reject the idea that news acts as an effective watchdog.[10] Surveys in many places with free and diverse news media find that majorities reject the notion that news media monitor and scrutinize powerful people and businesses, as we see in the Reuters Institute *DNR 2019* (figure 5.3).[11]

Our survey of U.S. news audiences showed slightly higher agreement across the board, but, again, few differences between news avoiders and other news consumers (figure 5.4). In short, it turns out that news avoiders

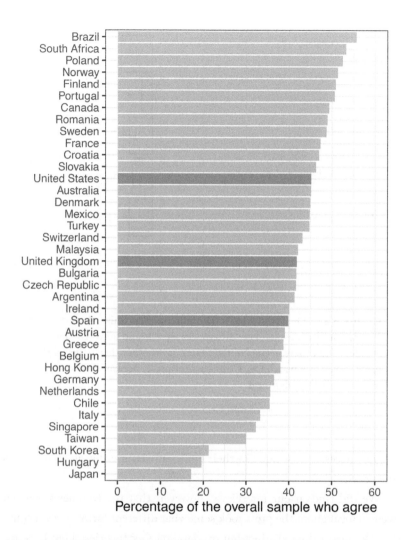

FIGURE 5.3. "The News Media Monitor and Scrutinize Powerful People and Businesses." Varying levels of agreement with the watchdog role of the press worldwide. "Tend to agree" and "strongly agree" responses have been combined.

Source: *Digital News Report 2019*, https://www.digitalnewsreport.org/survey/2019/.

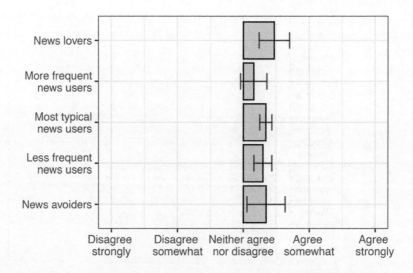

FIGURE 5.4. "The News Media Monitor and Scrutinize Powerful People and Businesses." Few differences were found between news avoiders and others in the United States on whether they believed the press served as a watchdog. Error bars reflect 95 percent confidence intervals for the subgroups.

Source: U.S. News Audiences Survey 2020.

are not necessarily unique in their cynicism about either government or the press.

We did find in our interviews, however, that the way news avoiders were cynical about the press took somewhat different forms in each country. We heard three distinct but overlapping folk theories about how and why news fails to hold politicians to account, which we explore in greater detail in the next few subsections. We present them as country-specific case studies because in each country one folk theory was usually more prevalent than the rest, but, in truth, all theories were present to some degree in each place. The details change, but the underlying criticisms are often the same.

THEY'LL DO ANYTHING TO SELL A STORY: AVOIDING TABLOID SENSATIONALISM IN THE UNITED KINGDOM

U.K. interviewees rarely mentioned politics explicitly, even Brexit, which was striking because the referendum had taken place only months before our interviews. When a few did mention Brexit, they used the same language Megan used when we asked what she thought was the most important issue facing the United Kingdom. She responded, "I don't know, probably Brexit at the minute, I'd say. I'm not really big into politics." In other words, interviewees knew other people considered Brexit important, but they mostly saw Brexit as an example of the kind of distant political issue they found uninteresting, confusing, and disconnected from daily life.

That U.K. interviewees rarely mentioned politics was consistent with their feelings of alienation from politics (see also chapter 2). But it also reflected features of the British media system and how interviewees were positioned in it. Many U.K. news avoiders did not immediately think of hard-hitting political news when they thought about news in general, and they rarely mentioned the BBC. Instead, they most often mentioned tabloids, such as the *Sun*, which they associated with grisly crime news, sports, and celebrity gossip. With the tabloids as their default idea of what news was like, British news avoiders consistently complained that when the news was not just trivial, it was too sensationalistic and negative, which they saw as a symptom of a profit-hungry press. As they explained, news outlets were commercial enterprises, so they could not be trusted to present the unvarnished truth—as a matter of course, they twisted and exaggerated to "sell stories." (The BBC, despite being a public-service broadcaster, rarely registered as an exception.)

This general impression of news coverage as massaged and sensationalized to maximize profit encompassed political news as well. Interviewees described politicians, like journalists, as profit seekers (which was consistent with news avoiders' tendency to think of journalism and politics as overlapping spheres). Amelia, for example, said she did not understand what the different political parties stood for, but she assumed that "they all kind of want to do the same thing, which is get rich." On the rare occasions when interviews turned to something like independent, watchdog journalism, U.K. participants were dismissive, usually citing it as another example of the kind of news they found tedious, sensationalized, and overly negative.

Time permitting, at the end of our interviews we asked participants to read and reflect on examples of recent news stories, sometimes about politics. For those who had not yet mentioned politics, it was often the moment when they said they disliked it. One of the articles, from the BBC, concerned opposition-leader Jeremy Corbyn's finances. Though not an in-depth investigative piece, the story covered a fairly typical watchdog topic, and reactions to the article were telling. Adam, for example, conceded that reporting about politicians' finances was "an important subject" but added, "I'm sick of hearing about it 'cause it's been dragging on so long. Whenever you do put the news on, there's always something about MPs' expenses, so it gets boring." For Nicole, the article inspired deep skepticism, not of the politician under investigation but of the news outlet doing the investigating:

> I just look at it, and I just think to myself, "I should be interested because it's telling me that he's not paying enough tax." But then I feel, deep down, whoever is writing it, are they trying to create a witch hunt against him? Why is it being written? Why is it being exposed? Also, why is it not being investigated by the proper sources? If he is tax avoiding, surely, the HMRC [Her Majesty's Revenue and Customs] should be looking into this rather than the BBC. . . . I question why somebody has written that. What's the ulterior motive to somebody writing something like that?

Not only did U.K. news avoiders appear not to value the BBC's scrutiny of a politician's finances, but, if anything, some, like Nicole, also saw it as inappropriate for a news outlet to pursue this kind of story. They seemed more suspicious of the news organization's motives than of the politician's. Perhaps their suspicion stemmed from an inclination to defend the Labour leader, but it was consistent with a broader belief, expressed throughout the

U.K. interviews, that news organizations were motivated primarily by their own economic interests, not by nobler notions of public service.

THE MEDIA COVERS UP A LOT OF THINGS: PARTISAN NEWS AND CORRUPTION IN SPAIN

We saw the same range of general attitudes toward politics in Spain—from indifference to dislike—but Spaniards talked significantly more about establishment politics than British participants did, for two main reasons. First, unlike the British, many Spaniards expressed an active frustration with politics in their country, frequently naming "the government," "corruption," or simply "politics" when we asked what they thought was the main problem facing Spain. Second, media outlets' alignment with political parties in Spain is widely recognized by both citizens and scholars.[12] Whereas tabloids usually came to British news avoiders' minds when they reflected on news, current events tabloids do not exist in Spain. Spaniards instead immediately thought of politically partisan news. And although interviewees in all three countries were suspicious about why different outlets reported the same story differently, almost every interviewee in Spain saw those differences as proof that news outlets were politically biased (*sesgados*) or outright manipulated (*manipulados*)—exhibit A for why you could not trust any of them. As Sofia summed up this belief, "All the news channels and the newspapers show information in their favor according to their politics or their way of thinking, so in the end you'll never get a 'virgin' piece of news. They can manipulate it however they want."

British news avoiders sometimes talked about manipulation, but among the Spanish interviewees the frustration was more pronounced, and the Spaniards, more so than the British news avoiders described earlier, saw a direct link between financial and political motives. It was not just commercial incentives that distorted news; it was old-fashioned corruption. For example, Oliver—a computer programmer who said if he wanted fiction, he would just watch Netflix (not news)—explained that it was impossible to separate political and economic influence behind Spanish news "because everything is intertwined." Right-leaning businesses placed advertisements in right-leaning newspapers and demanded positive coverage in exchange. "In general, in Spain we all get mad about corruption," he said. "It bothers everyone that politicians put money in their pockets, but who hasn't paid for something without the value-added tax? And who hasn't done an invoice for a friend?"

Oliver here referred to some of the common ways that ordinary Spaniards technically cheat the system to save a little money or help out someone. He connected the partisan and economic manipulation of news back to what he saw as a broader cultural problem of widespread corruption in Spain. He was not alone: many Spanish interviewees saw the political partisanship of news as an example of precisely the kind of pervasive graft that, in theory, a watchdog press should be weeding out but that, in practice, was so deeply rooted in the culture at large that it encompassed the news media as well. As another Spaniard, José, explained, "I think the media covers up a lot of things—that, because of ideology or whatever, they cover up a lot of things so maybe you only get half the information, you never get all the information. I think they keep some things for their own benefit because the government doesn't want it known or different people don't want it known."

The frustration Spanish participants felt about news that they perceived as distorted by powerful interests was thus just part of a broader narrative they told of frustration about corruption and ineptitude that, they argued, was endemic to the country. And just as the U.K. interviewees had done with Brexit, in Spain interviewees consistently cited the biggest political news story in their country, the Catalonian independence referendum, as an example of these trends. Interviewees saw it as an issue that got way too much news coverage—most likely, they believed, to cover up or distract from more important issues that politicians could not resolve, such as unemployment, or that they would benefit from hiding, such as their own malfeasance.[13] As Silvia explained, "For example, the Catalonian problem—it's been in the works for ages, and the politicians and news media are all obsessed with it. And in the end, what happens? I think they're like, 'Look, we're going to focus on this because people's real problems—work, education, health care—in the end, we can't fix them.' And those are the things people really care about." Reflecting on it, she concluded, "The things that really affect you and are important, you have to look for that information yourself."

IT'S TOO MUCH OPINION, TOO LITTLE FACT: POLARIZATION AND PARTISAN BIAS IN THE UNITED STATES

Like the Spanish news avoiders, Americans often pointed out that different news outlets showed different versions of the same stories, so it was hard to know which to trust. Like the British news avoiders, Americans were turned off by what they saw as sensationalism for profit. What differentiated the U.S. news avoiders from the others was the degree to which they talked about all of this playing out against a backdrop of growing division and incivility in not just the political sphere but also the entire country. As Brian put it, "Instead of everybody uniting and trying to fix problems, I feel like the country's—they're very separated, and I just don't get that."

U.S. news avoiders saw evidence of growing political divides all around them, from politicians continually yelling and bickering (as David put it, "That's not a debate; that's people being snarky") to political conversations among people they knew, which many said they preferred to avoid because they didn't want to get into fights. In contrast to news lovers and their more extensive news communities (see chapter 4), news avoiders often said that their social circles were either indifferent to politics or included people who had strong opposing views, leaving the news avoiders feeling awkwardly stranded in the middle, wishing everyone would shut up. It felt like an up-close-and-personal version of the ugly divisiveness gripping the country more broadly. For example, Dion explained that not staying up-to-date on politics gave her an excuse to avoid political conversations. She said, "My fiancée is totally on one side, my parents are totally on the other, and I guess it's a cop-out, or I can just be like, 'Oh, I don't have the information to have an educated argument with you,' and I just get out of it."[14]

Most news avoiders we interviewed saw news as contributing to the problem of polarization rather than offering any kind of solution to it. The contribution was in part a matter of tone—they felt news echoed and magnified the shrill, snarky voices at the top—but also a matter of what they continually diagnosed as partisan bias or "too much opinion" in news. As Charlie concluded, "I feel that news outlets today, they're [motivated by] political agendas, and that's not journalism. Journalism is a watchdog for the people. That's not being a watchdog; that's serving your own interests. That's wrong." Here the examples that most quickly came to mind for news avoiders were cable networks such as Fox and CNN. Melanie, for example, said she disliked CNN because "I feel it's very biased. I mean, I think a lot of news is biased as to who's presenting the story. So, like I said, if there was just a way to just have the facts rather than any opinion in it, that would be nice."

Cable news came to mind first not because interviewees saw it as an exception but rather because they saw it as a good example of a widespread trend. This is a key point: although journalism scholars like us usually think of cable news as belonging to a different category of news provider—one that presents some straight news as well as programs that are commentary *by design* and therefore not expected to be neutral—news avoiders made no such distinctions. They did not see a clear difference between cable news and other news outlets or between programs designed to be commentary and others designed to report more objectively. They embraced the folk theory that *all* news blended fact and opinion to an unacceptable and confusing degree.

As we explained earlier, many news avoiders we interviewed said they were strictly apolitical. Without a strong partisan identity to help them differentiate between sources, they felt somewhat rudderless to navigate the options they encountered. However, in some cases, partisanship, or ideological leanings, did play a role in the United States in shaping how news avoiders assessed the worthwhileness of the available news media choices. Among news avoiders who had more defined partisan identities, these political attachments helped them make sense of what they perceived as a polarized information environment. Conservatives avoided news because of perceptions of widespread anti-Trump biases, while liberal-leaning news avoiders were turned off by any coverage of Trump at all. As Johnny put it, "I don't like seeing a bunch of Trump stuff, but that's almost unavoidable."[15]

Elite partisan rhetoric played a role here as well, with a number of U.S. news avoiders referring to messages they had heard about news being "fake."[16] Recall William, for example, from chapter 2, one of the U.S. news avoiders we interviewed who did not consume much *mainstream* news but did follow conservative voices on social media, including Trump. When we asked him his opinion on journalists in general, he said he often turned to InfoWars on Facebook or YouTube as an alternative. Much like news avoiders in Spain and the United Kingdom, William saw news organizations as obstacles to government effectively serving the public's interest rather than as independent guardians of democracy. Sites such as InfoWars were a potential antidote, he thought, but the problem was with the system as a whole. "There's a lot that gets hidden from the public," he said. "I wish somebody would let it all loose."

In sum, folk theories about why news was more lapdog than watchdog differed in the three countries we studied. In the United Kingdom, news avoiders blamed commercial incentives. In Spain, they said the press was distorted by political corruption. And in the United States, "too much opinion" poisoned news in a relentlessly polarized climate. In all three countries, however, news avoiders concurred that news was much more a contributor than a solution to the problem of government failing to respond to citizens' needs.

INTERNAL POLITICAL EFFICACY AND THE IMPORTANCE OF POLITICAL NEWS COMMUNITIES

As we showed in the previous section, many news avoiders in all three countries had low external efficacy. That is, they saw politics as unresponsive to citizens' needs, sometimes for different reasons in different countries. But many people feel this way generally, as the survey data we presented also indicates. So in this section we return to the question of what differentiates news avoiders from news lovers when it comes to their ideological beliefs. Yes, as we explained in the first section, news lovers found politics and political news interesting and intelligible, while news avoiders did not. But news lovers also found news important—vital even—despite not always feeling politics was responsive to their concerns. In this section, we explore why and how they retained that belief.

Our survey data showed some differences between news lovers and news avoiders regarding political efficacy overall, but the differences were much more apparent when we looked specifically at questions designed to measure *internal* efficacy, or people's confidence in their own abilities to effect change and participate in political life. These questions included two that political scientists typically use to tap political efficacy's internal dimension: whether respondents agree or disagree with the statements "People like me don't have any say about what the government does" and "Sometimes politics and government seem so complicated that a person like me can't really understand what's going on." Sure enough, people who consumed less news were significantly more likely to agree that they lacked such influence or abilities (figure 5.5).

These differences were even more stark on a third question we included—a question more directly tied to how engagement with news relates to internal efficacy. When respondents were asked to evaluate the statement "There's no point in watching the news because it deals with things I can do nothing about," news avoiders were the only group on average to agree (figure 5.6), a clear contrast with news lovers and other groups.

This sense of not being able to influence politics was echoed repeatedly in our interviews with news avoiders and interwoven throughout their broader narratives about news. Many made observations similar to Jane's (United Kingdom) that when it comes to politics, "I don't think that there's much I can do to change things, so I just don't bother listening or reading or anything in the first place." Or as Gracie (United Kingdom) explained, it was all too frustrating "because I can't change it. Especially reading the newspaper. That's not gonna get you anywhere." News avoiders often threw down similar comments as a kind of trump card to prove definitively that following news, political news in particular, was a waste of time.

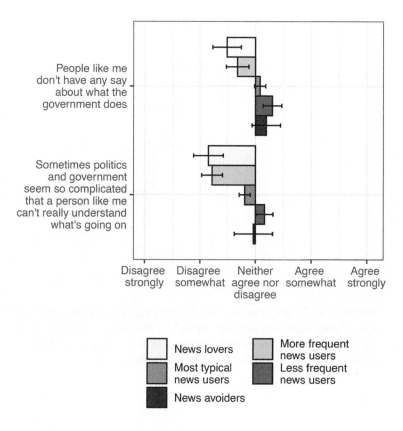

FIGURE 5.5. Differences in Internal Efficacy. News avoiders exhibited lower levels of "internal efficacy"—perceptions that they could have an impact on political and civic life. Error bars reflect 95 percent confidence intervals for the subgroups.

Source: U.S. News Audiences Survey 2020.

Where does a sense of internal political efficacy come from, specifically the belief that news can help one engage politically in an effective way? It is at least in part a question of how one is socialized, which is strongly influenced by one's station in life—that is, the intertwined forces of socioeconomic class and the communities to which one belongs. As we argued in chapter 4, being enmeshed in news communities (social or professional or

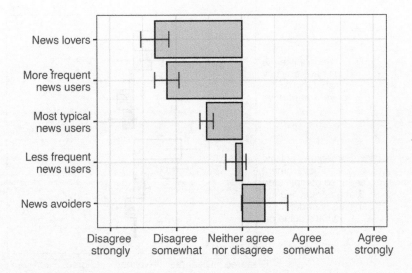

FIGURE 5.6. "There's No Point in Watching the News Because It Deals with Things I Can Do Nothing About." Differences were more evident for internal efficacy, specifically with respect to the news. Error bars reflect 95 percent confidence intervals for the subgroups.

Source: U.S. News Audiences Survey 2020.

both) that demand that members keep up with news also helps news lovers sustain the belief that doing so is an important civic duty. We can now add that these communities also help news lovers feel empowered to engage politically by providing psychological and practical support for that engagement.

For the news lovers we interviewed in Iowa, social encounters were often saturated with discussion of news about political affairs. This was, no doubt, magnified by caucus season: they also described being contacted continually by the presidential campaigns and pressing hands with candidates at political events. Like news avoiders, they saw discussion about politics as a minefield and sometimes avoided conversing with people who held opposing views to avoid unpleasant altercations. But they often took comfort in conversations with people who shared their political views. Barb, for example, said she couldn't discuss anything with her mother, a Trump supporter ("It's forbidden. It's a guaranteed argument"), but she saw conversations with like-minded liberal friends as an essential outlet—not fun, exactly, but cathartic because they all cared so much about the issues. For news lovers, attending political events was easy and even enjoyable in part because such events were an extension of their social lives; they valued them as opportunities to chat with people who shared their views. Mike, for example, a gregarious father of four, described the Iowa caucus he attended as "a neat community event" where he enjoyed running into people he knew and getting to "share who you're supporting and why." He insisted, "There's some good conversations that come from that."

For news lovers, the social aspect of news had important practical implications. Many news lovers we interviewed also said they socialized with elected politicians and other political professionals ranging from school board and city council members to former governors and presidential staffers, naming them as people they could contact directly with questions or concerns about policy matters. For example, when we asked Carolyn, a former political operative, if she felt she was informed enough about current events, she said, "I have a lot of friends still in DC and here in the State House and friends in city council that I can ask."

For news lovers like Carolyn, being close to political inner circles was helpful in a practical way, as a source of information, but it also helped in a more abstract way because it made politics seem close to home and less mysterious, reaffirming the news lovers' belief that they could make an impact. Unlike news avoiders, who thought of politics as a distant realm open only to an elite political class, news lovers thought of politics as a decision-making process that not only included them but also was vitally important and could even be fun. Lance, a young father who worked in the agriculture business, never doubted that politics affected him: his job was directly affected by even international policies such as Chinese tariffs. His group of friends enjoyed debating politics, and he said he sometimes had trouble sleeping because his head was on fire over the rhetoric coming out of Washington. When we asked if he ever felt helpless to influence politics, he responded, "I would say yes, but what's funny is one of the guys in my group felt the same way, and then he ran for city council and won." Another news lover, Rachel, was running for city council when we initially interviewed her. By the time we did the follow-up interview, she was a newly elected city councilwoman.

News avoiders not only often lacked partisan identities to help them navigate political news but also, as we detailed in the previous chapter, typically lacked connections to news communities where they could regularly converse about political stories in the news. As news lovers' experiences show, such communities provide multiple forms of support: serving as a resource for questions about politics, offering social incentives for following politics closely, and, most of all, building up their confidence that they were capable of understanding and participating in political life. News avoiders sometimes said they did not know *anyone* who knew more about politics and current events than they did, and even when they did know someone like this, they felt at best ambivalent about political discussions and at worst actively turned off by what they saw as pointless arguing. News avoider Bethany (United States), for example, tried and failed to cast a vote in the local Iowa caucus because she did not know in advance that the process takes hours, which in her case would require arranging for childcare. She had a conflicting appointment later that evening. "It was the first time I've ever done that," she explained. "I didn't know exactly what I did, or anything." By contrast, we spoke to news lovers who had carefully strategized in advance with their partners about how to manage their kids at the caucus. They knew what to expect, and if they had not known, their political community could help them figure it out.

News avoiders also had little to no contact with politicians or people who worked in politics, even in passing. In most cases, there was simply no overlap between their social circles and those of professional political actors at all. With very few exceptions, that was even true for news avoiders in Iowa during caucus season, where crossing paths with a presidential candidate is not uncommon for even marginally engaged citizens, and registered voters are bombarded by political appeals from the various campaigns.

This disparity between news lovers and avoiders in their connections to political communities is also reflected in our survey data from the United

States (figure 5.7). News avoiders were far less likely than other groups to say they knew a politician personally; only 18 percent of news avoiders compared to 48 percent of news lovers. And none of the personal ties that news avoiders did have were with a close friend or family member.

This disparity also extends to contact with journalists. News avoiders not only lacked close ties to political actors but also had fewer direct experiences

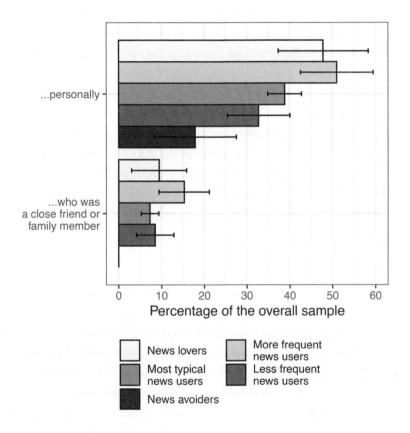

FIGURE 5.7. Percentage Who Have "Known a Politician . . . ." Differences between news avoiders and others in the United States were evident with respect to whether they said they personally knew a politician. The percentage of news avoiders who knew a politician as a close friend or family member was zero. Error bars reflect 95 percent confidence intervals for the subgroups.

Source: U.S. News Audiences Survey 2020.

with journalists and rarely knew any personally. Meanwhile, the opposite was true for news lovers. Not only did they run in the same circles as politicians, as we described earlier, but they also had relatively frequent contact with journalists, especially compared to news avoiders. We can see this distinction in our U.S. survey data as well (figure 5.8). News avoiders are significantly less likely to have been interviewed for a news story (10 percent said they had been, compared to 48 percent of news lovers), known a journalist personally (20 percent compared to 38 percent), or contacted a journalist with ideas or feedback (10 percent compared to 36 percent).

In sum, not being integrated into a political news community has both practical and more abstract implications for facilitating political participation and in turn for making political news seem relevant. In practical terms, people gain important information about how to participate in political life from political campaigns, from news content, and from those around them who follow political news. Just as important, in more abstract terms, being enmeshed in a news community can help individuals sustain an interest in politics and can help to reinforce beliefs on a gut level that they can make a difference in politics and that news can help them do so.

* * *

As we have argued in this chapter, rather than seeing news about political officials as serving the public interest, news avoiders tend to view such coverage cynically as motivated primarily by a single-minded pursuit of profit, as in the United Kingdom; distorted by economic *and* political corruption, as in Spain; or defined by a growing partisan divide that engenders pervasive political bias, as in the United States. However, these folk theories about the failings of the press—how it serves to facilitate rather than temper the excesses of an unresponsive, out-of-touch system of government—are not unique to news avoiders. Low external efficacy—the sense that politics is not responsive to people's concerns—is widespread, and the belief that news media fail to hold politicians to account is a part of that sense. What sets news avoiders apart has more to do with their *internal* political efficacy, their sense of their own lack of power to effect change. Although both news

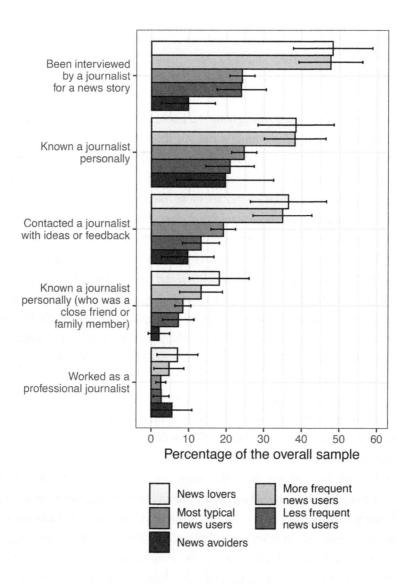

FIGURE 5.8. Interactions with the News Media. Differences were evident between news avoiders and others in the United States for other kinds of interactions with journalists. Error bars reflect 95 percent confidence intervals for the subgroups.

Source: U.S. News Audiences Survey 2020.

lovers and news avoiders may concede that they have limited ability to influence major political decisions, the news lovers we interviewed were far more confident in their ability to try—thanks in part to stronger partisan identities and connections to communities of other politically oriented people.

As we have argued throughout the book, the factors that help people build and sustain news communities are shaped by patterns of socialization that are inextricably bound up with social class. People with higher levels of education are more likely to have jobs and social circles that require them to keep up with news and are more likely to come into contact with or even belong to a professional political class. That proximity can help people sustain ideological beliefs about the political system, including the beliefs that paying attention to politics through news is important, that one can make a meaningful impact in politics, and that the former can help with the latter. Being part of those circles can also make even distant matters seem close to home for them because other people in their social circles not only find those issues relevant but also believe that as individual citizens they are able to—and actually *can* in some cases—affect the way problems are addressed and rectified.

News avoiders' conviction that they cannot make a difference politically and that news certainly will not help them do so is the core of many news avoiders' media choice narratives. Why follow news when it cannot help you change any of the problems news highlights? But that belief propels a cycle. The more people avoid the news, the harder it is for them to feel informed enough to engage politically. Should they decide they want to try, it can feel extremely hard to get up to speed if they have checked out of political news for many years or all their lives. Moreover, both news organizations and political actors have little incentive to attend to the concerns of the disengaged. After all, generally speaking, the disengaged do not pay for news or see advertisements in news or pressure their representatives or vote.[17]

If news avoiders usually lack empowering news communities *and* distrust news media to provide independent, reliable information about politics, what might this mean against a backdrop of growing populism across much of the world? News media that the public perceives as less trustworthy than politicians or in the same untrustworthy camp are an attractive target for populist figures who lump the news media into a group with political and economic elites and claim for themselves the role of public defender. Indeed, our findings suggest that news avoiders might be receptive to such appeals, especially if the appeals are made through alternative media channels. Although most news avoiders we interviewed did not yet embrace populist movements, they already more or less embraced a populist view of the news media as the enemy—or, at least, not the friend or defender—of the people. We saw hints that even the more apolitical among them might see the appeal of political rhetoric that attacks the authority of the press as an independent institution even when that rhetoric originates from far away. For example, at the end of each interview we asked if interviewees thought it was "important to be informed about the news." We had the following exchange with Hollie (United Kingdom):

> *Hollie:* Yes, but what else I was reading on Donald Trump was how he was saying that certain news are fake, and when you read stuff like that, you think, if he's saying it, and he's the president of the U.S. now, you just never know what's going on. Do you know what I mean? So, it's like, I don't know.
>
> *BT:* How do you make sense of all the different sources of information?
>
> *Hollie:* I just don't trust anything, to be honest.

In this chapter, we have explored how political ideologies can shape people's views of the news media and be used to justify their news avoidance. How people think and feel about news is also strongly influenced by the infrastructures that make different forms of media available to them and give them different options for managing information. We explore these dynamics in the next chapter.

6

INFRASTRUCTURES

How Media Platforms and Pathways
Shape News Avoidance

R ecall Mike from chapter 4. A devout Catholic in Iowa, Mike talked about the importance of the church in his life and how his religious identity shaped his relationship with news. When we asked him to name the issue that most concerned him day to day, he said he saw it as his family's "mission as Christians" to raise kids to be "good people and have them go to heaven." Mike was also a news lover—at least as defined the way we define it in this book by how frequently he accessed news. Much of his news consumption was on Twitter. He was drawn to "that constant buzz almost, addiction almost, of just always consuming something." But Mike was not the kind of news lover devoted to journalism. He didn't like the way it made him feel dependent, out of control. As he put it, "The Israelites were slaves to the Egyptians, and we're slaves to the news, streaming, information, sweets, alcohol, you name it. We're slaves to all this stuff."

Between our first and second interviews, Mike did something unusual. For ninety days before the Easter holiday, he cut out virtually all news from his life. Cold turkey. He found he had to stop himself from tapping on Twitter "out of reflex" ("It's like a muscle," he said), but he soon found he could resist the urge and "hardly even thought about it." He went from news addict to news avoider in just two weeks. And he liked it—more than he thought he would. Sounding every bit like a news avoider, he said changing his media habits helped him feel "*freed* of not having to even think about it." Instead of being bombarded by doom and gloom, he explained, "I don't have to worry about the things that don't impact me and/or I can't influence or change."

In previous chapters, we focused on how statements like these function as powerful media choice narratives: explanations for behaviors informed by folk theories around the worthwhileness of news (or its lack thereof). We underscored the importance of how people's *identities* (who they are) and *ideologies* (what they believe) intersect in ways that shape the news communities they are (or are not) a part of, socializing and reinforcing practices around news use and perceptions about its value in their lives. Indeed, when Mike curtailed his use of news, he still found that his news community, especially his news-loving wife and talkative coworkers, helped him stay informed enough about the stories that mattered to him. It allowed him to thrive.[1]

But Mike's relationship to news was not only defined by these social factors and beliefs but also shaped by the tools and technologies he used (or avoided)—that is, by media *infrastructures*. These infrastructures have loomed large throughout the book, and in this chapter we examine them more directly. We focus specifically on people's experiences with and folk theories about infrastructures (as opposed to the material characteristics and affordances of these infrastructures), and we use the term broadly to encompass digital platforms such as Twitter, Facebook, Google, and WhatsApp as well as other offline pathways people may use to discover and make sense of information. The latter include legacy modes of media, such as radio and television, but more generally the habits and routines that structure people's lives and establish the conditions under which they are exposed to news and (especially) conversations about it. Many of the tools, technologies, and techniques people use to find, access, and navigate the contemporary information environment are different from even a few years ago, and the current phenomenon of news avoidance cannot be understood without them.

In this chapter, we consider people's experiences with media infrastructures in two ways. We begin by describing how news avoiders think about them. Specifically, we detail three folk theories about how the contemporary media environment works that we heard repeated by many news avoiders and that guided their behaviors toward news: (1) "news finds me" via *incidental* exposure to information as opposed to daily routines specifically devoted to consuming news;[2] (2) if news does not just appear on its own, "the information is out there" and just a Google search away; and (3) "I don't know what to believe," an expression of frustration that some (but not all) news avoiders shared about what happens when news does *not* find them or on the rare occasions when they went looking for it. We found that information-gathering strategies that were heavily reliant on digital tools and technologies but not forged in strong, trusting relationships with news outlets often left news avoiders struggling to make sense of what they saw and heard. Not knowing what to believe when they encountered news often reinforced the notion that it was best not to care about it at all.

In the second half of the chapter, we focus on how news lovers differ from news avoiders in the ways they find, access, and navigate the contemporary information environment. The folk theories we capture in the first half of the chapter—"news finds me," "the information is out there," and "I don't know what to believe"—are not unique to news avoiders. But news lovers, unlike news avoiders, have developed specific routines involving a narrow selection of trusted sources that best match their preferences and suit the circumstances of their lives. These well-developed curation strategies allow them to navigate the media landscape more confidently and even to enjoy it. Understanding how news lovers relate to media infrastructures suggests ways that news avoiders might be empowered to engage more effectively with news on their own terms.

FOLK THEORIES OF INFORMATION DISCOVERY

FOLK THEORY 1. "NEWS FINDS ME": PATHWAYS TO INCIDENTAL EXPOSURE TO NEWS

One of the most common folk theories we heard repeated by news avoiders was that carving out specific times in the day for consuming news was old-fashioned. Instead, as Cameron (United Kingdom) put it succinctly, "News should come looking for me; I shouldn't go looking for it." Given the contemporary digital media landscape, they saw it as unnecessary to fit reading the newspaper, watching the news on television, or browsing news websites into their routines because in their experience any important information would reach them all by itself as they went about their lives. Indeed, many interviewees described feeling as if news were almost always "in the air," an ambient part of daily life.[3] Libby (United Kingdom), a hospital administrative staffer, said most people she knew "kind of absorb" news from the radio or the internet. As a result, she explained, "most people are, kind of, aware of things that are happening." This "daily feed of news," as she described it, happened almost through osmosis; it did not require active information seeking. News avoiders felt this was an easier, more efficient way to stay informed—or at least informed *enough* about what they cared to know—than seeking out news directly from the source.

This "news finds me" folk theory, well documented by a growing number of academic studies,[4] took various forms, but many news avoiders expressed versions of this sentiment. Indeed, when we surveyed U.S. news audiences about the statement "I don't worry about keeping up with the news because I know news will find me," those who said they accessed news the least frequently were the most likely to agree (figure 6.1).

Of course, there is reason to doubt whether adopting a "news finds me" attitude toward information really works as a strategy for being well informed (more on that when we get to the third folk theory). Indeed, studies have shown that digital algorithms are less likely to deliver news content to those least interested in clicking on it,[5] and people who express "news finds me" perceptions also tend objectively to know less about politics.[6] But when most news avoiders referred to news finding them, they were not suggesting that their brief exposure to it gave them in-depth knowledge, only that it helped them be aware of what the "big stories" were at any given moment. After all, some pointed out, they had learned about terrorist attacks and other major stories in the past without taking the time to look for them. Even if they did not want to hear about Brexit, Donald Trump, or Catalan independence, as Celeste (Spain) noted, finding out about those huge stories was all but inevitable: "There's one [piece of news]

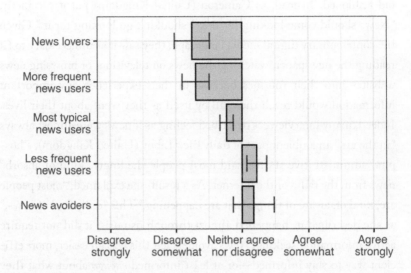

FIGURE 6.1. "I Don't Worry About Keeping Up with the News Because I Know News Will Find Me." People who use news more often are somewhat less likely to agree that "news finds me," whereas news avoiders and less frequent users of news are somewhat more likely. Error bars reflect 95 percent confidence intervals for the subgroups.

Source: U.S. News Audiences Survey 2020.

that is impossible to not know about, even if you don't look at anything at all, it's impossible, and that's Catalonia, the independence thing. Because if you go to a store to look at a dress, you're hearing two ladies behind you talking about it. It's not that I'm interested in what people are talking about, but you just hear it. Or you're in a bar having a drink at one table, and the group of friends at the table behind you are talking about it."

As this example illustrates well, although some news avoiders may have felt as if they were simply absorbing news stories through osmosis, they in fact relied on incidental exposure to news through different combinations of online and offline sources to stay informed about the big stories of the day. Some of the news they encountered was "firsthand news," or news produced by professional journalists, but much of it was what we came to think of as "secondhand news" (borrowing a phrase from an interviewee), or conversations about news they either participated in or overheard. For example, Rodolfo, a twenty-six-year-old web developer in Spain, said political corruption was an important topic to him. When we asked how he got wind of information about this issue, he responded, "The same as almost everything I've told you. From clips that someone sends on WhatsApp, some story, word-of-mouth conversations, and the TV at coffee hour at work." Rodolfo did not seek out current events information—he thought he learned "practically 90 percent" of his current events news through joke memes circulating on WhatsApp—but time had taught him he could rely on these sources to incidentally expose him to major news stories. In the United Kingdom, Caleb described a different set of pathways to information, but the effect was similar. He recalled learning the news that Trump had won the 2016 U.S. election first because he walked by protests in Leeds, and then "Facebook lit up about it, so there were a lot of that I had to scroll past, and then a lot of the newspapers, you know, when I got on the bus, and I had a little cheeky glance: Trump."

As these examples illustrate, for news avoiders today, even in a highly digital world, old-school forms of incidental exposure to firsthand news via broadcast TV, radio, and cable television do still take place.[7] These pathways to exposure often involve specific social ties: some news avoiders we interviewed lived with or visited someone—often a parent or grandparent—who liked to watch news on TV. Others described the classic incidental exposure scenario of catching bits of news on TV between preferred programs or on the radio in the car before they changed the station. Exposure to firsthand news in public places was also fairly common. Interviewees described catching, as Caleb put it, a "cheeky glance" at newspaper headlines on public transit or in line at the supermarket or glimpsing TV news in hospital waiting rooms, bars, or cafés, sometimes against their will. For example, in Spain Pedro said he ate lunch every day in a restaurant where the TV was tuned to news and found himself sucked into coverage of political corruption despite his best efforts to avoid it. He explained, "You see the headlines, you see the subtitles, you see the stories, and of course you get upset even if you don't want to. . . . I sit with my back to the television, but of course you hear comments."

And, notably—again, even in a highly digital environment—old-fashioned offline word of mouth was the most common form of second-hand news that came up in our interviews. As discussed in chapter 4, many news avoiders relied on a spouse, family member, or close friend who followed news more closely than they did to keep them informed. What they described was similar to the "two-step flow model" developed by media researchers in the 1950s to capture how we are often influenced by people we know and trust, who get much of their information from the media.[8] Even the most disengaged news avoiders who did not encounter news in any other way said they found out about major events from other people. As Iris, a stay-at-home mom in Spain, explained, "Many times I've said to my husband, 'One of these days we're going to get up, and there will be a war, and we won't know about it.' I mean, if someone doesn't tell us, we don't find out about things; that's the truth."

Although these old-school forms of offline incidental exposure do still occur, for many news avoiders the belief that "news finds me" was especially tied to their use of social media and messaging platforms such as Facebook, Twitter, and WhatsApp. As Caitlin (United Kingdom) explained, "It's Facebook. It's always Facebook. I think that's how people communicate and find out things nowadays, rather than watching the news." She added that conventional ways of paying attention to news were too time-consuming, so "Facebook's an easy way to keep up with it." Although most of the news they saw online was secondhand discussion, some did bump into firsthand news on digital media via headlines through alerts, apps, or widgets that "just popped up" on their phones either by default or because they had inadvertently installed them, encounters they mostly described as intrusive and bothersome. For example, Daniel (United States) said Apple News sometimes appeared on his phone when he swiped the icon by accident "just because I haven't spent the time to figure out how to shut it off." Brian (United States) recalled getting occasional alerts from a local TV news affiliate on his phone. He explained, "I signed up to win, like you sign up to win a prize ticket somewhere," and he had never bothered deleting the app.

Although our news-avoiding interviewees were sometimes exposed to firsthand news, they relied mostly on secondhand sources to keep them informed. But that meant they wound up missing a lot. Most recognized that they were hearing only a limited set of news stories: as we noted earlier, these stories were usually the *huge* news stories of the day, such as Brexit, Trump's election, and Catalan independence, as well as anything so sensational or so close by that "everyone was talking about it." That left out a lot of news that makes for less compelling gossip: policy discussion, for example, or the less juicy contextual material that helps people make sense of the big stories they do encounter. Alex (Spain), for example, had seen joke memes on WhatsApp about the Catalan leader Carles Puigdemont, so he was able to recognize him, but he admitted he did not know much beyond "that he's named Puigdemont and that they're looking for him to put him in jail and [laughs] nothing else." Awareness of basic political information like this can be useful, but as a basis for engaging meaningfully in political life, it clearly has limitations.

Indeed, most news avoiders we spoke to were aware of the many gaps in their knowledge about the news. As we detailed in earlier chapters, many did feel as if they lived in their "own little bubble." But some were very happy in that bubble. When they were not, they could always fall back on a second folk theory that structured their attitudes about the importance of paying attention to news.

FOLK THEORY 2. "THE INFORMATION IS OUT THERE": ACCESSING THE NEWS THAT DOESN'T FIND YOU

When news-avoiding interviewees described the relatively rare occasions when they wanted to know more about a specific piece of news-related information, many articulated an additional set of beliefs and practices that we colloquially call the idea that "the information is out there." That is, they believed there was an infinite expanse of facts available at everyone's fingertips if ever they chose to seek them out. Central to this folk theory is the belief that if one should want more information about an issue, this information will in fact be both available and easy to find whether via social media or search engines or other sources. As Annabelle (United Kingdom) put it, "I feel like it's all out there. It's all out there." Or as Gracie (United Kingdom) said, "The internet is so incredibly vast. There must be information on there somewhere." This folk theory manifested in a couple of different ways, often alongside two complementary statements repeated in interview after interview: "I just Google it" and "Do your own research." When news did *not* find them, news avoiders explained, these options were the essential strategies, made possible because, again, the information was all around, available, and waiting to be found. By comparison, they saw sitting back and trusting the news provided by professional news organizations as not only inefficient but also dangerously naive.

A confidence that "the information is out there" led many interviewees to say they preferred Googling information periodically rather than consuming news regularly because the search engine gave them greater control over their own news exposure and allowed them to be more selective about the sources they used. They felt they could dive into civic and political affairs with a laserlike focus when they really needed to but also go about living their lives above the fray the rest of the time. News avoiders also described feeling empowered by digital technologies and the access they afforded to these "vast" ecosystems of information. Brianna (United Kingdom), for example, compared using online search to "an encyclopedia, books, and things like that" but "so much easier." She said, "So, that's probably my first call. It would depend on what I was looking for and how serious or how deep I want to go," but generally her first instinct was to use a search engine: "Google, yeah! Yeah, you can Google everything." For many interviewees, "Google" was shorthand for how to navigate this expanse of information: a helpful tool for precise extraction of facts on reserve in the internet's endless repository of knowledge. The (unprompted) references to the search engine were a near constant refrain in our interviews. As Silvia (Spain) summed it up, "The things that really affect you and are important, you have to look for that information yourself. Now, for example, we have the easiness of Google. But if we didn't have that, where would we be?"

As Silvia's statement suggests, the second part of the "information is out there" folk theory is another notion: it is not only advisable but imperative to "do your own research" if you really want to be informed.[9] As we described in previous chapters, news avoiders tended to see professionally produced news as molded and twisted by unseen commercial and political forces that packaged the news to suit their own agendas. It was therefore incumbent upon individuals to seek out the real story by digging deeper on their own, whether on Google or elsewhere, rather than accept information from journalists at face value. Many expressed versions of what researchers have referred to as "generalized skepticism" toward all sources of information,[10] but especially toward information that they felt was being actively pushed on them by professional sources, whom they suspected of having ulterior motives. David (United States) said he knew he had to be skeptical of any news he encountered "unless I seek it out or unless I am doing my own independent research." He went on, "If I'm being force-fed, I just don't trust it."

When it came to doing their own research, the information that news avoiders often had in mind as being "out there"—whether they actually tapped into it or not—was primary or "official" information, which they said they could get directly online from government agencies and which they saw as more trustworthy than individual news articles. For example, when Isabella (United Kingdom) described looking for information about a new government program for childcare subsidies, she said she would go first to government websites rather than to news stories. She explained, "I'd probably just Google it, and then there would be some sort of form to fill in or some sort of . . . there would be information on there where to get it." Ed (United States) described seeking out "meeting minutes" from city council meetings ("it's like the raw data") to better understand what was happening locally, whereas "me watching the news and feeling stuff about the news ain't going to do anything."

In some extreme cases, when it came to "doing their own research," a small number of news avoiders said what they had in mind went beyond searching online and involved conducting their own interviews with subjects in the news itself. Ironically, some described practices not dissimilar to journalism. Reggie (United States), for example, said if he was "passionate" enough about a subject, he would "go out and talk to people involved with it," verifying information with original sources directly. He didn't think professional news organizations could be trusted to do this work fairly on their own.[11] "I got into an argument with somebody one time about why I don't watch the news, and they're like, 'Well, why don't you watch the news?' I was like, 'Because I don't think. . . .' It came to where I was saying I would research it, and they were like, 'Well, how would you research it?' 'I would go out and actually do this stuff myself.' And they're like, 'Wouldn't you just watch a different news station?' Really, just hear yourself! Like, no, no, no! That's not going to work."

It is worth underscoring that the "information is out there" folk theory is deeply intertwined with specific changes in media infrastructures, especially the rise of the web and search engines. As we showed in the previous section, the "news find me" folk theory likewise involves newer digital platforms, including social media and messaging applications that enable incidental exposure and easy sharing and forwarding of all sorts of content. But that folk theory *also* relies heavily on older forms of media infrastructures, including television and radio, as well as on offline conversations with friends, family, and colleagues. One can imagine news avoiders in a pre-digital environment believing that news would "find them" simply through word of mouth. By contrast, the belief that the "information is out there"— that everything is, at least in principle, only a click or a few search queries away—is a much more contemporary idea, specific to current media infrastructures and what people imagine they make possible.

Of course, a belief that the "information is out there" does not mean that information is as easily findable in practice as news avoiders might expect or that they necessarily seek out that information using the various alternatives they said they could use. There is a big difference between saying one can just "Google it" and actually doing so. But this second folk theory captures how contemporary digital media infrastructures often interact with deep-seated ideas about the nature of news media. When news avoiders not only believed information was easily accessible *but also* held deeply suspicious views toward news itself, most saw turning to Google to independently research information as the more responsible way to navigate the current environment. This belief, the confidence that many expressed that the real information was out *there* rather than attributable to reporting by professional journalists, thus reinforced tendencies to avoid news. Not only were finding and engaging with information online empowering and easily done—at least in theory—but relying on such strategies was also an important defense against otherwise unavoidable efforts by media organizations to manipulate and mislead.

FOLK THEORY 3. "I DON'T KNOW WHAT TO BELIEVE": WHAT GETS MISSED AND MISUNDERSTOOD?

The combination of the "news finds me" and the "information is out there" folk theories helped many news avoiders we interviewed feel untroubled by their relative lack of attention to news. Most did not feel *well* informed, but through being incidentally exposed to news online and offline and by relying on internet search engines to do their own research (or knowing that they had that option, whether they used it or not), many were convinced they could stay informed *enough* about the bits of information in the news they cared about.

That said, a considerable number of the news avoiders we interviewed also described feeling frustrated and uncertain when they tried to put such strategies into practice. We call this third folk theory "I don't know what to believe." Not all news avoiders expressed it. Those embedded in more robust news communities often felt they had more tools at their disposal to navigate the information environment (see chapter 4). But many could also point to specific moments when they had felt entirely out of the loop—when news had not, in fact, "found them," and they could not find it. Yes, the information might be out there, but knowing how to sort through it was another matter, and some said they had mostly given up trying. As Gracie (United Kingdom) said, it would require searching through "the whole of Google to find the unbiased news. . . . I just can't be bothered." Similarly, Jane (United Kingdom) said she felt overwhelmed by a "black hole of information." Before trailing off, she went on, "I don't try to make sense of what's going on, to be honest. I mean, I know knowledge is power, but. . . ."

The "I don't know what to believe" folk theory captures how it can feel for people who see all sources as equally suspect to try to navigate media infrastructures and information pathways in contemporary life. News avoiders had trouble sorting through the vast quantities of available sources they found online in part because they so rarely felt they could place their trust in any particular source to help them decipher what was true and false. Most had never developed any kind of habitual relationship to specific news sources, so they all seemed equally credible—and equally incredible—and, for some, conventional news sources were the least credible of all.[12] This distrust felt justified by the fact that news sources reported the same stories so differently (see chapter 3). "You can look in newspapers and stuff, but you don't always get the right answer," Alicia (United Kingdom) said of her experiences looking for information online. "One newspaper says one thing, and one says another. Can't always rely on 'em."

News avoiders often expressed versions of this folk theory when we pressed them to describe what happened when they felt they needed more information about specific issues. Terri (United States) concluded, "I just need to figure out more reliable websites," adding that when she had tried using Google, "that doesn't help" because "I don't know who to trust anymore." Likewise, Olivia (United Kingdom) said she wasn't sure she would be able to parse through stories online: "I'd need to learn that skill if I was going to get into the news. I'd need to . . . if I was going to actually, like, do something about this, I don't know, I'd have to learn the skills. There's a lot of conflicting things."

This sense of not knowing what to believe is closely tied to the way news avoiders navigate digital media infrastructures, but it also relates to the form of news itself, a phenomenon the journalist and public intellectual Walter Lippmann famously observed nearly a hundred years ago. He argued that news items are constructed such that the individuals featured in them, the issues they cover, the processes at play, and the vocabulary used is unfamiliar, even alien, to much of the public. It makes sense only to those who are continuously engaged and who understand the background context. As such, Lippmann wrote that newspaper readers often "arrive in the middle of the third act and [leave] before the last curtain, having stayed just long enough, perhaps, to decide who is the hero and who the villain of the piece."[13] That metaphor is still pertinent today. News coverage makes a host of assumptions about how familiar people are with, for example, politics, the actors and institutions involved, and the language in which they operate—assumptions that are sometimes, even often, not warranted. (Tellingly, in 2016 *after* the United Kingdom's referendum on its membership in the European Union, Google reported that searches for "what is the eu" and "what is brexit" started climbing across Britain late into the night.[14])

Contemporary digital audiences consume news in an even more disjointed and disconnected way than in Lippmann's era. One does not even need to enter a "theater"; we instead catch bits of dialogue broadcast in an endless stream directly to the devices in our pockets. Such snippets are often devoid of context, so we must try to make sense of them with the tools at our disposal. Our interviews suggest that for consistent news avoiders the feeling is not unlike dipping into the middle of the sixth episode of the fourth season of *Game of Thrones* and expecting to be able to rely on Google to piece together what's happening and why it matters. It is theoretically possible, but in practice even grasping who the heroes and villains are can be a challenge. You *may* find vast streams of messages online about the latest events in the news, but much of the information is contradictory, so it is hard to know for sure what transpired, who any of the characters are and why they matter, or what to think about any of it enough to feel invested in the story's resolution. And jargony terminology remains a challenge: not everyone will know what "inflation" means, what the Dow Jones is, what, if anything, the adjective *natural* says about gas, and so on.

News avoiders often saw digital platforms such as Facebook and Google favorably as useful tools for making sense of news stories, but just as they expressed skepticism about news outlets, they also said the digital tools could not be blindly trusted, either. Some speculated about the indirect role that platforms and their algorithms played in shaping the information they encountered. Kali (United Kingdom), for example, said she thought her exposure to news stories was related to her past browsing behaviors, noting, "I assume that's based on searches that I've done and cookies that have been on my site—that that's been picked up."[15] Many expressed concern that Facebook's algorithm encouraged infighting and disagreement.[16] Isabella (United Kingdom) offered, "I think what happens on Facebook is one thing gets shared, and then everyone thinks they're a little bit of a politician, so they all start sharing it and having their opinions." These beliefs and uncertainties about the unseen forces that shaped the news that news avoiders did and did not see via digital platforms only reinforced their view that it was safer to be distrusting toward all professionally produced news, whether they encountered it via platforms or straight from the source, and instead to stay informed through secondhand news from trusted friends and acquaintances.

The folk theories "news finds me" and the "information is out there" probably seem familiar, even empowering, to many readers of this book. Some news avoiders saw them that way as well. But as we have shown in this section, a reliance on these media pathways also left many news avoiders feeling uncertain, expressing versions of the "I don't know what to believe" folk theory. As Hollie (United Kingdom) recounted when describing her information-seeking processes when looking for information about Brexit, she would "Google it"; more specifically: "'The latest on Brexit,' that's what I would Google. Or, like, 'What will the British pound be worth?' 'What changes are going to happen to the economy?' That's what I'd Google, probably." But Hollie was also quick to point out that professional news sources were especially to be avoided and discounted. She said she would turn to "articles from independent researchers . . . not, like, news" because news itself was automatically suspect. She concluded, "I just feel like you just don't know. Look how people are saying it's fake. It's just fake, isn't it?"

NEWS LOVERS' CURATED MEDIA DIETS
OF TRUSTED SOURCES

The three folk theories described in this chapter—"news finds me," "the information is out there," and "I don't know what to believe"—capture different ways news avoiders see the media infrastructures they rely on. Many more typical news consumers will relate to these ideas—the first two at least, if not the third at times as well. In this concluding section, we focus more specifically on how news lovers, as opposed to news avoiders, thought about and navigated their information environments. We do so to assess what is distinct about their relationships with media that allows them to find, access, and navigate information more easily. We focus on two points that came up repeatedly: their use of news was largely a function of habit involving a distinct set of carefully curated sources, and, in a reversal of the experience many news avoiders described, placing their trust in those specific sources made it easier and more enjoyable for news lovers to pay attention to news. This complementary pair of strategies made news something they could love rather than avoid.

CURATING A PERSONALIZED MEDIA HABIT

One of the most obvious differences between the ways that news lovers and news avoiders navigated the information environment was that the former had particularly well-defined habits related to news. As many scholars across disciplines have highlighted, habits by definition begin as deliberate actions that are found to be rewarding and are repeated until they become rote.[17] Habits take much of the active decision making out of our media choices. They are often no longer experienced as individual choices but rather as routines. Many news lovers experienced news in that way: when we asked Jerry (United States) to summarize the main reasons he consumed so much news, he responded, "By now, probably a good portion of it is just habit. I would say something that I've been doing for maybe fifty-plus years."

For many news lovers, habits involving news consumption made it easier to stay informed in part because they did not need to "make time" to follow news. News was already built into the way they lived their lives. Automatic. They enjoyed it in part because it was a reliable, reassuring touchstone of daily life. As Paul (United States) said, "I'll get up, get a cup of coffee, and I'll listen to the news." Or Bob (United States): "I'm just kind of repetitious. I do the same things all the time." These news habits were often quite detailed but easy for news lovers to describe because they always followed the same pattern.[18] They were also highly personalized and varied dramatically from person to person. Consider Fred and Nancy, the conservative farmer and left-leaning grandmother we wrote about in chapter 5 as examples of news lovers in the United States with clear partisan identities that allowed them to navigate between sources more easily. Both had developed a finely tuned palette with many carefully considered preferences about specific sources of news they either liked or disliked. In contrast to the news avoiders described in the previous sections who lumped most news together as equally unappealing, news lovers like Fred and Nancy curated their news media repertoires to reflect their specific preferences:

> The first thing I do is look at the weather radar and see what's coming or what isn't coming, and then I get the *Des Moines Register*; they have a little synopsis, and I read that, and then I go to the national news and see what's there, read Farm Futures, [which] has an internet page, and then I have a marketing firm out of Spencer, Iowa, and they usually have a thing, and so by the time I get through all of those, and I click on maybe a link or something to read. Like this morning, Japanese beetles are really bad, so I click on that link, and here's what you need to look for, what sprays work, those kind of things. So by the time you get it all, it's an hour.
>
> —Fred (United States)

> My morning is . . . I'll have my morning cup of coffee, which is about as long as it takes to read the [*Des Moines*] *Register* cover to cover. That includes doing the puzzle. Then, during the day, I will try to work my way through both the entire *Washington Post* and the entire *New York Times* online, *Atlantic* magazine. I get a lot of alerts. I subscribe to Thomas Friedman, David Leonhardt, different columns, and so I get those every day. I kind of sprinkle that through the day. I don't really watch television. We don't have cable. We have a Roku box instead. We have Sling TV, which includes CNN and MSNBC, so I will watch those when I can or when I feel like I want to.
>
> —Nancy (United States)

Many news lovers echoed aspects of "the information is out there" folk theory, insisting that it was important to do one's own research, but they treated the latter as a supplement rather than a replacement for the conventional news they turned to regularly. They saw in journalism a professionalism that made news sources superior to the research they could do on their own. They believed that the infrastructures of digital media may have made it easier to keep up with what was happening in the world, but the information, if it was out there, did not just appear on its own. It took the work of trained professionals to pry it loose and make it available to the public. As Lance (United States) put it, repeating a joke he had heard, the idea of Googling for answers on the internet was "basically the same as going to Walmart and just randomly asking twenty people," adding that in his view it was crazy not to turn to "a qualified professional." (News lovers are somewhat exceptional in this respect; such attitudes toward journalism are markedly less common among the broader public.)[19]

Although their favored sources varied, Jennifer's (United States) case was fairly typical of news lovers. She relied so much on National Public Radio (NPR) as her primary source of news, listening regularly in the car and throughout the day, that she said her husband would often joke with her, "Of course you heard it on NPR. Yes, you heard it on NPR." It was a deliberate choice, she said, because she felt there was "a little bit more thoroughness in the reporting, a lot more . . . not as sensationalized. There's a lot more root to the story" than the clickbait she saw elsewhere. A former journalism major, she also felt personal research was important and was concerned that by relying so heavily on one source, she hadn't "necessarily done all of the work to get the full story on much of the news that's going on." But trusting NPR so much allowed her to stay informed without feeling the need to Google everything she heard. That trust was freeing.

REAPING REWARDS FROM TRUSTING NEWS (SELECTIVELY)

As is evident in Jennifer's example, one of the keys to news lovers' carefully curated news habits was that they had decided to trust some news sources over others—a clear contrast to most news avoiders. This trust, seen as so naive and dangerous by many news avoiders, was often quite liberating for news lovers, allowing them to navigate the media environment with far less effort, confidently filtering the sources around them, embracing some while dismissing others. As news lover Barb (United States) put it when explaining why she regularly watched the morning show on CBS, "It's routine. It's ritual, if you will. It's consistent." She agreed that for "more important stories you have to do your own research on [them]. You can't just listen to the news," but she trusted her favorite news source to "give you the best-rounded view that they can from different sides." She felt sufficiently informed without needing to dig deeper. The "black hole of information," as Jane (United Kingdom) had described the contemporary media environment, felt manageable.

Prior research on trust in news has underscored its advantages to individuals as a useful heuristic, or shortcut, that allows people to differentiate more confidently and efficiently the sources of information they might encounter as they go about their lives.[20] Its benefits may be particularly acute in the digital environment, where people may be especially likely to come across news from outlets with which they were previously unfamiliar[21]—that is, if they manage to recall where the information came from at all, which people are less likely to do when browsing the web via intermediaries such as social media or search engines.[22] At its core, placing one's trust in journalists and news organizations to report the news fairly and accurately requires a willingness to be vulnerable. It is risky to assume that the source of that information has no ulterior motives, that it is not aiming to manipulate or mislead. Those who consume news less often and engage less deeply with it are less likely to recognize individual news outlets as familiar and consider them worthy of trust. As we see with some news avoiders, lack of trust does not require being actively hostile toward the media; *indifference* toward news can also breed suspicion.[23] Those who use news most frequently, in contrast, are not simply blindly trusting everything they see, as news avoiders sometimes imagine. Rather, the news lovers we interviewed knew *which sources* they did and did not trust.

These dual factors—habit and trust—made it easier, enjoyable even, for news lovers to navigate the information environment. The importance of these factors became even clearer when we did follow-up interviews with some news avoiders. Between our first and second interviews, a handful of them had started consuming more news. They had not fundamentally altered their views toward news and journalism—they were still wary of news media in general—but, like news lovers, these newly news curious had identified specific forms and sources of news that fit into their daily routines, had chosen certain media platforms to use, and had decided (cautiously) to trust them. Carly (United States), for example, described making room during her morning commute for a news podcast from the Skimm, a digital news organization that markets itself to young women in big cities throughout the United States.[24] She had been turned on to the podcast by her sister, who thought it might help her make better sense of Trump's impeachment proceedings, which she had taken an interest in. With limited time to focus on news while working full-time and raising two young kids, Carly said listening to the podcast while driving felt like a manageable, accessible way to keep up. "I like that I can listen to it rather than read," she said. "It's pretty well explained, and it's kind of written and produced by women of my millennial generation, for women, and I appreciate that."

Brian (United States), a forty-something father of three school-age kids, was another revealing example of a news avoider who developed a news habit after previously calling himself "more of a headline guy." After signing up for a free subscription to satellite radio, he started listening to cable news broadcasts in his car on his way to work. "I think a part of it is just so I'm more informed [about] what's going on in the U.S.," he said, adding that if his boss, who "chats all the time" about divisive political topics, was going to inundate him, "I want to hear both sides." He planned to listen to both Fox and CNN, "so that way I can get a better understanding of what both sides are saying. And I'm sure somewhere in the middle is the truth."

Fast-forward several months, Brian's life had changed. "I listen to it all the time; that's probably my favorite thing to do in the car," he said, estimating that he listened to *Fox News* 90 percent of the time, flipping over to CNN during commercials or seeking out sermons from a "Christian station" if he felt he needed a break. Brian had something of a born-again convert's appreciation for the practice. "I definitely enjoy it; I feel like I'm more informed," he said. It made him more confident about his own ability to hold his own in conversations with others and engage in political life.

> I used to think [my boss] was smart or something, and then I'm like, "No, he just listens to CNN." You can tell it's usually CNN because—it's funny, because I said I flip back and forth—he'll bring up something, and I'm like, "Yeah. I just heard that on the radio coming in." And that's all he's doing! [He] is repeating what he heard on CNN. And me, I'm like, "I just heard that same thing." Or he'll read it in the *Des Moines Register* or something. I'm like, "Oh. He's not really that informed." I mean, he is, but he's just regurgitating what he either read in the *Des Moines Register* or listened to on CNN.

For all his newfound interest in news, though, Brian had not become any less distrustful about what he perceived as pervasive problems with the mainstream news media in general. In our first interview, he had said he thought journalists were biased against people like him. "If I say anything about being a Christian, I'm a bad guy; or if you're a Trump supporter, you're automatically labeled as racist." Listening to hours of *Fox News* each day had only reinforced such beliefs. "I think I'm more aware of that because I didn't really listen to it as much. And now that I see it, I notice how [most news is] very pro-Democrat." But he also perceived benefits from consuming news more regularly. Like Carly—and like all the news lovers we interviewed—by developing a news routine centered around specific trusted sources, Brian had found a way to fit news into his life that felt easy and automatic rather than burdensome.

* * *

In previous chapters, we examined how who news avoiders are (*identity*) and what they believe (*ideology*) shape their relationships with news. In this chapter, we have focused on a third factor that intersects with the other two: the media platforms and information pathways that people rely on to navigate the contemporary media environment (*infrastructures*). These increasingly digital, distributed means by which people find, access, and make sense of information in their daily lives also play a key role in defining their relationships to news. To understand that role, we focused on three folk theories we heard repeated in different combinations across our interviews with news avoiders: "news finds me," "the information is out there," and "I don't know what to believe." These ideas about how the contemporary media environment works and how one ought to operate within it helped explain why so many avoiders adopted a defensive skepticism toward all sources of news they might encounter, often preferring instead to rely on "secondhand news" from trusted friends and family. This generalized lack of trust in all sources of news, however, made their efforts to parse through competing narratives and seemingly diametrically opposed perspectives online arduous or even bewildering, like trying to dive into a story midway through it. Publishing more of the same kinds of news will do nothing to address such concerns. To many news avoiders, the vast array of sources online already feels more like a "black hole of information" than a reassuringly rich trove of resources. News lovers, by contrast, have carefully curated habits involving select sources they have chosen to trust, which makes consuming news relatively easy, automatic, and even pleasurable.

Decades ago, many people turned to their local news outlets as a primary resource for navigating everyday life—a "daily instrument or guide," as the media researcher Bernard Berelson put it in his famous newspaper study from the late 1940s.[25] But, little by little, many of the services these resources once offered have been parceled out and replaced by more efficient, more timely digital alternatives. When people want to know about local school announcements, local weather, the latest traffic updates, or the latest restaurant openings and closings, how many of them today turn to their smartphone and its many apps and services? At the same time, the unique value proposition of authoritative, independently produced journalism has become increasingly contested—rightly so, perhaps, given its many well-documented shortcomings when it comes to serving the entirety of the public.[26] In media environments where people have access to so many digital tools to solve many of the problems in daily life that traditional news outlets once solved—what Anne Schulz in her work on how people navigate their local communities has called "the great unbundling"[27]—news itself as a product can seem antiquated and passé, and it's easy to see why many news avoiders view it that way.

Despite relying on many of these same media infrastructures, news lovers often hold fast to the idea that journalism, now more than ever, still provides an essential service. We tend to agree with them, although admittedly such views may say more about our own convictions about the state of the world and our place in it as engaged citizens than they do about the state of the news media. Such views are also, perhaps, increasingly anachronistic. In the final chapter, we synthesize our findings and consider how news organizations might respond to news avoidance today. Many of the obstacles and beliefs about news that make it difficult for avoiders to see value in conventional news are encountered and shared more widely, which makes developing strategies to address them all the more existential for news organizations and essential for society more broadly.

7

NEWS FOR ALL THE PEOPLE?

Frrom news for the few and the powerful, to news for all the people."
That is how Juan González and Joseph Torres describe the historical
"grand arc of the American press."[1] Many journalists and editors across
all the countries we study here have fought hard to bend that arc toward
more diverse and inclusive news that serves the whole public. But even in
an age of abundant supply and unparalleled ease of access, millions of people still consistently avoid the news, and, as we have shown, that behavior
does not occur at random among the public. It is especially prevalent among
younger people, women, those who are most socioeconomically disadvantaged, and those least interested and engaged in political life. This strati-
fication in avoidance is a problem: for journalism's aspiration to be for the
whole public, for those who believe in equitable participation in civic life,
and for a significant part of the citizenry who miss out on what journalism, despite its many imperfections, has to offer. To the extent that news
avoidance is growing—as some research suggests it is—it is also cause for
concern for journalists and for already-struggling news organizations whose
existence depends on cultivating future generations of engaged news
consumers.[2]

Paying close attention to the experiences of consistent news avoiders provides insights into how journalists and news media—if they want to prioritize it—might close the gap in the "grand arc" and strive to ensure that news *is* for everybody. The first step is to understand that people do not simply choose to consume or to avoid news. Their choices are shaped by interlocking forces of identity, ideology, and infrastructure—by how people see news based on who they are, what they believe, and how they access media.

This means that consistent news avoidance is only in part a response to news content. Many of the news avoiders we interviewed saw seemingly insurmountable barriers preventing them from becoming more regular news consumers. Sometimes those barriers were rooted in people's identities: the communities to which they belonged, their roles in those groups, and social expectations around keeping up with news. In other cases, the barriers were rooted in political ideologies that saw journalism as a corrosive institution working in concert with a corrupt class of political elites rather than as an independent watchdog on the side of the public. People's identities and ideologies further interacted with their relationships with the media infrastructures that shape the environments in which they encountered and engaged with news. Although many were confident, at least in theory, that they could use digital tools to find information they needed and that essential news stories would "find them" via those same tools, they lacked the habits and heuristics used by news lovers to make sense of that information, so they often felt uncertain what to believe.

It is important to be clear that although we have argued (in line with decades of research) that following professionally produced news helps people stay more informed and politically engaged,[3] many news avoiders do not see their (distant) relationship to news as a problem. Some of our interviewees, yes, were ambivalent or even regretful about not consuming news more regularly. They did not feel they knew where to begin to change that behavior. But many others not only were satisfied with their lack of news use but also told us explicitly that they felt happier and more empowered without it. We respect both views. Our interviewees were curious, capable people who were weighing demands on their time and energy. Some preferred to concentrate on matters close to home that they felt they could influence, and in their limited free time they opted for media choices that helped them recharge. This may sound familiar even to highly engaged news users. Facing the stresses of events such as the COVID-19 pandemic with its attendant health and economic threats, even ardent news lovers like those we interviewed in Iowa found themselves turning away from news at least occasionally. News hurts, and many are already hurting.

All of this means that simply offering more of the same kind of news will not in itself convince most consistent news avoiders to engage with journalism. The *New York Times*, the *Times* of London, and *El País* could double the size of their newsrooms and expand their output, but that would do nothing to change the many complex social and contextual factors that often play a decisive role in whether people choose to consume news or not. NPR, the *Guardian*, and *El Diario*—all highly regarded news organizations that currently offer digital news for free to all who want to access it—could invest millions more in their journalism, but that investment would not in itself ensure more universal inclusion.

No, addressing news avoidance is not a question of supplying an even greater abundance of news content (the supply already feels overwhelming) or making access easier (it is already only a click away). It requires taking people's relationships with news seriously and recognizing how combinations of identity, ideology, and infrastructures lead a significant minority of the public not to engage with news because they do not feel that news has anything to offer them worth the time and energy it demands—or that it really cares about people like them, anyway.

In the remainder of this closing chapter, we highlight key takeaways from our research first for scholars, then for journalists. Then we conclude by proffering—cautiously—five practical suggestions for how consistent news avoidance might be addressed. We were hesitant to offer them. If anything, our research reveals how complex a phenomenon news avoidance is, and we recognize that news organizations are already facing many challenges. But one of our interviewees' most consistent complaints about news was that it highlights problems without giving them any hope or ideas about how to take action, and that same criticism could easily apply to much academic research as well. There is no question that finding ways to attract and serve consistent news avoiders poses a daunting challenge to news organizations, but it is not impossible, and we want to offer some possible strategies.

TAKEAWAYS FOR SCHOLARS: FOLK THEORIES, MEDIA CHOICE NARRATIVES, AND NEWS COMMUNITIES

We hope not only that the substantive findings in this book will contribute to the growing body of research on news avoidance but also that our inductive method and research design will be helpful for scholars interested in different ways to study how people relate to news and media more broadly. Scholars who study media audiences often call for comparative qualitative research and mixed-methods comparative work, but that kind of work is rarely done because it is complex and difficult, requiring many skills and many trade-offs. We hope that our study, for all its imperfections, will be generative for researchers interested in doing this kind of work, and in that spirit we highlight in this section what we consider to be some of the most important takeaways for them.

If we want to understand why people choose to engage with some kinds of media but not others, narrowly utilitarian approaches that focus only on information supply and demand and sociological approaches that focus only on the role of social structures—relegating the kinds of phenomena that we study here to "nonuse"—tend to be impoverished. They are liable to miss out on the importance of the social and technological factors that shape demand and, eventually, habit. As we have shown, news avoidance is not simply a matter of deliberate individual choice. It is clearly influenced by social structures such as gender and (especially) socioeconomic class, which shape action in ways that people often cannot control and that they may be unaware of. But news avoidance is *also* a habitual behavior that results from cumulative choices made in response to news supply in light of how individuals consider their own personalities, social worlds, life circumstances, and media alternatives. In other words, news avoidance must be understood as occurring through a complex interplay of structure, media supply, and media habits.

As summarized in figure 7.1, folk theories, media choice narratives, and news communities are the theoretical tools we use to study that interplay. We began our research knowing that we wanted to understand news avoiders' folk theories of journalism. During the interview process, we came to realize that we were collecting not just individual folk theories but also folk theories strung together in explanatory stories people used to understand and justify their news use—that is, media choice narratives. We identified the concept of news communities at the analysis stage, when it became clear that news lovers were enmeshed in the very kinds of groups that news avoiders lacked—groups that created social incentives around the consumption of news. These three concepts thus became the essential lenses through which we learned how news avoiders related to news. But they are especially useful to focus on because they are not *only* theoretical concepts but also social phenomena that influence how people relate to news, part of Ann Swidler's "cultural tool kit."[14] They do not determine what media people use or how people use them, but they provide reasons and resources that help

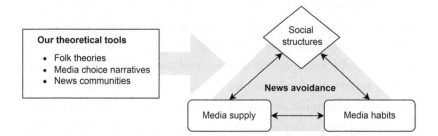

FIGURE 7.1. Our Theoretical Tools and Our Objects of Study. Folk theories, media choice narratives, and news communities are the theoretical tools used to study the interactions between social structures, the supply of media, and individual habits around using such media.

people navigate media and make some media habits more likely than others. In other words, folk theories, media choice narratives, and news communities are helpful tools for us to understand news avoidance precisely because they are also tools that news avoiders use to conceive of, build, and maintain their media habits.

By examining these theoretical concepts or cultural tools, we found that news avoidance resulted from the ways people assessed news through the filter of their identities, ideologies, and infrastructures (and that these assessments occurred in and could perpetuate an environment of inequality). The combination of these three factors is central to understanding consistent news avoidance. But these factors can also help account for other kinds of media use because, in the end, *all* forms of news and media use are social and only partially intentional. That goes for media behaviors that may appear more extreme, like those of both news lovers and consistent news avoiders, as well as for behaviors that are more widespread, such as the habits of "daily briefers" who express at least some interest in news and use it daily.[5] Informational content and utility play a role, but a whole host of assumptions, expectations, and preconceptions underpin and shape the choices we make and the value that we do or do not see in news. This is as true for subscribers who religiously read upmarket newspapers as for those who would not read them even if they were free.

We think our approach could be useful for studying many kinds of media use, but as sociologists have long argued, studying people who behave very differently from what scholars consider "normal" helps us understand not only others but ourselves as well. As always, studying the unfamiliar provides a way to unfamiliarize the familiar. We began this study thinking consistent news avoidance was both extreme and troubling, but we found that our interviewees' folk theories and media choice narratives sounded more and more familiar over time and resonated with us far more than we had expected, just as they likely do with many readers. Meanwhile, viewed through the lens of how consistent news avoiders talked and thought about news, our own behaviors, assumptions, and preconceptions began to look more and more curious to us. If our explicit question to those we interviewed was "Why don't you use the news?," their implicit question for us was "Why do you use the news so much?"

Folk theories, media choice narratives, and news communities can help us here, too. Believing that following the news helps us understand the world and is part of what it means to be an informed citizen, telling any-one who asks that this belief is part of why we follow the news, and mov-ing in circles where others share and validate this belief and such stories are surely among the reasons many of us follow the news on a daily basis—above and beyond any intrinsic or instrumental value of the news content. Those reasons also happen to validate our choices as not just right for us personally but also righteous in a broader, more public sense.

If paying close attention to what news avoiders say about their relation-ship to news shows that they are less strange and their beliefs less extreme than we and many other consistent news consumers might have thought, it also challenges one of the central assumptions of journalism and journal-ism studies: that journalism is, as John Hartley puts it in a much-quoted passage, "*the* sense-making practice of modernity."[6] Is it? We certainly believe that journalism *can* be *an* important sense-making practice, a pro-fession and a set of institutions that can help people understand the world beyond personal experience. Many more privileged people engage with news in what the media scholars Nick Couldry, Sonia Livingstone, and Tim Markham have called "action contexts," where news not only provides them with information but also plays a role in their communities and, at least sometimes, deals with things that they might, at least in principle, act on.[7] As the sociologist Pierre Bourdieu put it many years ago, upmarket news media provide some people and some communities with a "sense of full membership in the universe of legitimate politics and culture."[8] But for news to perform that function effectively, audiences must perceive themselves as having a significant role to play in the worlds depicted in the news.

The news avoiders we interviewed generally did not get this sense from news media. They often saw much of "legitimate" (i.e., elite) politics and culture as at best indifferent and at worst hostile to people like them. For news lovers and many daily briefers, news use is underpinned by daily routines and a sense of individual and collective validation—you matter, people like you matter, and you can take meaningful action to address problems you see in the world. In other words, their approach to news as shaped by their identities, ideologies, and infrastructures leads them to value it in part because they feel valued by it. We found that news avoiders do not feel either of those things. They see the news as not simply irrelevant or of little use—in addition to often being depressing—but also as fundamentally uninterested in people like them.

TAKEAWAYS FOR JOURNALISTS: MEETING PEOPLE WHERE THEY ARE, LITERALLY AND FIGURATIVELY

Consistent news avoidance may be one of the starkest expressions of how the implicit social contract between journalism and much of the public is fraying. But it is not the only sign. News today is central to some people's identities and relationships, but that is simply not the case for most people.[9] News avoidance is on the rise in many countries, trust in news is in decline, and the number of people who say they are interested in the news is likewise falling.[10] In this and the following section, we distill the main takeaways our research offers for news industry professionals who are concerned about these kinds of trends and seeking ways to address them.

We want to be very clear that we recognize that individual journalists, editors, and news media executives already operate in a very challenging environment. They are dealing with the ongoing disruption of their traditional business models while trying to cover powerful actors who employ increasingly professionalized public-relations and many digital channels to circumvent the news media. And they are doing all of this while facing active hostility from some politicians and parts of the public. That said, it is also important to emphasize that the news industry is not the "little guy" when it comes to consistent news avoidance. Unlike situations where powerful politicians, corporate titans, and even scholars safely ensconced in the academy are questioning journalism professionals' work from positions of privilege, most news avoiders who are critical of journalism are punching up. They feel small and powerless relative to journalists and news organizations, and in many ways they are. Furthermore, the fact that journalists and editors have a lot on their plates does not make news avoidance go away, and as we have shown in this book, news avoidance is a different kind of problem from other challenges the industry is facing, so it will require different solutions. Creating new funding models, empowering journalists to counter spin, and reducing political attacks on journalism might free up resources, but they will not address any of the root causes of news avoidance.

Journalists and those who care about journalism's role in our societies and especially its ambition to be for "all the people" have to be prepared for the possibility that consistent news avoiders are just the tip of the iceberg. News is a small and shrinking part of media use overall. Many find it depressing, irrelevant, and biased, and barely half the public believes journalism does any of the basic things journalists insist are what sets them apart from strategic communications or anything else on the internet—such as independently verifying the information they report and trying to remain independent of the agendas of powerful politicians or commercial interests.[11] However unwelcome (and sometimes unfair) many of the folk theories we have identified here may seem to industry insiders, they resonate far beyond the minority of consistent news avoiders and are rooted in much wider swaths of the public. What we called "the oyster problem" in chapter 1 is real, and it is a problem the profession and industry need to confront. It poses a fundamental cultural and social challenge to journalism.

One possible response is to retreat from the ambition that news should be for all the people. Journalists could focus on ensuring the continued supply of the kinds of journalism they are often most proud of (accountability journalism, investigative journalism, watchdog journalism, etc.). They could accept that the funding models that enable this kind of award-winning journalism are based primarily on engaging with a privileged minority— that journalism's wider public value is premised on the idea that the broader citizenry benefits from it even if many people do not engage directly with it and may even disavow and avoid it. There is historical and contemporary precedent for this approach. Journalism originally mostly served small, niche, elite audiences, and much prominent journalism today continues to do the same. Maybe the future of journalism is to double down on this approach and believe—as many who commit their lives to academic work, classical music, or fine arts no doubt believe—that the whole endeavor serves a public purpose whether the public agrees or not.[12] Few journalists would explicitly say that their ambition is to provide "news for the few and the powerful," as Gonzalez and Torres phrase it.[13] But some of the world's most respected news media do exactly that, and they would no doubt argue that they nevertheless serve the public interest.

Another possible response to the challenge of news avoidance is to recommit to the idea of popular journalism, to "news for all the people," and to make it a central professional ambition to overcome the barriers to delivering on that goal. Our research suggests a good starting point is to embrace the idea that to reach people who are not already engaged, you have to meet those people where they are. We mean this both literally and figuratively. First, literally with regard to infrastructure. As many digital journalists have long understood, news organizations must appreciate the value of "off-site" reach, meaning they must connect with people on social media, via search engines, and so on, not just "on-site" through the channels that news media own and operate.[14] There are many complications that come from relying on for-profit platform companies with their own interests and agendas that are at best only partially aligned with those of news media.[15] But we need to be clear: many people do not, and probably never will, rely primarily on direct access for news. Journalists who want to reach them will *have* to meet them where they are—however ambiguous or even problematic the platforms people use may be.

Second, figuratively: meeting people where they are requires recognizing the identities and ideologies that shape how people think about and engage with media and how these factors in turn often cast journalism in a very different light from how the profession might prefer to see itself. Indeed, the people we interviewed for this book make very clear that journalistic work does not "speak for itself." The value (and values) of journalism must be both demonstrated and communicated. To successfully make their case, journalism practitioners need to try to recognize and engage with the folk theories, narratives, and communities that people draw on to make sense of what they see and are told. Denying the existence of widespread folk theories or getting overly defensive about them is not a good strategy for engaging an already disengaged population. Working from people's preconceptions is also not the same as pandering to their prejudices. True, it *can* take that form; for example, some self-styled populist media have leveraged the widespread folk theory that the "mainstream media" are profoundly biased in order to cast themselves as the only "fair and balanced" show in town. But it does not *have* to take that form. Instead of dismissing or ignoring the beliefs and cultural currents that some partisan brands and alternative sources actively cultivate, other forms of journalism could seek to engage with them in their own ways by actively making the case for what fairness and balance means for them, how they practice it, and why.

Public journalism and other reform movements in the profession that seek to integrate journalism more actively in the democratic process and their more theoretical counterparts articulated by various academics seek to do some of this work.[16] Community journalism projects have long sought to focus specifically on underserved groups.[17] The increasing use of audience analytics in newsrooms at least in principle offers the possibility of being more attuned to audiences' preferences, as do editorial approaches that aim to put user needs at the center of their work.[18] Advocates of constructive journalism and solutions journalism are focused on two of the central complaints expressed in our interviews: that the news is relentlessly depressing and does not provide any meaningful ways of acting on what it covers.[19] (Whether most disengaged members of the public are aware of these efforts is a different story, though, an issue we address later.) All of these reform movements in journalism embrace the idea that a recommitment to truly popular journalism requires going beyond focusing on formal political processes and current audiences, practices that often just engage the already engaged. We hope news industry reformers find our analysis useful in their important efforts.

It is up to journalists, editors, and news media executives to decide how important it is for them, relative to the many other challenges they face, to address news avoidance. News professionals in different types of media organizations—whether upmarket commercial news media, mass-market titles, public-service media, or nonprofit media with various funding structures—will face consistent news avoidance and the more widely fraying social contract from different starting points. We hope many of them will want to continue to bend the arc of journalism toward news for all the people. As we have shown throughout the book, news avoidance is influenced by many factors, including some that journalists have little or no control over, and there can be no one-size-fits-all solution for it. But it is neither natural nor inevitable.

We finish our book with five ideas drawn from our research about what can be done to address consistent news avoidance. They are not a call for top-down social engineering to prop up existing forms of journalism. They are based on what we have learned from studying people who feel news has little to offer them—people whom many journalists in principle would like their profession to reach and serve better.

FIVE THINGS THAT CAN BE DONE TO RESPOND TO CONSISTENT NEWS AVOIDANCE

RESPONDING TO HOW NEWS FEELS

Let us start with news content and the way it is presented. We have shown throughout the book that news avoidance is not *only* a response to content. But make no mistake: content is still a big part of the problem. When so many people explain their news avoidance by saying, "It's not me, it's news," a first response should be to look closely at the coverage that turns them off. *Many* people—not just consistent news avoiders—say that news is depressing, irrelevant, and unintelligible and that there isn't anything they can do about the problems they see, hear, or read in the news anyway. These complaints are a starting point for meeting people where they are culturally.

If our goal is to address consistent news avoidance, it fundamentally does not matter whether these beliefs are fair or accurate. What matters is the social fact that millions of people hold these views and that these preconceptions lead some to systematically avoid the news and many others to approach it only hesitantly.

It does not have to be this way. A news organization could say, "We hear you." It could differentiate itself from an abundance of relentlessly depressing news as usual by stating clearly and explicitly, "We want to be different," and telling people—over time *showing* people—that it is not afraid to lead with news that is uplifting, closer to people's lived experience, presented in more accessible ways, and focused on things they can influence. We are aware that calling for more accessible news may trigger some well-worn complaints from self-styled intellectuals and media critics, such as concerns about the "dumbing down" of news. But the core of the matter here is not intelligence; it is *intelligibility*. Political journalism, especially, tends to make assumptions about what audiences know about political actors and processes that are impossible for all but the most dedicated news lovers to live up to. This results in coverage that is about as meaningful for many potential news consumers as sports journalism of a specialized game would be for those who have little conception of the stakes, norms, or rules—with the crucial difference that political news is not a game.

Another likely objection is that integrating more constructive, down-to-earth, and solutions-based approaches in editorial routines risks reducing otherwise serious, hard-hitting news to feel-good puff pieces and superficial service journalism. It is hard to take this objection seriously. Only those who refuse to contemplate the idea of change cannot see that journalism already does plenty of this "puffy" stuff, but its "puffy" stuff is focused primarily on the famous, powerful, and rich. Elite news organizations rarely lead with this stuff at the top of their apps or websites, but it is in plentiful supply, at least for privileged audiences. Surely, it cannot at the same time be perfectly compatible with journalism's core values to have plenty of news dedicated to expensive cars, investing, private education, real estate, and "high" culture aimed at the well-to-do or a weekly supplement called "How to Spend It" full of service journalism and actionable content for the most affluent (with lucrative ads to boot) but antithetical to those same values to help everybody else live their lives.

Actionability seems especially important here. News avoiders we interviewed too often felt that the "how this could affect you and what you can do about it" statement in most news was implied or missing, which left them trying to fill in that gap on their own. And without the clear articulation of that link to their lives, many news avoiders saw little reason to consume news that would just upset them. Structuring stories explicitly to highlight rather than to bury or elide how those stories could directly affect audience members' lives and how they might respond would counterbalance the feeling that news is pointlessly negative. It would also address frequently invoked folk theories that much news, especially about politics, has no bearing on ordinary people's lives.

TAKING COMMUNITIES AND IDENTITIES SERIOUSLY

Those who want to engage news avoiders need to keep in mind that, as we have argued throughout this book, the meaning and value of news to individual citizens is deeply relational, tied in with their identities and the communities to which they belong. In that regard, efforts to address consistent news avoidance need to begin by systematically examining whether media organizations do in fact serve those groups most likely to avoid the news—younger people, women, and less privileged parts of the public—as well as journalists would like to claim they do. Making it a goal to represent, reflect, and respect groups that have historically been poorly served by the news will require trying to understand these specific publics better—not what they click on or how much time they spend on a web page, but their daily routines, priorities, and broader beliefs about how consuming news directly from news sources stacks up against other alternatives available to them.

Research has long shown that a sense of community helps enhance the value of almost any media practice, from romance reading to fan fiction to online gaming.[20] Cultivating a sense of community is also central to other long-standing practices, including community organizing, political mobilization, and religious proselytizing, just as it is to much of today's "creator culture."[21] Consistent with those practices, our findings point to the importance of community in helping people to maintain a news habit, and we found that even the most hardened news avoiders usually conceded that there were some *social* benefits to being informed about news. They often said they wished they could participate in conversations and even games that required knowledge of current events and felt people who did so came across as smart, cultured, and simply well prepared in social situations (at least when they didn't seem pompous and ridiculous).

We therefore believe that a good way to help people see more value in news is to try to emphasize the social benefits of news use and to foster new and more inclusive news communities where few or none exist. Journalists and news media cannot travel back in time to change news avoiders' childhood socialization, but they can work to make news consumption a more sociable experience in the present. Up to this point, journalism has, with some exceptions, not engaged with this idea of community building around news consumption. Some marginal experiments aside, the dominant approach is still "we publish, you read," involving limited interaction with readers' comments and maybe some social media debate. Outside-the-box interventions that emphasize news's social benefits, especially those that cultivate and increase the visibility of news communities and the wider benefits of news use, might range from outward displays of news consumption (such as lifestyle branding used in membership drives) to fostering book-club-like news-reading and news-viewing groups, which could also help with creating and maintaining news communities. The building of news communities also dovetails nicely with the idea of making news more actionable. More privileged audiences and news lovers already tend to be embedded in news communities that provide a built-in action context. But many people do not. Journalists could try to show people how and where they can change the world by taking action—on their own or with like-minded others.

To be effective, these approaches would need to be tailored to different kinds of groups. There is still a tendency for many news organizations to apply one-size-fits-all approaches that worked in a low-choice environment dominated by a few mass media but are unlikely to work in a high-choice environment where even more media use is differentiated along social lines and communities of interest. Making these changes will be a challenge. We also recognize that approaches aimed at playing up social benefits and community aspects of news are unlikely to quickly change the minds of news avoiders who do not trust news or have other complaints about news content. (Many of our interviewees felt media organizations would do anything to sell a story, were intertwined with partisan political interests, and led with opinion rather than with factual reporting; if journalists think these news avoiders are wrong, they need to convince them otherwise.) However, emphasizing social benefits to news use could help to counterbalance some of the costs and downsides that news avoiders associate with news consumption. Such an emphasis is especially important for news avoiders who have never formed a news consumption habit or seen the point of dedicating time to it.

Again, before the idea of playing up social benefits of news communities is rejected as incompatible with everything that journalism stands for, it is worth pointing out that many news media already do versions of this in their service journalism—though again, almost invariably, only for the most affluent consumers or those most narrowly tied to their commercial interests. They curate bespoke LinkedIn groups for readers with common interests, for example, and woo them with consumer product reviews and travel sections linked to affiliate fee and advertising revenue streams. In those and so many other ways, news media already tell elite audiences that they matter and provide them with a sense of belonging and efficacy. Surely it is possible for news media to do the same for other parts of the public. Indeed, the historical roots of journalism include many examples of work that foregrounded people's agency—for example, as part of the feminist movement, the labor movement, and the civil rights movement. Ensuring that all kinds of people feel their identity is reflected and valued in news— indeed, that news can empower them to take meaningful action—is clearly not impossible.

PACKAGING AND DELIVERING CONTENT
FOR CONSISTENT NEWS AVOIDERS

Many news avoiders said they felt news was too time-consuming, a poor fit with daily routines, and incompatible with their caretaking responsibilities at home. These concerns are also actionable. Beyond the editorial changes discussed earlier, even just packaging existing reporting differently for different audiences could help. Simple summary pieces to accompany longer in-depth pieces could better serve different people's needs. Some upmarket brands take pride in their "smart brevity." The frequency with which our interviewees said they struggled to understand news when they came across it highlights the unmet need for "simple brevity" for those who do not already consider themselves in the know. Current content and formats are not meeting this need. On the content side, the problem involves assumptions made about people's familiarity with actors and processes—in politics or elsewhere, as noted earlier—but on a more basic level this problem is one of language. The U.S. Department of Education estimates that more than half of adult Americans have a prose literacy level below sixth grade, but much news seems to assume high-school-level, if not college-level, proficiency *as well as* contextual knowledge.[22]

Online widgets—which some news organizations are experimenting with—can provide background and context for those who are new to a story or issue. Personalization, at least in principle, provides further opportunities. Loyal returning users may be perfectly happy with incremental updates on ongoing stories they are assumed to be following. But that is not the right starting point for everyone. In the future, personalization might offer not just different story selections but also stories matched to individual users' interests and prior levels of background knowledge. (After all, Spotify does not offer the same front page to all users, whereas most news organizations still do.)

Delivery also matters. Editorial innovation is often heavily focused on what news organizations offer on their own websites and apps. That is understandable. These channels are where media have the most control (and they are the most valuable for commercial organizations). But the reality is that most consistent news avoiders and many other people rarely if ever go specifically to the websites and apps of news media. So as complicated and fraught as the relationship between publishers and platforms remains, reaching the least engaged members of the public will require continued effort to meet them where they are in terms of infrastructures: on social media, messaging applications, video platforms, and the like.

The way we see it, when people say that they believe the news will "find them," news organizations have two options: they can respond by saying, "No, it won't; you'll have to find it on our websites and apps" (which our research shows is highly unlikely), or they can respond by maximizing the chance that news *will* find people. Each option reflects different priorities. Likewise, when people say that the information is "out there," news organizations can respond by saying, "No, it isn't, so you should subscribe in order to access our archive" (which, again, our research suggests that consistent news avoiders are very unlikely to do), or they can respond by maximizing the chance that people will find credible news when searching. Again, each option reflects different priorities. If meeting people where they are in terms of delivery and infrastructure is an unappetizing prospect for upmarket commercial news providers focused on developing their own on-site audience, it may be particularly important for public-service and nonprofit media to think about how they can do so on different platforms and thereby avoid just superserving already well-served, privileged audiences.

NEWS MEDIA LITERACY AND COMMUNICATING THE VALUE OF JOURNALISM

For a profession and industry almost entirely premised on communications, journalism and the news media can come across as curiously inept at getting across the point of their own work. News, at its best, offers real value to people and real social benefits for communities and society at large. But it is important to explain and advertise these contributions. All the innovations we have discussed so far and others that news organizations are already experimenting with will appeal to news avoiders or other potential news audiences only if people know about them. Our interviewees sometimes said they might consume more news if only it came in a more digestible format or covered X, Y, or Z—options that *we* knew existed already, but *they* did not. If news organizations develop ways to deliver news that are efficient and digestible and that foreground why people should care—as some already have—they need to find better ways to promote those formats beyond their loyal customer bases.

It is also clear from our study that when people explain and justify their news avoidance, they often base their arguments on limited familiarity with or discernment about the range of options already available to them, on broad folk theories of journalism, and on misinformation about how and why news gets made. Sometimes they invoke folk theories that have been deliberately propagated by actors intending to dissuade people from trusting news. As a result, news avoiders find it difficult to distinguish between professionally produced journalism and other information floating around online and off. As such, we see an important role for improved and expanded efforts at basic news media literacy (NML) as a way to empower citizens and address news avoidance. Because news habits formed early in life are relatively stable, such efforts would ideally be a required part of school curriculum starting in primary school,[23] and news organizations would therefore do well to actively partner with schools and do more educational outreach. Of course, NML is not important just for schoolchildren, and efforts to assist the rest of the public to navigate the contemporary media environment are also vital.

Experts argue that NML should cover the role of journalism in democracy; the basics of news production, content, and structures; and critical skills such as how to seek out diverse sources, analyze content, and understand context.[24] Indeed, most of our interviewees did not have much knowledge or feel confident in these areas. It is possible that procedural interventions—including the various forms of labeling based on specific criteria being developed by initiatives such as the Journalism Trust Indicators, the Trust Project, and others—could help over time, but the precondition for these interventions to have much meaning to people is a stronger basic understanding of editorial practices than most people, including our interviewees, currently have. For example, we found that consistent news avoiders rarely felt they knew much about how news gets reported, making it difficult for them to distinguish between sources that produce news and sources that just regurgitate it with a twist. That uncertainty appeared to contribute to their feeling that all news was too opinionated. They also did not seem familiar with the enormous range of news options available to them or the differences between them. And while most did not believe that news media held politicians to account, many also seemed unfamiliar with the idea that they were even *supposed* to. It is particularly important here to focus on forms of news and media literacy that not only cultivate critical faculties but also help people make positive choices for themselves—to decide which news media, with all their imperfections, are good enough for their own present purposes.[25]

To these more established subjects within news media literacy, we would also recommend specifically addressing widely circulating folk theories of journalism: what these theories are; in what ways they are accurate and in what ways they are misleading; and why some actors might be deliberately propagating them. This recommendation overlaps with our fifth idea, discussed next. Throughout the book, we have concentrated on trying to understand our interviewees' folk theories of journalism rather than on judging their accuracy, but it must be said that some of these folk theories are just plain wrong. All mainstream news is not fake news. All news sources are not equally biased and untrustworthy. All news media outlets are not acting only in their own self-interest.

Insofar as some of these folk theories serve as vocabularies of motive to justify news avoidance—sometimes even to the point of making news avoidance seem like the only rational, intelligent approach to news—they can be dangerous when actively weaponized by some prominent public figures.[26] Under the guise of wisdom, these notions dissuade people from becoming more active, critical news consumers. Some of these folk theories, in other words, work in direct opposition to the goals of NML, and while they circulate unchecked, they can effectively nullify it. Folk theories of journalism often have some basis in truth: many news outlets obviously do publish sensationalistic pieces, have a partisan slant, or lead with opinion, for example. Effective NML interventions should therefore dedicate time to closely examining these folk theories, understanding what aspects of them might be accurate and in what ways they may be overly simplistic or misleading, and learning how they are sometimes deliberately spread by people who benefit from their embrace by the public.

(RE)AFFIRM EDITORIAL VALUES AND DEFEND PROFESSIONAL STANDARDS

While our previous recommendations are aimed at news organizations' traditional functions in that they concern the production of news, its role in communities, and how it is packaged, presented, and delivered, our last suggestion departs more from journalistic business as usual. In an environment where it has become increasingly difficult to differentiate professionally produced news from other media *and* where the industry itself is regularly under attack from political actors and corporate interests deliberately trying to discredit it, journalists and the news media cannot just wait around for people to see the virtue of their work or for NML interventions to cultivate trust in the next generation. A large-scale public-relations campaign at an industry level may be needed to alter people's notions about what journalists do. Many people want things from journalism that journalists would like to offer: accurate reporting that holds power to account and is independent from undue commercial and political influence. They just do not believe such journalism exists or know where to find it. News organizations, not only individually but also *collectively*, must more proactively explain what they are doing, communicate its value, and defend themselves against some of the most pernicious folk theories about journalism, or they risk even more people turning their backs on news altogether. If they want alternative ideas about journalism to take hold to counter the negative ones, those arguments will not all by themselves simply propagate or "find" people.

A coalition of journalism-oriented academic and nonprofit organizations and news outlets is probably best positioned to mount this effort to reaffirm editorial values and defend professional standards before the public. This task will not be easy. It will require, first, taking seriously the fact that there are many media organizations that do *not* live up to the hallowed ideals exalted in journalism school classrooms and industry awards banquets (not to mention the many organizations that try to meet these ideals but sometimes fall short). Uniting as a profession and confronting bad-faith criticism requires grappling with the many elements of the news media whose editorial values are not in fact the same. Sometimes these differences and inconsistencies exist within an individual media organization, which can seem baffling if not outright hypocritical from the outside. You can forgive the public for being confused or untrusting when Tucker Carlson, then a *Fox News* host, called the rest of the media "cringing animals who are not worthy of respect,"[27] even as his employer lobbied with the *New York Times* and others through industry associations such as Digital Context Next, or when the *Daily Mail* describes *The Guardian* as possessed by a "psychotic hatred of the commercially viable free Press,"[28] even though both are represented by the News Media Association. (Regular *New York Times* and *Guardian* readers as well as *Fox News* and *Daily Mail* regulars might also be confused by these alliances.)

Not all news sources are equally worthwhile or deserving of consumption—as all journalists would agree. Yet there is a hesitancy at an industry level to draw lines around what the minimum requirements are for something to qualify as journalism rather than clickbait. That hesitancy is understandably rooted in a desire to remain impartial and above the fray (e.g., at *work*, not at *war*), but it can also be traced to a more ambiguous and even problematic kind of "honor among thieves," a reciprocal arrangement where the implicit agreement is, as the former *Guardian* editor Alan Rusbridger puts it, "We won't cover you if you don't cover us."[29] But if journalism is a public good (and at its best we think it is), it deserves a well-articulated coordinated public defense. That will require a clear and explicit demarcation of the lines that separate news specifically from content more broadly, including content from organizations that fail to uphold basic professional standards. The fact that journalists and news media are shy about publicly discussing the real or perceived shortcomings of colleagues and peer institutions isn't exactly stopping politicians, pundits, or opinion leaders from loudly criticizing the industry. The silence from the profession itself can come across as a bit conspicuous.

As we try to imagine what a coordinated public defense of journalism might look like, useful comparisons can be made between the public perception of the news media in contemporary democratic societies and public skepticism regarding other industries. Big banks, big tobacco, big oil, big tech, big pharma—these industries and specific brands within them face both collective and individual challenges in negotiating their standing with the public. Journalists may feel that they enjoy, or ought to enjoy, more public trust and support than these industries, but they generally do not, as survey after survey has documented. News organizations, rightly or wrongly, often find themselves in the same predicament as these other industries, but, unlike them, news media sometimes seem to be in denial about how they are seen and have rarely banded together in an effective way to try and change the public's attitudes about their products' contributions to the greater good. Journalists tend to think their values are self-evident, but they are not—certainly not to news avoiders and not to many others.

Journalism and the news media like to say they operate in the public interest. If so, they need to explain how they do so, addressing existing preconceptions and concerns about what it is that journalists do, while recognizing, naming, and holding to account those parts of the profession and the industry that routinely fall short in demonstrating their commitments to shared values and standards. Convincing the public that the rest of the profession and industry *is* delivering on their mission and living up to their principles requires making that case again and again in word and in deed.

* * *

Throughout the book, we have tried to highlight the powerful role that individuals' media choice narratives and broadly shared folk theories can play in justifying and normalizing attitudes toward media and media practices in general as well as toward news and news avoidance in particular. A rich and growing body of research looks at different forms of news avoidance and factors contributing to it. By taking a comparative, mixed-methods approach, we aimed to contribute to that conversation by offering a holistic view of the phenomenon that takes into account how infrastructures, identities, and ideologies interact with individuals' life circumstances to contribute to how they experience news avoidance.

There is still much we do not know about how folk theories of journalism are born and spread and how they might be effectively countered when they are damaging. That we found such similar folk theories in all three countries we studied underscores how frictionlessly they can cross borders and shape how people living in very different cultures, political contexts, and media systems relate to the news media. In that regard, both folk theories of journalism and comparative qualitative research of news audiences, especially beyond the Western media systems that we studied, are ripe areas for future research.

By some measures, the breadth and depth of news options available to the public has never been greater. That will not matter if people do not know or believe that those options exist or do not have the tools to take advantage of them. Adjustments to the form and content of news may help entice some news avoiders to take up a news habit, but they will not address the fact that most citizens who are already disengaged from news will probably not even know that those changes have taken place and may not believe news has anything of value to offer them anyway. Ultimately, addressing news avoidance will require confronting a much larger cultural problem that journalism now faces—that millions of citizens do not see consuming it as a practice worth pursuing in light of the time, effort, and even discomfort it requires, much less as a necessity. The only people with a clear and pressing need to actively address this problem are those who believe that news matters and that it needs to serve everybody, not just comparatively easy-to-reach, often privileged, existing audiences. That's what we believe, and we hope this book will help journalists, media professionals, and others in the difficult, challenging, and necessary work ahead.

APPENDIX A

STUDYING NEWS AVOIDANCE USING INTERPRETIVE METHODS

I n presenting our findings, we were forced to make difficult editorial choices. As is frequently the case with qualitative data, this often meant pruning or cutting out the larger context in which quotes were expressed while entirely excising ourselves from the dialogue. One could come away with the feeling that the quotes and ideas we have included in the book emerged all by themselves. But, of course, we were there every step of the way, making decisions—decisions that were consequential over time and decisions that others might have made differently—about how to design the study and interpret what our interviewees said. This methods appendix is our effort to be transparent about those decisions. We detail many of the methodological choices behind our qualitative data collection and analysis, which spanned more than half a decade. This explanation is organized into two parts. We begin with how we defined and recruited news avoiders; then we focus on how we carried out interviews and analyzed our data to arrive at our findings.

OUR INITIAL QUESTIONS AND HOW WE
RECRUITED NEWS AVOIDERS

This study began with a gnawing curiosity. In the first several years that the Reuters Institute fielded the *Digital News Report*, the survey screened out any respondents who said they accessed news "less often than once a month" or "never" because the surveys focused on attitudes and practices of news *consumers*. (The Reuters Institute stopped excluding these respondents in 2022.) Although the percentage of people consuming so little news was relatively small (in 2016, the year we began our study, it was just 3.5 percent on average),[1] it still constituted a lot of people. It seemed strange— impossible, even—that anyone could consume so little news when "news" was defined broadly as "national, international, regional/local and other topical events accessed via any platform (radio, TV, newspaper, or online)." How could it be true that some people consumed no news whatsoever? What about on social media, even incidentally? Were they expressing some rejection of news but still consuming it? Were they intentionally avoiding news, or did they just never develop the habit? Above all, why *not* news?

DECIDING WHICH NEWS AVOIDERS TO TALK TO

The questions we most wanted to answer were about subjective experience, so the research design clearly called for qualitative methods that would allow people to answer at length and in their own words. Because media choices and news routines are also highly personal, we quickly landed on in-depth one-on-one interviews as our best option. The next questions were whom to interview and where. As is typically the case for social science research, our decisions were based on a combination of theoretical and practical concerns.

From the start, we knew we wanted to understand people like those excluded from the *DNR*, so we decided to use the same screener question ("Typically, how often do you access news?") to identify people for our study and the same "less often than once a month" cutoff. Because such low news consumption is uncommon among older adults and people of higher socioeconomic status,[2] and because we were particularly concerned about how news avoidance might further disadvantage people in lower socioeconomic strata, we decided to recruit working- to middle-class people ages eighteen to forty-five who fell in this category. We weren't sure yet whether these individuals really constituted "news avoiders," but defining the population in this way provided a consistent sampling frame we knew we could apply across different countries.

We decided to do a first round of interviews in the United Kingdom for several reasons. At the time, approximately 7 percent of adults in the United Kingdom consumed news less often than once a month—low, but still higher than in most countries, so we thought that would make recruitment easier.[3] Ben, who had been hired as a postdoctoral researcher at the Reuters Institute to study news avoidance, was based in the United Kingdom, and language barriers were less of a concern there than elsewhere (although local accents could at times pose a challenge).

More importantly, we knew this study might end up being comparative, and the United Kingdom's media environment offered an advantageously varied news landscape. The United Kingdom has a very strong public-broadcasting arm in the BBC, high levels of ownership regulation, and a wide-reaching commercial print press that runs the gamut from elite broadsheets such as the *Telegraph* on the right and *The Guardian* on the left to mass-market tabloids such as the *Sun* and the *Mirror*.[4] So the British media system presented something of a middle-ground option compared to neighboring countries in northern and southern Europe but also compared to the United States.[5]

The possible importance of these characteristics became evident soon after Ben began the U.K. interviews. Interviewees often referred to features specific to the British media system, especially British-style tabloids. Moreover, Ben did the interviews at the end of 2016 and the beginning of 2017, when the country was still reeling from the Brexit vote, and it was especially revealing to speak to people who consumed so little news during a period when news was completely dominated by one issue with wide-reaching implications for many citizens. These circumstances led us to embrace the logic of expanding this project to other countries because comparative studies are ideal for understanding these kinds of contextual factors.

Comparative studies using qualitative methods are rare in part because they are logistically and theoretically tricky to justify and pull off, starting with the choice of which countries to compare. Following best practice, we knew the key was to choose countries where we could replicate the U.K. study as closely as possible. They also needed to be similar but also different enough for the comparisons to be revealing.[6] Comparing, say, North Korea and the United Kingdom makes no sense because they are distinct in so many ways; finding differences related to news avoidance would tell us little. Without unlimited resources, we decided to narrow our focus to two additional countries whose media systems contrasted with the United Kingdom's but were still large, wealthy Western democracies. We rejected many countries, in particular the Nordic countries, because news consumption in those places tends to be consistently high, making recruitment near impossible (see figure A.1 for a comparison of these rates over time in the three countries we chose). We settled on Spain and the United States.[7] We knew we could replicate the U.K. study as closely as possible in those countries because we could do all the interviews and data analysis: Ruth lived in Spain and spoke Spanish, and Ben had been hired at the University of Minnesota, so he would soon be based in the United States.

As is typical of southern Europe, the media system in Spain is characterized by relatively low levels of journalistic professionalism (in terms of journalists' autonomy and shared professional norms) and extremely high levels of political parallelism, meaning that news outlets tend to openly embrace a particular political orientation, a fact that is widely known in Spain.[8] TV is by far the most popular news source (as it is in the United Kingdom and the United States). Spain's newspapers have historically been more oriented toward an elite readership, and today the press landscape is dominated by several elite, national newspapers that have distinct ideological orientations (*El País*, *El Mundo*, and *ABC*), a couple of digital newspapers (*elDiario.es* and *El Confidencial*), two very popular sports newspapers (*Marca* and *As*), and some big regional dailies. Glossy weekly magazines chronicle the lives of the rich and famous, but Spain has no tabloids in the British mold.

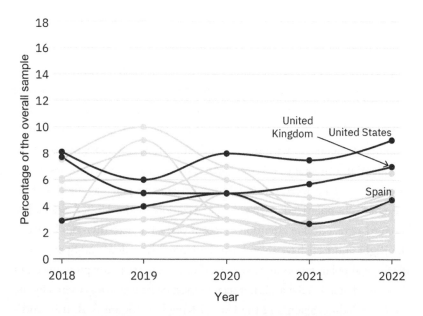

FIGURE A.1. Rates of Consistent News Avoidance Over Time by Market. The percentage of consistent news avoidance over time by market (Spain, the United Kingdom, and the United States are highlighted).

Sources: Digital News Report from 2018 to 2022, https://www.digitalnewsreport.org.

Meanwhile, the U.S. media system is characterized as having relatively higher levels of journalistic professionalism (especially compared to Spain) but much weaker public broadcasting (especially compared to the United Kingdom). Unlike in Spain and the United Kingdom, for the past century and a half the U.S. print landscape has been dominated not by national newspapers but by local newspapers that are not typically aligned with a political party or ideology. However, the rise of cable news channels such as *Fox News* and *MSNBC* that openly adhere to a particular political perspective has led to a news landscape that scholars rank alongside the United Kingdom in terms of political parallelism (but still well lower than Spain's media system).[9]

The three countries are of course distinct from each other in other ways as well, especially politically. While the United States and the United

Kingdom share an Anglo-Saxon, Anglophone history and culture and long histories of uninterrupted democracy (at least on paper), Spain transitioned to democracy only in 1975 after thirty-six years of Francoist dictatorship. Spain also obviously differs linguistically. In many respects, however, the three countries are more alike than different. They all are high-income Western democracies with high levels of press and political freedom and political stability. Although Spain and the United Kingdom are parliamentary democracies with many political parties, as opposed to the U.S. presidential democracy and two-party system, in all three countries power largely swings between two established parties in practice, and all three are relatively polarized. Growing polarization in the United States has received a great deal of attention in recent years, but deep divisions between the Right and Left have riven both the United Kingdom and Spain.[10] But ideological polarization in trust toward news is particularly pronounced in the United States, a dynamic not seen in most other countries covered by the *DNR*, including Spain and the United Kingdom (figure A.2). It is worth noting that in all countries those who "don't know" where to place themselves on the left–right ideological spectrum tend to be the least trusting toward news.

While Brexit was a unique, impossible-to-replicate event in the United Kingdom, repeating the study in Spain and the United States enabled us to conduct interviews in these other countries at moments immediately before and after major elections dominated the news. We did the interviews in Spain immediately after the Catalan independence referendum of 2017, widely heralded as the biggest political crisis in Spain since its transition to democracy in the late 1970s. In the United States, we did the interviews in the months before and immediately after the first presidential primary votes in Iowa in 2020.

RECRUITMENT AND CONTEXT

Finding news avoiders to interview was the first challenge. Oxford, with its highly educated population, might seem like the last place to look for people who consume little to no news in the United Kingdom. Yet the city's

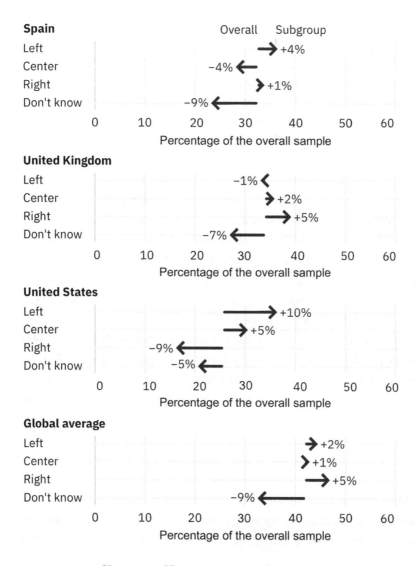

FIGURE A.2. Variation in Trust in News by Political Ideology. Differences in the percentage who agreed that "you can trust most news most of the time" among those who said they "don't know" their political ideology compared to those who identified as left wing, centrist, or right wing. Levels of trust in Spain, the United Kingdom, and the United States were considerably lower than the average (42 percent) across the forty-six global markets.

Source: Digital News Report 2022, https://reutersinstitute.politics.ox.ac.uk/digital-news-report/2022.

outer ring does include some communities that the U.K. government defines as among the most economically deprived in the country. So, at least initially, Ben began recruitment efforts there. He tried a variety of approaches with modest success. Armed with an iPad for screening potential participants, he struck up conversations in public places such as pubs and community centers; he reached out to churches, community groups, and local community newspapers; he posted flyers in targeted neighborhoods; and he even contracted with the postal service to send leaflets to ten thousand homes in select neighborhoods, offering £40 (approximately U.S.$50) for completing an hour-long interview. These efforts yielded just three volunteers. As it turned out, people who consume little to no news tend not to be out and about in the places where Ben was looking. They were busy at work or at home caring for kids or other family members. The same structural obstacles in people's lives that keep them from devoting time to the news also make them hard to find.

As researchers with the backing of an established institution, we were in the privileged position of being able to throw money at the problem, so we did. We contracted with a multinational market research firm (Kantar) with access to hard-to-reach populations to help recruit people who fit our study's parameters. We also expanded our search to Leeds and Manchester, postindustrial cities with diverse socioeconomic populations. This new approach yielded an additional forty individuals, and Ben completed a first round of interviews between November 2016 and March 2017. After Prime Minister Theresa May called a snap election that spring, we decided Ben should return to do follow-up interviews with ten people to see if the heightened atmosphere surrounding the election affected anyone's relationship to news.

In the other two countries, we applied versions of the same research design and recruitment procedures.[11] We had not seen signs in the United Kingdom that the characteristics of the city (such as size) particularly influenced news avoidance, so in Spain participants were recruited from the greater Madrid area, mostly for the practical reason that Ruth lived there.[12] She conducted the Spanish interviews from October 2017 to February 2018, when the ongoing movement for independence in the northeastern region of Catalonia was at a moment of peak tension.[13] In the United States, we decided to recruit in Iowa in part because it was relatively near where Ben lived in Minnesota but also because we could do the interviews there at a time of heightened political tension and media coverage around an election.[14] Because of its "first in the nation" status in the presidential nomination process, Iowa is the focus of intense campaigning and media coverage starting the summer prior to the state's "caucuses."[15] We conducted the first round of Iowa interviews in the summer of 2019, when the divisive politics of Donald Trump had reached a boil. Much like we had done in the United Kingdom, we returned to Iowa for follow-up interviews in February, just after votes were tallied—and just before much of the world went into lockdown due to the coronavirus pandemic.[16]

By the time we reached the U.S. stage of the study, we also made the strategic decision to recruit a complementary group of people we began to call "news lovers." We wondered whether some of our news avoiders' complaints about news were fairly widespread, even among those who heavily consumed the news. We could use survey data to compare news avoiders' attitudes to other groups' attitudes, but we wanted to capture these alternative perspectives with the same kind of depth we were able to apply to news avoiders. We screened for news lovers using the same question adopted from the *DNR* but focused on the other end of the response scale: on people who said they accessed news ten or more times a day. Because we knew from past research that people in this category tend to be older and of higher socioeconomic status, we eliminated the eligibility requirements related to age and income.[17] Only a lack of time and resources prevented our going back to interview news lovers in the other two countries as well.

In table A.1, we summarize our multiple stages of fieldwork across the three countries and provide basic demographics and other details about the participants, which are based on brief surveys we administered on iPads at the end of each qualitative interview. In appendix B, we also include detailed tables listing our participants by their pseudonyms and describing them, which readers may find useful as a reference guide.

TABLE A.1 Summary of the Qualitative Fieldwork and Demographics of Participants

	NEWS AVOIDERS			NEWS LOVERS
	UNITED KINGDOM	SPAIN	UNITED STATES	UNITED STATES
Location	Leeds, Manchester, Oxford	Madrid	Iowa (Des Moines, Cedar Rapids)	Iowa (Des Moines, Cedar Rapids)
Dates of fieldwork (and follow-ups)	Nov. 2016– Mar. 2017 (June 2017)	Oct. 2017– Feb. 2018	July 2019– Aug. 2019 (Feb. 2020)	July 2019– Aug. 2019 (Feb. 2020)
Number of participants	43	40	25	25
Number of interviews	53	40	35	35
Gender (%)				
Women	84	45	52	44
Age (%)				
18–34	68	65	48	0
35–44	32	30	40	20
45+	0	5	12	80
Class				
College graduates (%)	38	23	48	84
Median household annual income range	£40,000– £44,999	€30,000– €34,999	$50,000– $54,999	$100,000– $149,999
Political Ideology (%)				
Left wing	25	23	32	60
Right wing	8	20	36	28
Don't know	50	23	4	0

Notes: A total of 163 interviews were conducted. Age and class data in the United Kingdom are based on responses from thirty-eight individuals for whom survey responses were collected. Respondents who said they did not know or preferred not to answer the question about their household income are excluded from these calculations. Additional social grade data were collected by the recruitment firm in the United Kingdom and Spain on the basis of household occupation.

INTERVIEWING NEWS AVOIDERS AT HOME
AND MAKING SENSE OF THEIR MEDIA
CHOICE NARRATIVES

We conducted the vast majority of the hour-long interviews as face-to-face conversations in participants' homes.[18] We decided to conduct interviews in people's homes in part to make it as convenient as possible for the interviewees to participate in the study but also, just as important, to gain broader insights into what participants' lives were like—what is sometimes called a more "ethnographic way of seeing."[19] Our goal was to get people to talk about their relationship to news—to elicit their media choice narratives—but we were also paying attention to everything else they did and did not say, to the complicated, culturally constructed, and sometimes contradictory forms these narratives take.

To be sure, interviewing people in their homes did have definite downsides. It required time-consuming travel, and safety could be a big concern. For women researchers especially, there is almost always a moment before entering a stranger's home to do an interview when it crosses your mind that you might get raped or killed there. We felt much safer because the interviews had been arranged by research firms that had done an initial vetting of everyone involved and knew where we were. And yet we had some experiences—Ruth in a windowless basement interviewing an increasingly manic news avoider, Ben dropping in on a domestic altercation culminating in a smashed car window—that made us wonder whether understanding news avoidance was worth these kinds of risks.

However, we found that interviewing people at home was invaluable. By talking to people at their kitchen tables or perched on the edge of twin beds in overcrowded apartments, by seeing what they saw outside their living-room windows, and by traveling the streets of their neighborhoods, we got a better understanding of how they lived, their daily concerns, and the ways media fit into all of that. These observations often informed the interviews. As opposed to employing a strict survey-based approach, we used a semistructured interview guide that allowed flexibility as conversations veered in unexpected directions. While we covered a range of consistent topics in all three countries—including daily routines and media habits; views about the most important issues in participants' lives, communities, and countries; and attitudes toward journalism (samples are provided in appendix C)—the most revealing exchanges often came from follow-up questions we could not have anticipated in advance. Those exchanges often benefited from talking to participants in person. For example, most participants had many demands on their time and emotions. On multiple occasions, interviewees fought back tears while talking about struggles with unemployment, the responsibilities of caring for sick family members, and their own challenges with substance abuse and mental health. Not only were these challenges clearer to us from the inside of their homes, but we also suspect many felt more comfortable talking about their personal obstacles in a private, familiar setting than they might elsewhere.

This method does run the risk of becoming unwieldy. Interviews can become unfocused; some go off on long tangents. With respect to the subject of news media, people often speak in generalities. To guard against these problems, we took steps to ground interviews in people's specific behaviors or in their responses to specific pieces of media.[20] For example, we included a "day-in-the-life" prompt, in which we asked participants to talk through their daily routines and reflect on where news did or did not fit into them.[21] In the United Kingdom, we also experimented with offering interviewees examples of news articles to read and discuss to anchor their responses in concrete examples of news content, but it was clear from the news avoiders' reactions that we were asking them to do something they very rarely or never did on their own. It felt artificial, even alien. Although that feeling was interesting in itself, the activity also told us little about their actual habits with regard to news, so we decided to cut out this part of the interview guide.[22] After all, we were aiming to understand the world as our interviewees saw it, not to impose our own understandings on theirs.

EXAMPLES OF AN "ETHNOGRAPHIC WAY OF SEEING"

To give a sense of the texture of these in-home interviews, in this subsection we provide two examples from Spain and the United States The first is an excerpt of the conversation Ruth had with Cristiano, a thirty-nine-year-old news avoider in Madrid. Only the first question in this excerpt (in bold) is from the interview guide. Seated at the dining table in his apartment, Cristiano gestured animatedly around the room as he described his life with his wife and two young daughters. Up until the previous year, he had worked doing maintenance for a professional soccer team, but he was let go when the team moved from first division to second. Since then, he had been struggling on multiple fronts. He found that many of his "friends" disappeared when he lost that job. He had been unemployed since then and recovering from stomach surgery that had left him feeling unwell much of the time. Money was tight. His wife was now the breadwinner, so he was the primary caretaker for his daughters. He loved spending time with them, but it was also exhausting. He described a very busy schedule that left no time for anything except looking for a job—but, in any case, he felt news was too depressing given his fragile emotional state. Although the conversation appears to veer off topic, these seeming tangents are in fact highly relevant for understanding how Cristiano thinks and feels about news. As is evident here, each interview really is, as the political scientist Ithiel de Sola Pool put it many years ago, an "interpersonal drama with a developing plot."[23]

> *RP:* **And do you have any specific sources for information that you trust to find out what's going on in the world?**
> *Cristiano:* No, the truth is I don't.
> *RP:* It sounds like you find out about what's going on mostly from other people.
> *Cristiano:* That's right, from people—or by, I'd say, at some point I might turn on the TV, and they're talking about what has happened.
> *RP:* Yes. But it's not something you have looked for?
> *Cristiano:* No. Because it was just on. And maybe I say, "Oh, well, look, I'm going to leave it on and watch it," but really I can't stand ten minutes watching a news report. I don't even find out about the weather. I don't find out anything.
> *RP:* And why do you say you can't stand it?

Cristiano: Well, because of what I'm telling you, because I have enough problems of my own to put on the television and see "A person has been murdered," "They have killed I don't know whom," "This happened." Maybe I am more sensitive now than I was before, and I don't feel like seeing anything.

RP: Because of being unemployed and that whole situation.

Cristiano: Yes, that's why.

RP: Sure. Sometimes people say—well, my brother has two kids, too. He says that after he became a father—

Cristiano: It changes your life.

RP: Well, he's gotten more sensitive.

Cristiano: Yes.

RP: Do you feel that way?

Cristiano: Well, yes. Look, the other day I don't know why we went to the movies—it was the *fiesta del cine*, and we went on one of the three days because I really can't afford it, and my father came in the morning—he's retired—and he went to get the tickets here in the [unintelligible], and he brought me the tickets for me, my wife, and my two daughters. And we were watching a movie about a dog that gets reincarnated as other dogs—it's called "My Best Friend"—and it had been years since I had gone to the movies, well, maybe once a year I think I go, and I just cried.

RP: Sure.

Cristiano: I saw the dog, and I saw what was happening, how they were telling the story in the movie and all, and I was crying like a Magdalena; I had a lump in my throat because I wanted to burst into sobs, but since there were people next to me—my daughter was there, the older one, holding my hand and everything, and I started in with some enormous tears and with that lump in my throat and these enormous tears falling, and I said, "Damn." I mean, before that might not have happened.

RP: Sure.

Cristiano: I mean, I wasn't as sensitive as I am now.

RP: I had something similar happen. I went with my brother to see a movie, and he shed some tears—

Cristiano: Well, I was crying like a Magdalena.

RP: And I thought, "Gosh," and he said, "Oh, well, since Benjamin was born—"

Cristiano: Sure, sure. Just like me. It reminded me that the day I got fired from [the soccer club], the day before, my dog had died. He had been with us for sixteen years, a little bitty poodle, and I have him here, and we had a—

RP: Where?

Cristiano: There in the urn. [He points to a tiny urn on a shelf.]

RP: Oh, I see.

Cristiano: And we had such a day, and I said, "Damn, look, everything happens at once. My dog dies on me, the next day they call me to fire me from [the soccer club]." And we had a vigil and everything for the dog, as if he were another member of the family, and we took him to get cremated, and my daughters were there, they were with him, and in the movie I was remembering that.

RP: Man, of course.

Cristiano: Everything happened to me at once, you know?

The conversation with Cristiano illustrates the value of doing interviews in people's homes. Not only was being in a safe and intimate space probably helpful for Cristiano to open up, but it also made it easier for him to communicate about his life. It was often helpful for interviewees, as it was for Cristiano, to see and indicate objects in their homes, such as photos, children's toys, and medical equipment, to trigger their memories and illustrate their points as they talked about their lives. The excerpt also demonstrates how active interviewing techniques, such as asking if different ideas resonate with participants, can elicit vivid narratives about interviewees' lived experiences.

Sometimes interviewees were home alone, like Cristiano, but children and spouses often came traipsing through and even chimed in during the interviews. Some interviewees were holding babies or wrangling toddlers the whole time. It was distracting, but it also gave us more insight into what people's lives were really like than responses to any questions we could have asked. In a second example, this time from Iowa, Ben interviewed Joanna, a mother of three small children. Her husband worked full-time, and Joanna's main concerns were raising their kids and managing their home-schooling. On a daily basis, her kids were her main interlocutors. In a follow-up interview excerpted here, she said she would not start seeking out information about the presidential candidates until much later in the campaign; she had her hands full in the meantime. As is evident in this excerpt, what goes on in between the questions from the interview guide (again, in bold) is at least as important as the way Joanna answers them.

> *BT:* **OK. So far, at least, there isn't any stories or new sources or sites that you've turned to for information, specifically about a campaign that you've found useful, or no?**
>
> *Joanna:* No, I wish I could tell you that there was.
>
> *Child 1:* Owl, owl, owl!
>
> *Joanna:* Life with a toddler. Uh oh! Go get it. Oh, OK.
>
> *Child 1:* (yells loudly)
>
> *Joanna:* Is your sister still down there?
>
> *Child 2:* He's too crazy.
>
> *Joanna:* [Child 2], why don't you see if—
>
> *Child 1:* (yells loudly)
>
> *Joanna:* Go see if there's something . . .
>
> *Child 1:* (yells loudly)
>
> *Joanna:* Go see if there is. . . . Hey guys, we're going to turn on a show that [Child 1] likes, OK? Turn on a *Bob Show*, *Tumbleweeds*, whatever. OK? Sorry.
>
> *BT:* That's OK.
>
> *Joanna:* You're never going to want to come back here. It's crazy.
>
> *BT:* Is there usually that much screaming?
>
> *Joanna:* No, no. I think it's a show-off mode thing or something. No, he's loud, but he doesn't scream like that.
>
> *BT:* That would be hard to listen to on a daily basis.
>
> *Joanna:* Yeah, yeah.
>
> *BT:* **Is the campaign or the elections, have you felt like you're needing to actively avoid it or tune it out in some way? Or is it just a matter of not seeking it out and not coming up that much?**

Joanna: I think it's more apathetic tendency than avoidance. It's just because I have not sought out information. Not because I don't want to, at some point, but I haven't placed a lot of value in that lately. As it gets closer, it'll be clearer.

BT: **Other than your husband, are there any other people that you feel like you'll probably have some conversations about the elections with that'll be useful to you?**

Joanna: Not ones that'll be useful.

Absent a fuller understanding of the rhythms and demands of Joanna's daily life, it would be easy to misinterpret her statements about not placing "a lot of value" in news about the election and to attribute this attitude to pure "apathy." That is (part of) Joanna's own narrative. But by watching her multitask as she juggled her kids' demands for attention while hosting a stranger in her home, it became clear that what is "useful" to Joanna in a day-to-day sense is necessarily constrained by many factors outside of her immediate control. Boiling down her lack of interest in news to "preferences" would only obscure the all-consuming manner in which her children quite literally prevented her from focusing on other matters. Although we might have captured some of these nuances by other means (say, a telephone call), seeing these aspects of her life up close—for instance, being loudly and repeatedly interrupted by her kids—made that reality plain and inescapable.

ANALYZING AND PRESENTING OUR INTERVIEW DATA

After completing each interview, we wrote memos to ourselves describing the main themes and details of the encounter to capture details from the exchanges that might not come through in the transcripts. In addition to these field notes, we also added entries to a spreadsheet documenting some of the basic characteristics of each participant, including the themes that immediately jumped out at us. These initial reactions, however, were just the first step in making sense of our data. All interview recordings were fully transcribed and added to a database in NVivo software, where two or all of us read and reread each one closely. Through a series of conversations about observations gleaned from poring over these transcripts, over time we collaboratively came up with "codes," or common themes we identified and cataloged across our interviews, and a framework for how they connect to each other. This process was iterative in the sense that we often added codes and went back into the transcripts to identify additional excerpts that we may have missed, and it was inductive in the sense that we allowed ourselves to be led by the themes we discovered over the course of the study—an approach that is similar to what is sometimes described as constructivist or "grounded theory."[24]

Throughout the interview and analysis process, we paid particular attention to our own positionality in relation to our interviewees, most of whom had backgrounds very different from our own. Both Ben and Ruth are American and did the interviews in the United Kingdom and Spain, respectively (they split up interviews in the United States). Ben was living in the United Kingdom at the time, and Ruth had been living in Spain for five years and had ties to the country going back twenty years. Our accents in the United Kingdom and Spain gave us away as foreigners, and there is no doubt that interviewing across cultures or languages can mean some nuances are lost. But we suspect our foreignness might have helped as much as it hurt. It diminished the most obvious cultural markers of class and prompted many interviewees to say things explicitly that they might have left unspoken if they were speaking to an insider.

That said, we are also white university professors with stable jobs and comparatively privileged lives. Our interviewees, at least the news avoiders among them, were often from the working class. Most did not have college degrees, and quite a few faced challenges in their personal lives that we could only imagine. Our differences in socioeconomic class, education, and life circumstances often felt like an elephant in the room, and sometimes we struggled to build rapport across those divides. By comparison, we noticed that talking to news lovers was often a breeze. We simply had more in common with them. In addition to our similarities to them in education and socioeconomic class, it was hard to avoid the fact that *we study news for a living*, which created a central point of commonality with the news lovers that we did not share with the news avoiders.

We were also concerned about social desirability effects and reactivity: that people might distort their answers based on what they thought they *should* say and what they thought they should say *to us* in particular. Some interviewees clearly did feel self-conscious about saying they did not follow news and current events more closely. One Spanish news avoider, for example, Olga, stopped herself after saying she found news "boring" and said she was "embarrassed" to admit it. "I don't want you to get a bad impression of me," she said, adding that she worried "maybe you're going to think, 'Fuck, what a disaster.'" As Ruth did in that instance, in an effort to put the study participants at ease we always reassured them that we were not judging them or trying to get them to change their behavior. But some interviewees (though certainly not all) had clearly internalized norms around news use, and the questions we were asking appeared to trigger those norms. For example, at one point during an interview with Annabell (United Kingdom), she said, "The more I talk to you, the more ignorant I can hear myself sounding."

Would someone like Annabell have expressed herself differently if conversing with someone else, someone she perceived as more like herself? No doubt. But insofar as we treated these exchanges as two-way conversations and tried to be cognizant of how our own presence affected what was said, we believe these factors do not negate the themes we ultimately identified. Our sense of who we are and what we believe about our place in the world is central to shaping our relationships—not only with news but with everything else as well—and these aspects of our interviews may have contributed to bringing these themes to the fore. That is, they are as much a feature as a bug.

We were also relieved to find that, overall, despite any professed hesitations due to social desirability, people were often very willing to speak openly and bluntly about quite personal matters. Sometimes, that openness also meant the views they expressed were objectionable, including at times some racist, homophobic, or xenophobic ideas. It can be a strange feeling, but when doing in-depth interviews, you do enter into a different, less judgmental mindset. In the moment, as a listener you try to be as empathetic as possible, but it can later be jarring to listen back to recordings and hear yourself just murmuring along noncommittally as an interviewee expresses views you would normally (you hope) shoot down in a heartbeat. We were especially conscious of the effort required to suspend judgment when interviewing Americans with political views that contrasted with our own, perhaps because, at least for Ruth and Ben, our own political views are largely rooted in the United States.

* * *

Ultimately, we have tried to do justice to the news avoiders and news lovers who were generous with their time and energy to share their stories with us. But there is no doubt that this book is our story about their stories. Here we pull back the curtain on how we constructed that story in ways that will shed light on our findings but also help future researchers who take on similar projects. To that end, in appendixes B and C we also provide brief details about each interviewee and our interview protocols, respectively.

APPENDIX B

SUMMARY TABLES DESCRIBING STUDY PARTICIPANTS

TABLE B.1 Description of News Avoider Participants in the United Kingdom

NAME	DATE OF FIRST INTERVIEW	MODE	LOCATION	GENDER	AGE	EMPLOYMENT STATUS	SOCIAL CLASS	NEWS USE FREQUENCY	DESCRIPTION
Adam	03/28/2017	In home	Leeds	Man	26–35	Employed full-time	Working class	Less often than once a month	Tech-savvy urbanite, works at an events company
Akpan	03/23/2017	In home	Manchester	Man	36–45	Self-employed	Middle class	Less often than once a month	African immigrant, sports fanatic
Alaina	03/24/2017	In home	Manchester	Woman	26–35	Stays at home to look after house/family	Working class	Less often than once a month	Stay-at-home mom, into competitions
Alicia	03/06/2017	By telephone	Leeds	Woman	36–45	Self-employed	Working class	Less often than once a month	Furniture restorer with four kids
Amelia	03/14/2017	In home	Leeds	Woman	26–35	Long-term sick/disabled	Working class	Less often than once a month	Young mother in council housing
Amy	03/15/2017	In home	Leeds	Woman	36–45	Employed part-time	Middle class	Less often than once a month	Suburban mom
Andrea	03/08/2017	In home	Leeds	Woman	36–45	Employed full-time	Working class	Less often than once a month	Full-time house cleaner with dream of being astrophysicist

Name	Date	Method	City	Gender	Age	Employment	Class	Frequency	Description
Annabell	03/13/2017	In person	Oxford	Woman	26–35	Employed full-time	Unknown (Did not ask)	Once a week	Works in court system, still adjusting to living on her own
Ava	03/06/2017	By telephone	Leeds	Woman	26–35	Employed full-time	Middle class	Less often than once a month	Full-time office worker with small child
Brenna	03/08/2017	In home	Leeds	Woman	26–35	Employed full-time	Middle class	Less often than once a month	Working class, confused by politics but concerned about community
Brianna	03/28/2017	In home	Leeds	Woman	26–35	Employed part-time	Working class	Less often than once a month	Social worker
Caitlin	03/16/2017	In home	Leeds	Woman	26–35	Employed full-time	Middle class	Less often than once a month	Single mom, former police officer, now working in retail
Caleb	03/14/2017	In home	Leeds	Man	18–25	Employed part-time	Working class	Less often than once a month	Family-oriented guy into looking for job
Cameron	03/08/2017	In home	Leeds	Man	26–35	Employed full-time	Middle class	Less often than once a month	Musician and video game enthusiast
Carleigh	03/16/2017	In home	Leeds	Woman	18–25	Employed full-time	Working class	Less often than once a month	Young support worker in council housing
Chelsea	03/07/2017	In home	Leeds	Woman	36–45	Employed full-time	Working class	Never	Long-distance runner, anxious busy-body mom

(continued)

TABLE B.1 (*continued*)

NAME	DATE OF FIRST INTERVIEW	MODE	LOCATION	GENDER	AGE	EMPLOYMENT STATUS	SOCIAL CLASS	NEWS USE FREQUENCY	DESCRIPTION
Emily	03/14/2017	In home	Leeds	Woman	26–35	Self-employed, long-term sick/disabled	Working class	Never	Anxious stay-at-home mother
Evelyn	03/24/2017	In home	Manchester	Woman	26–35	Employed part-time	Working class	Less often than once a month	Part-time courier, mother
Gemma	03/23/2017	In home	Manchester	Woman	26–35	Employed part-time	Middle class	Less often than once a month	Young mother, works part-time, uninterested in news
Gracie	03/16/017	In home	Leeds	Woman	26–35	Self-employed	Middle class	Less often than once a month	Works in antique sales, no kids
Haylie	03/24/2017	In home	Manchester	Woman	36–45	Employed full-time	Middle class	Never	Personal-injury lawyer, self-help fanatic, yoga instructor
Heidi	11/07/2016	In person	Oxford	Woman	18–25	Full-time student	Unknown (Did not ask)	Up to 5 times a day	Foreign student studying film (interviewed along with Kelley)

Name	Date	Method	City	Gender	Age	Employment	Class	Frequency	Description
Hollie	03/07/2017	In home	Leeds	Woman	18–25	Employed part-time, full-time student	Working class	Less often than once a month	Student distrustful of fake news
Isabella	03/10/2017	By telephone	Leeds	Woman	26–35	Employed part-time	Working class	Less often than once a month	Support worker with two kids
Jane	03/15/2017	In home	Leeds	Woman	26–35	Employed full-time	Middle class	Less often than once a month	Aspiring fashion designer, works in food service industry
Jennifer	03/28/2017	In home	Leeds	Woman	36–45	Employed full-time	Middle class	Less often than once a month	Upper middle class, pregnant, educated
Jessica	03/28/2017	In home	Leeds	Woman	18–26	Employed part-time	Working class	Less often than once a month	Council housing resident, caring for child with rare disease
Jodie	03/23/2017	In home	Manchester	Woman	36–45	Employed part-time	Middle class	Less often than once a month	Mother of three, works at nearby school
Kailey	03/09/2017	By telephone	London	Woman	18–25	Employed part-time, full-time student	Working class	Less often than once a month	Young student, distrustful of media
Kali	03/06/2017	By telephone	Leeds	Woman	26–35	Stays at home to look after house/family	Working class	Less often than once a month	Full-time caregiver to two kids, one with autism, and another kid on way

(*continued*)

TABLE B.1 (*continued*)

NAME	DATE OF FIRST INTERVIEW	MODE	LOCATION	GENDER	AGE	EMPLOYMENT STATUS	SOCIAL CLASS	NEWS USE FREQUENCY	DESCRIPTION
Kate	03/28/2017	In home	Leeds	Woman	18–25	Employed full-time	Middle class	Less often than once a month	Works in travel customer service, recently married
Kelley	11/07/2016	In person	Oxford	Woman	18–25	Full-time student	Unknown (Did not ask)	2–3 times a month	Foreign student studying film
Lexi	03/10/2017	By telephone	Manchester	Woman	36–45	Employed full-time	Working class	Less often than once a month	Animal-rescue worker, single with no kids
Libby	03/13/2017	In person	Oxford	Woman	26–35	Employed full-time	Na	Once a week	Admin worker at hospital, politically active
Lilia	03/23/2017	In home	Manchester	Woman	26–35	Employed full-time	Middle class	Less often than once a month	Recent grad, lives in expensive area of town, keeps to self
Megan	03/16/2017	In home	Leeds	Woman	26–35	Employed full-time	Middle class	Less often than once a month	Human resources staffer, lives with boyfriend in suburbs
Nicole	03/07/2017	In home	Leeds	Woman	26–35	Employed full-time	Working class	Less often than once a month	White-collar worker in construction industry with plans to move abroad

Name	Date	Interview type	City	Gender	Age	Employment	Social class	Frequency	Description
Olivia	03/14/2017	In home	Leeds	Woman	26–35	Unemployed	Working class	Less often than once a month	Unemployed and depressed, living in student area
Patrick	03/24/2017	In home	Manchester	Man	26–35	Self employed	Working class	Less often than once a month	Vegan personal trainer, self-professed believer in conspiracy theories
Robert	03/15/2017	In home	Leeds	Man	18–25	Employed full-time	Working class	Less often than once a month	Engineer from working-class roots, living with girlfriend
Rosemary	03/10/2017	By telephone	Manchester	Woman	26–35	Employed part-time	Working class	Less often than once a month	Support worker with one kid, actively trying to get better informed
Ryan	03/07/2017	In home	Leeds	Man	36–46	Stays at home to look after house/family	Middle class	Never	Cynical stay-at-home dad
Sarah	03/15/2017	In home	Leeds	Woman	36–45	Stays at home to look after house/family	Working class	Less often than once a month	Unemployed single mother, lives on same street grew up on
Tessa	03/08/2017	In home	Leeds	Woman	26–35	Long-term sick/disabled	Middle class	Less often than once a month	Professional on leave from work due to chronic fatigue

Note: In the United Kingdom, the recruitment agency measured social class on the basis of occupation. Na = "not applicable"; we did not collect that information.

TABLE B.2 Description of News Avoider Participants in Spain

NAME	DATE OF FIRST INTERVIEW	MODE	LOCATION	GENDER	AGE	EMPLOYMENT STATUS	DESCRIPTION
Adriana	02/28/2018	In home	Madrid	Woman	26–35	Employed full-time	Admin at a driving school, lives with her partner
Alex	01/25/2018	In home	Madrid	Man	18–25	Full-time student	Chatty physical education student, devoted to longtime girlfriend
Andrés	12/16/2017	In home	Madrid	Man	18–25	Full-time student	Garrulous fourth-year software engineering student
Antonio	11/20/2017	In home	Madrid	Man	18–25	Full-time student	Aerospace engineering student from pueblo in Extremadura
Aria	02/05/2018	In home	Madrid	Woman	18–25	Full-time student	College student studying primary-school education, newly awakened feminist
Blanca	12/16/2017	In home	Madrid	Woman	36–45	Employed full-time	Four kids, works in a bank
Celeste	01/17/2018	In home	Madrid	Woman	26–35	Employed full-time	Laconic hotel receptionist
Cristiano	10/20/2017	In home	Madrid	Man	36–45	Stays at home to look after house/family	Stay-at-home dad of two small girls, looking for work
Emilia	11/08/2017	In home	Madrid	Woman	26–35	Employed full-time	Soft-spoken admin living with parents
Gonzalo	02/24/2018	In home	Madrid	Man	36–45	Employed full-time	Mattress salesman, father of a one-year-old, dislikes reading
Ignacio	11/04/2017	In home	Madrid	Man	18–25	Employed full-time	Recently heart-broken barrista

Name	Date						Description
Inés	10/23/2017	In home	Madrid	Woman	36–45	Employed full-time	Hospital accountant, likes to travel
Iñigo	02/26/2018	In home	Madrid	Man	26–35	Employed full-time	Young taxi driver, lives with parents, likes video games
Irene	02/28/2018	In home	Madrid	Woman	26–35	Employed full-time	Young administrator, lives alone in Orcasitas
Iris	12/16/2017	In home	Madrid	Woman	36–45	Stays at home to look after house/family	Sensitive mother of two, busy, worries about making ends meet
Isaac	10/25/2017	In home	Madrid	Man	26–35	Employed full-time	Young electrician from Córdoba, lives with four roommates in semibasement apartment
Javier	02/26/2018	In home	Madrid	Man	36–45	Unemployed	Excon handyman, lives in basement apartment with three dogs
José	12/15/2017	In home	Madrid	Man	18–25	Full-time student	Only child, studying to be a PE teacher
Juan	11/03/2017	In home	Madrid	Man	26–35	Employed full-time	Voice-over actor, loner and happy that way (except for a slightly lonely heart)
Laura	02/23/2018	In home	Madrid	Woman	36–45	Employed part-time	Busy working mother of three small kids
Manuel	11/20/2017	In home	Madrid	Man	18–25	Employed full-time	Good-natured young accountant with a blind poodle
Mara	01/26/2018	In home	Madrid	Woman	18–25	Employed part-time	Adventurous young woman, spends half the year working in Ibiza
Marco	10/20/2017	In home	Madrid	Man	18–25	Full-time student	Young engineering student and handball player, lives with parents

(continued)

TABLE B.2 *(continued)*

NAME	DATE OF FIRST INTERVIEW	MODE	LOCATION	GENDER	AGE	EMPLOYMENT STATUS	DESCRIPTION
Marta	11/11/2017	In home	Madrid	Woman	36–45	Employed full-time	Mortgage broker in poor health, works a lot, anxiety prone
Miguel	11/11/2017	In home	Madrid	Man	18–25	Employed part-time	Young man, hopes to move to Denmark
Nico	02/26/2018	In home	Madrid	Man	26–35	Employed full-time	*Star Wars* fan from a pueblo in the Sierra, lives and works in North Madrid
Olga	02/23/2018	In home	Madrid	Woman	36–45	Employed full-time	Mother of a teen, cares for mom with Alzheimer's
Oliver	10/25/2017	In home	Madrid	Man	36–45	Employed full-time	IT worker, separated father of two, currently living with parents in the home where he grew up
Paco	10/25/2017	In home	Madrid	Man	36–45	Unemployed	Extroverted stay-at-home dad
Paloma	11/03/2017	In home	Madrid	Woman	36–45	Employed full-time	Chatty director of studies at a public high school, with two-year-old
Patricia	01/25/2018	In home	Madrid	Woman	26–35	Employed full-time	Talkative accountant, husband listened in and sometimes interjected
Pedro	11/11/2017	In home	Madrid	Man	36–45	Employed full-time	Busy father of two, wife and kids came into interview midway, lots of cats

Raquel	02/24/2018	In home	Madrid	Woman	18–25	Employed full-time	Young admin, works for family company, long commute
Rodolfo	11/11/2017	In home	Madrid	Man	26–35	Employed full-time	Cheerful young web developer
Rodrigo	10/23/2017	In home	Madrid	Man	26–35	Employed full-time	Young father of three, works as a stock boy, huge football fan
Rosana	12/13/2017	In home	Madrid	Woman	18–25	Full-time student	Friendly graphic design student, lives with parents
Silvia	10/21/2017	In home	Madrid	Woman	26–35	Employed full-time	Young married working mom expecting second child in Vallecas
Siva	10/20/2017	In home	Madrid	Man	36–45	Employed full-time	Yoga teacher in search of enlightenment
Sofia	02/28/2018	In home	Madrid	Woman	18–25	Full-time student	Disaffected but articulate young Argentinean Spaniard
Susana	08/11/2017	In home	Madrid	Woman	26–35	Employed full-time	Spanish Filipina young mother of five-year-old, sells insurance

Note: In Spain, class was determined by the participant's head of household. In the United Kingdom, the recruitment firm supplied the breakdown of social class and frequency of news use, but in Spain it did not, which is why we do not include that information here.

TABLE B.3 Description of News Avoider Participants in the United States

NAME	DATE OF FIRST INTERVIEW	MODE	LOCATION	GENDER	AGE	EMPLOYMENT STATUS	EDUCATION	NEWS USE FREQUENCY	DESCRIPTION
Arman	07/17/2019	In home	Des Moines	Man	26–35	Employed full-time	Four-year college graduate	Less often than once a month	Fast-talking, sports fan engineer, close group of diverse friends who disagree about politics
Bethany	08/14/2019	In home	Cedar Rapids	Woman	26–35	Employed full-time	Some college	Less often than once a week	Mother of two young kids, interested in becoming more engaged with news but struggles to find the time
Brian	08/22/2019	In home	Des Moines	Man	36–45	Employed full-time	Advanced degree	Less often than once a week	Athletic and religious father, distrustful of news on ideological grounds but highly educated
Bruce	08/22/2019	In home	Des Moines	Man	36–35	Employed full-time	Four-year college graduate	Less often than once a week	Religious family man, considers himself mainly libertarian, rejects most conventional news sources as untrustworthy (married to Katie)
Carly	08/07/2019	In person	Cedar Rapids	Woman	26–35	Employed full-time	Four-year college graduate	Less often than once a month	Young mother, interested in liberal politics, limits media intake due to anxiety, anger with parents who watch a lot of *Fox News*

Name	Date		Location		Age	Employment	Education	Frequency	Description
Charlie	08/08/2019	In home	Cedar Rapids	Man	36–45	Employed full-time	Community college	Never	Very talkative Trump supporter who had previously been a Bernie supporter in 2016, ideologically opposed to most conventional news
Colleen	08/20/2019	In home	Southeast Iowa	Woman	26–35	Employed part-time	Community college	Never	Young woman, working two jobs and raising four kids, very much a caretaker, little time or interest in news
Daniel	08/13/2019	In home	Cedar Rapids	Man	36–45	Employed full-time	Some college	Never	Young working-class father, shared custody of kids, ambivalent about his lack of interest in news
David	08/09/2019	In home	Cedar Rapids	Man	36–45	Employed full-time	Four-year college graduate	Less often than once a month	Thoughtful, intellectual professional, quit following news as active choice after September 11, 2001
Dion	08/09/2019	In home	Cedar Rapids	Woman	26–35	Employed part-time	Four-year college graduate	Less often than once a month	Mother of special-needs child, avoids knowing more about the news to get out of conflictual arguments about politics
Ed	08/13/2019	In home	Cedar Rapids	Man	26–35	Employed full-time	Advanced degree	Never	No-nonsense, engineer mentality, quit following news largely because he saw it as a distraction in his carefully regimented time

(continued)

TABLE B.3 (continued)

NAME	DATE OF FIRST INTERVIEW	MODE	LOCATION	GENDER	AGE	EMPLOYMENT STATUS	EDUCATION	NEWS USE FREQUENCY	DESCRIPTION
Heather	08/20/2019	In home	Des Moines	Woman	26–35	Employed part-time	Four-year college graduate	Less often than once a week	Young mother of two kids, wife of a pastor, educated and interested in news but actively decided to take self off social media, so learns about news mostly through her husband
Joanna	08/23/2019	In home	Des Moines	Woman	26–35	Homemaker	Community college	Less often than once a week	Young mother, religious, home-schooled, found news makes her feel anxious
Johnny	07/18/2019	In person	Des Moines	Man	18–25	Employed full-time	Four-year college graduate	Less often than once a month	Recent college grad, working as an accountant, most apolitical of all the people he knows
Joyce	08/21/2019	In person	Des Moines	Woman	46–55	Not employed/ disability	Advanced degree	Less often than once a week	Educated, talkative, middle-aged woman, alienated from politics and in conflict with her family, worked part-time jobs to get by
Karl	08/14/2019	In home	Cedar Rapids	Man	26–35	Employed full-time	Technical/ vocational school	Never	Apolitical factory worker who had relocated to Iowa from the South, adjusting to feeling like a fish out of water
Katie	08/22/2019	In home	Des Moines	Woman	26–35	Employed full-time	High school graduate	Less often than once a week	Talkative, actively avoids news due to anxiety, interested in conspiracy theories (married to Bruce)

Name	Date	Mode	City	Gender	Age	Employment	Education	News frequency	Description
Lynn	08/23/2019	In home	Cedar Rapids	Woman	46–55	Self-employed	Some college	Never	Very talkative, middle-age former nurse with a teenager at home, preoccupied by conflicts with family members
Maggie	08/06/2019	In person	Des Moines	Woman	26–35	Employed full-time	Some college	Less often than once a month	Service industry worker in recovery, distant from family, exposed to some news on social media
Melanie	08/21/2019	In home	Des Moines	Woman	26–35	Employed full-time	Community college	Never	Suburban housewife, married to a committed partisan and Warren supporter, but disengaged from politics
Patricia	08/12/2019	In home	Cedar Rapids	Woman	46–55	Employed full-time	Community college	Less often than once a month	Soft-spoken mother recovering from cancer, dislikes politics though she is surrounded by it
Reggie	08/09/2019	In home	Cedar Rapids	Man	26–35	Employed full-time	High school graduate	Never	Working-class factory worker, small growing interest in politics
Sid	08/09/2019	In home	Cedar Rapids	Man	26–35	Employed full-time	Some college	Never	Spiritual father of young girl and in recovery for substance abuse
Terri	08/12/2019	In home	Cedar Rapids	Woman	26–35	Employed full-time	Advanced degree	Never	Young professional saddled with large student loan debt, forced to move back in with her parents
William	08/19/2019	In home	Des Moines	Man	26–35	Employed full-time	Community college	Less often than once a month	Father of three, works in construction, fan of InfoWars and other right-wing indie news sources

Note: In the United States, class was determined by a combination of household income and education, so we include the education information here.

TABLE B.4 Description of News Lover Participants in the United States

NAME	DATE OF FIRST INTERVIEW	MODE	LOCATION	GENDER	AGE	EMPLOYMENT STATUS	EDUCATION	NEWS USE FREQUENCY	DESCRIPTION
Barb	07/30/2019	In home	Des Moines	Woman	36–45	Not employed/ disability	Some college	More than 10 times a day	Artist with ADHD on long-term disability, loves routine
Bob	07/19/2019	In home	Des Moines	Man	66–75	Self-employed	Four-year college graduate	More than 10 times a day	Semiretired medical head hunter, bachelor, no kids, watches MSNBC all day
Carolyn	07/17/2019	In home	Des Moines	Woman	56–65	Self-employed	Four-year college graduate	More than 10 times a day	Upper-middle-class political operative, married to a campaign manager, highly engaged in local politics
Charles	07/22/2019	In person	Des Moines	Man	46–55	Employed full-time	Four-year college graduate	More than 10 times a day	Financial adviser who reads news for his job, tries to limit news at home
Clint	07/24/2019	In home	Des Moines	Man	36–45	Employed full-time	Some college	More than 10 times a day	Recently divorced (soon to be remarried) father of two, works in construction, loves local news, and watches a lot with his kids
Debra	07/16/2019	In home	Des Moines	Woman	36–45	Employed full-time	Advanced degree	More than 10 times a day	Busy, divorced mother of two with tons of like-minded friends

Name	Date	Location	City	Gender	Age	Employment	Education	Frequency	Description
Elizabeth	07/16/2019	In home	Des Moines	Woman	66–75	Employed part-time	Advanced degree	More than 10 times a day	Talkative semiretired schoolteacher, lives with husband on flood-prone property
Frank	07/23/2019	In home	Des Moines	Man	56–65	Employed full-time	Advanced degree	More than 10 times a day	High school social studies teacher, NPR lover, has strong commitment to civic duty
Fred	07/17/2019	In home	Des Moines	Man	66–75	Self-employed	Four-year college graduate	More than 10 times a day	Farmer devoted to family, has listened to Rush Limbaugh for thirty years
Gloria	07/17/2019	In home	Des Moines	Woman	56–65	Employed full-time	Four-year college graduate	More than 10 times a day	Progressive grandmother who works in a lab diagnosing cancer, lives in a semiretirement community
Jennifer	07/19/2019	In home	Des Moines	Woman	36–45	Employed full-time	Four-year college graduate	More than 10 times a day	Athletic young professional, highly interested in news, dating back to her time as a journalism major in college
Jerry	07/19/2019	In home	Des Moines	Man	56–65	Retired	Four-year college graduate	More than 10 times a day	Retired former small-town newspaper publisher, committed to newspapers and *Wonkette*
Joshua	07/17/2019	In home	Des Moines	Man	46–55	Employed full-time	Advanced degree	More than 10 times a day	Father of five boys, works at a school, surrounded by conservatives, somewhat guarded about his own political views

(*continued*)

TABLE B.4 (continued)

NAME	DATE OF FIRST INTERVIEW	MODE	LOCATION	GENDER	AGE	EMPLOYMENT STATUS	EDUCATION	NEWS USE FREQUENCY	DESCRIPTION
Ketrick	07/31/2019	In home	Des Moines	Man	38–45	Employed full-time	Advanced degree	More than 10 times a day	Political science professor who also teaches media, self-described "news hound"
Lance	07/23/2019	In home	Des Moines	Man	26–35	Employed full-time	Advanced degree	More than 10 times a day	Engineer, father of three, with a diverse group of friends and colleagues who discuss politics
Linda	07/16/2019	In home	Des Moines	Woman	46–55	Employed full-time	Four-year college graduate	More than 10 times a day	Articulate office worker, listens to CNN all day long at work on her phone, highly alarmed by Trump
Matt	07/16/2019	In home	Des Moines	Man	46–55	Employed full-time	Technical/ vocational school	More than 10 times a day	Former union worker, father to two teenage boys, works long hours at the airport to get by
Mike	07/18/2019	In home	Des Moines	Man	46–55	Employed full-time	Four-year college graduate	More than 10 times a day	Devout Catholic, Republican father of four who works in sales
Nancy	07/19/2019	In person	Des Moines	Woman	66–75	Self-employed	Advanced degree	More than 10 times a day	Very politically engaged older woman, sees herself as a networker in the community and is highly connected to the local political establishment

Name	Date	Location	City	Gender	Age	Employment	Education	Frequency	Description
Paul	07/16/2019	In home	Des Moines	Man	66–75	Self-employed	Advanced degree	More than 10 times a day	Retired conservative libertarian, lives on a farm in the country, obsessively follows politics on cable TV, hates liberals
Rachel	07/18/2019	In home	Des Moines	Woman	36–45	Homemaker	Advanced degree	More than 10 times a day	Liberal news-obsessive mother of three girls, urban planner running for city council
Randall	07/18/2019	In home	Des Moines	Man	56–65	Unemployed	Some college	More than 10 times a day	Anxious, older gay man, married, unemployed, dealing with health issues, listens to television news all day long
Ronald	07/18/2019	In home	Des Moines	Man	46–55	Employed full-time	Four-year college graduate	More than 10 times a day	Well educated, professional, intellectually curious, enthusiastic about sports, absorbs information "like a sponge"
Sharon	07/30/2019	In home	Des Moines	Woman	66–75	Self-employed	Four-year college graduate	More than 10 times a day	Works-from-home tax accountant, once ran for mayor, very politically engaged and liberal
Susan	07/24/2019	In home	Des Moines	Woman	46–55	Employed part-time	Advanced degree	More than 10 times a day	Preschool teacher, mother of two teens, relies heavily on Blaze TV

Note: In the United States, class was determined by a combination of household income and education, so we include the education information here.

APPENDIX C

INTERVIEW PROTOCOLS FOR
IN-DEPTH INTERVIEWING

News Avoiders Interview Protocol: English (United Kingdom and United States)

Introductions

1. Introduce self and review information sheet.
2. Answer any questions about the study.
3. Is it okay if I record this interview?

Background

1. Tell me about yourself generally.
   a. [Listen for whether describe work or home life, etc.] What about [work]?
2. [If telephone:] Where are you located?
3. Where did you grow up?
   a. What was it like growing up?
4. How did you end up living in [___]? Or staying in [___]?
5. Have you thought about living anywhere else?
   a. What stopped you?

6. Who are the people you are closest to?

    a. Same/different as the people you spend the most time talking to regularly?

Most Important Problems

1. What do you see as the most important issues in your own life day to day?

    iii. [If needed . . .] Survey researchers often ask people to rate what issues they think are important but don't always know which concerns/problems to include. We want to hear from you, in your own words, what YOU think is important.

2. How about in [your community]?

    a. What kinds of things are your neighbors worried about?

    b. What about your coworkers?

    c. What about friends/family?

3. How about most important problem facing the United Kingdom/Spain/ the United States right now?

4. Do you feel like you have all the information you need to know enough about what's happening in your community?

    a. What kind of information would you like more of typically?

5. Where do you turn to for information about what's happening in your community?

    a. Thinking about people you're closest to, do you talk about these issues?

6. Are there specific people or sources of information you rely on?

Routines

1. What's a typical day like for you?

    a. If you have one, take me through your morning routine.

        i. Do you drink tea or coffee? Eat breakfast usually?

        ii. Are you the type who is usually rushing or taking your time?

        iii. Watch or read anything in particular?

        iv. Check email or anything?

    b. Commuting?

    c. Who do you interact with regularly?

    d. During the day, do you set aside time to watch or read anything?

    e. At end of day, as you're winding down, any kind of evening routines? Watch or read anything before going to bed?

2. [If working], what's it like where you work?

    a. Every minute busy or have some time in between tasks to yourself?

    b. Do you work with computer at a desk or on your feet working with your hands, etc.?

    c. Do people socialize much at your work?

       i. What do they talk about?

In the Past

1. Growing up, did anyone in your family read the newspaper or follow the news?

2. Previous times in your life when you paid more attention to the news?

News Reactions

1. What's the last story you can remember coming across in the news? [Doesn't have to be particular article or TV segment, just a topic that's been in the news.]

    a. What was it about?

    b. Who were the people involved?

    c. How did you come across it?

    d. Did you talk to anyone about it?

    e. Did you follow up on the story at all? Seek out more information?

2. Does the news pay enough attention to people like yourself?

    a. Too much attention to some people?

3. Do you know anyone who has been featured in news stories before?

4. What do you think of journalists?

    a. Do you know anyone who works in the news business (for a newspaper or website or television)?

5. Do you know anyone who pays a lot of attention to the news?

    a. What do you think of [him/her/people like that]?

6. Would you say it is important to stay informed about the news?
   a. For being a good citizen?
   b. For being able to navigate the world you live in?

Complete iPad Survey [when possible]
I have a short survey on this iPad. Would you mind filling it out?

Closing
1. Some people use a lot of news, others don't. How do you think about your own habits relative to other people?
2. What would you say are the main reasons you don't pay attention to the news more?
3. Can you think of anything that might make you pay more attention to the news?
4. Interest/willingness for follow-up interview?
5. Anything I left out that you think is important?

NEWS LOVERS INTERVIEW PROTOCOL (UNITED STATES)

Introductions
1. Introduce self and review information sheet.
2. Answer any questions about the study.
3. Is it okay if I record this interview?

Background
1. Tell me about yourself generally.
   a. [Listen for whether describe work or home life, etc.] What about [work]?
2. [If telephone:] Where are you located?
3. Where did you grow up?
   a. What was it like growing up?
4. How did you end up living in [___]? Or staying in [___]?

5. Have you thought about living anywhere else?
   a. What stopped you?
6. Who are the people you are closest to?
   a. Same/different as the people you spend the most time talking to regularly?

Most Important Problem

1. What do you see as the most important issues in your own life day to day?
   a. [If needed . . .] Survey researchers often ask people to rate what issues they think are important but don't always know which concerns/problems to include. We want to hear from you, in your own words, what YOU think is important.
2. How about in [your community]?
   a. What kinds of things are your neighbors worried about?
   b. What about your coworkers?
   c. What about friends/family?
3. How about most important problem facing the United States?
4. Do you feel like you have all the information you need to know enough about what's happening in [the United States/your community/your neighborhood]?
   a. What kind of information would you like more of typically?
5. Where do you turn to for information about what's happening in your community?
   a. Thinking about people you're closest to, do you talk about these issues?
6. Are there specific people or sources of information you rely on?

Routines

1. What's a typical day like for you?
   a. If you have one, take me through your morning routine.
      i. Do you drink tea or coffee? Eat breakfast usually?
      ii. Are you the type who is usually rushing or taking your time?
      iii. Watch or read anything in particular?
      iv. Check email or anything?
   b. Commuting?
   c. Who do you interact with regularly?

    d. During the day, do you set aside time or take breaks to watch or read anything?

    e. At end of day, as you're winding down, any kind of evening routines? Watch or read anything before going to bed?

2. [If working], what's it like where you work?

    a. Every minute busy or have some time in between tasks to yourself?

    b. Do you work with a computer at a desk or on your feet working with your hands?

    c. Is it noisy or quiet?

Socialization

1. Growing up, did anyone in your family read the newspaper or follow the news?

    a. Any peers?

    b. Any particular memories stand out?

2. Did people TALK about events in the news?

    a. Any particular memories stand out?

    b. Do you remember participating in those conversations?

    c. Talk about politics?

3. Was news ever talked about when you were in school?

    a. Examples of experiences among classmates? Among friends? In classes?

4. Did you ever get out of the habit of consuming news? Can you talk about that a bit?

    a. Do you remember how/why you got back in the habit?

News Reactions

1. What's the last story you can remember coming across in the news? [Doesn't have to be particular article or TV segment, just a topic that's been in the news.]

    a. What was it about?

    b. Who were the people involved?

    c. How did you come across it?

    d. Did you talk to anyone about it?

    e. Did you follow up on the story at all? Seek out more information?

2. Does the news pay enough attention to people like yourself?

   a. Too much attention to some people?

3. Do you know anyone who has been featured in news stories before?

4. What do you think of journalists?

   a. Do you know anyone who works in the news business (for a newspaper or website or television)?

How News Feels

1. Was there a time you can recall where you couldn't access news? What was that like? What did you miss about it?

2. Have you ever felt the need to take a break from the news? Deliberately changed your media habits?

   a. When? Why? How did you do it? How did it go?

3. Which aspects of the news/topics [do] you like the most? Aspects or topics you dislike?

Community Norms

1. Some people use a lot of news; others don't. How do you think about your own habits relative to other people?

2. Thinking about the people you said you were closest to, would you say their news habits are similar to yours?

   a. What do they think about your news habits?

3. Do you know anyone who pays almost no attention to the news?

   a. What do you think of [him/her/people like that]?

4. Do you TALK about or SHARE a lot of news with others?

   a. In person or online?

   b. What kinds of reactions do you get from others?

   c. Do people ask you for information about the news?

   d. How do you feel about that?

5. Would you say it is important to stay informed about the news?

   a. For being a good citizen?

   b. For being able to navigate the world you live in?

6. [If relevant] What kind of news habits would you like your children to have?

Complete iPad Survey [when possible—explain question about follow-up interviews]

Closing

1. Anything I left out that you think is important?
2. What would you say are the main reasons you pay so much attention to the news?
   a. Despite all the things you dislike about?

NEWS AVOIDERS FOLLOW-UP INTERVIEW PROTOCOL (UNITED KINGDOM)

Catching Up

1. Tell me about anything new in your life since last time we talked.
   a. Changes to job or home life?
   b. Changes in the lives of people you are closest to?

Election 2017

1. Did you follow the election at all?
   a. How did you pay attention if at all? News?
   b. Were you drawn in to paying attention to the news more so than in the past?
   c. Recall how you became aware that the election had been called?
2. Did you vote? Or think about voting? Why or why not?
   a. (If applicable) Walk me through your experience voting—where, when, etc.
   b. Do you think it's important to vote?
3. Election night itself: Did you watch or read about the results as the returns came in?
   a. Were you surprised at all by the results? What did you expect?
   b. Why do you think May/Corbyn won?
   c. Tell me about the rest of your day on Thursday . . .

4. Do you recall any conversations you participated in or overheard about the election?

    a. People you know who were particularly interested in the election?

5. Any contact with campaigns or candidates? Rallies or door knocks, etc.?

    a. Did you hear about any campaign events, maybe on social media or word of mouth?

6. What would you say were the main issues debated in the election?

    a. Are there things you think should have been addressed by the candidates?

7. Impressions of Teresa May? Jeremy Corbyn? Any other political figure in the news?

8. Did you look for more information about candidates or parties or the election itself?

    a. How did you go about looking for information?

        i. Walk me through how that went . . . were you successful, etc.?

    b. Did you rely on any people in your life and/or sources of information online/offline?

    c. Any news sources or stories you found helpful (or unhelpful) in making sense of the election?

    d. Things that confused you over the course of the campaign?

    e. What would you like to know? Things you feel would have been helpful to know?

9. How do you feel about the results?

    a. What would you like to see happen?

10. Do you think you'll be any more or less likely to get involved politically in the future?

Terrorism

1. Regarding (*a*) the London Bridge attacks or (*b*) the attacks in Manchester over the last month . . . do you remember how you learned about it?

    a. Where were you when you heard about it? How soon after it had occurred?

    b. How did you feel about learning about it when you did? [So immediately? Or so long after it had occurred?]

2. Did you look for any more information about either event?

   a. Walk me through how that went . . .

3. Did you discuss it at all with others? Why or why not?

   a. With your kids? Parents? Partners? Coworkers?

   b. Tell me about those conversations . . .

4. Do you have lingering questions about either event?

   a. How important is it to you to know these details?

5. How did news about either of these events make you feel?

6. Was anyone you were close to affected by the news?

   a. Did you or they change any behaviors as a result of the news?

Ask for Feedback on Past Statements

As we go through all of the interviews we've conducted and other information we've gathered, we are focusing on a few different factors that help explain why some people pay close attention to the news and others mostly avoid it. We'd like your thoughts about some of these.

1. Perceptions of news: (*a*) celebrity gossip, (*b*) irrelevant political bickering, (*c*) doom and gloom (crime and terrorism)

2. Ambivalence about importance of following the news

3. "Information is out there" or "I'll just Google it"

4. "News finds me" incidentally online through social media or offline through friends and family

5. "I don't know what to believe"

NEWS AVOIDERS AND NEWS LOVERS FOLLOW-UP INTERVIEW PROTOCOL (UNITED STATES)

Catching Up

1. Tell me about anything new in your life since last time we talked.

   a. Changes to job or home life?

   b. Changes in the lives of people you are closest to?

    c. Changes to your daily routine?

    d. Changes to your media habits?

Impeachment

1. How closely have you been following the impeachment trial and all that?

    a. How have you been getting information?

    b. News alerts, television, etc?

2. Are the people you're interacting with regularly following it?

    a. Do people you know generally agree?

The 2020 Campaign

1. Did you follow the election at all?

    a. [If no] Did you end up coming across information about it? Social media, TV ads, etc.?

    b. Did you rely on any people in your life and/or sources of information online/offline?

    c. Any news sources or stories you found helpful (or unhelpful) in making sense of the election?

    d. Did you pay attention to the news more so than in the past?

       i. Did you find yourself taking extra steps to AVOID exposure?

       ii. [If yes] Did your strategies for avoiding news change at all?

2. [For Independents and Dems only] Did you participate in the caucuses? Or think about doing so? Why or why not?

    a. (If applicable) Walk me through your experience—where, when, etc.

    b. Do you think it's important to participate?

3. Over the course of the campaign, did you feel well enough informed?

    a. What kind of information did you want to know more about?

    b. How informed were other people you interacted with over the course of the campaign [or who were participating at the caucuses]?

    c. How did you go about looking for information?

       i. Walk me through how that went… were you successful, etc.?

4. Do you recall any particular conversations you participated in or overheard about the election?

    a. People you know who were particularly interested in the election?

    b. How did you feel about those discussions?

5. Any contact with campaigns or candidates? Rallies or door knocks, etc.?
   a. Did you hear about any campaign events, maybe on social media or word of mouth?
6. What did you feel were the most important issues in the election?
   a. Are there things you think SHOULD have been addressed more? Or should have been addressed less?
   b. By the candidates? By the media?
   c. Things that confused you over the course of the campaign?
   d. What would you like to know now, thinking back? Things you feel would have been helpful to know?

Caucus Results

1. Election night itself: Did you watch or read about the results as the returns came in?
   a. Were you surprised at all by the results? What did you expect?
   b. Why do you think [CANDIDATE] did as well [or poorly] as they did?
   c. Tell me about the rest of that day . . .
2. How do you feel about the results?
   a. What would you like to see happen now?
3. Do you think you'll be any more or less likely to get involved politically in the future?
4. Did the election affect the way you think about the news in any way? Will you change any of your habits going forward?

Ask for Feedback on Past Statements

As we go through all of the interviews we've conducted and other information we've gathered, we are focusing on a few different factors that help explain why some people pay close attention to the news and others mostly avoid it. We'd like your thoughts about some of these.

1. Personality differences such as openness to different ideas and perspectives, how private or focused inwardly a person is?
   a. How anxious a person is?

2. Stressful circumstances: raising kids, grappling with mental or physical health issues, emotional burden of following news is too much?

3. Social/community expectations to follow and discuss what's happening in the news?

4. Internalized norms about the importance of following the news as citizens? Reinforced in school growing up or at home or day to day by the communities you belong to?

NOTES

1. IS IGNORANCE BLISS?

1. In the Reuters Institute *Digital News Report 2022*, a survey of 93,000 people in forty-six markets around the world, 38 percent of respondents said they "sometimes or often actively avoid news," up from 29 percent in 2017. Numbers ranged from 14 percent in Japan to 54 percent in Brazil. In the countries we studied here, 42 percent in the United States, 46 percent in the United Kingdom, and 35 percent in Spain said they sometimes or often avoid news. See Nic Newman, Richard Fletcher, Craig T. Robertson, Kirsten Eddy, and Rasmus Kleis Nielsen, *Digital News Report 2022* (Oxford: Reuters Institute for the Study of Journalism, 2022), https://reutersinstitute.politics.ox.ac.uk/digital-news-report/2022.

2. Studies have found that these occasional and situational forms of news avoidance were common following Brexit and the election of Donald Trump in 2016. See Nic Newman, Richard Fletcher, Antonis Kalogeropoulos, and Rasmus Kleis Nielsen, *Digital News Report 2019* (Oxford: Reuters Institute for the Study of Journalism, 2019), 25, https://reutersinstitute.politics.ox.ac.uk/sites/default/files/2019-06/DNR_2019_FINAL_0.pdf; María Wagner and Pablo Boczkowski, "Angry, Frustrated, and Overwhelmed: The Emotional Experience of Consuming News About Trump," *Journalism* 22, no. 7 (2021): 1577–93, https://doi.org/10.1177/1464884919878545. Studies have also found that following an initial "COVID bump" in news consumption in the early weeks of the pandemic, news avoidance became a common strategy for dealing with the stressful circumstances. See Richard Fletcher, Antonis Kalogeropoulos, and Rasmus Kleis Nielsen, "News Avoidance in the UK Remains High as Lockdown Restrictions Are Eased," Reuters Institute

for the Study of Journalism, July 2020, https://reutersinstitute.politics.ox.ac.uk/news
-avoidance-uk-remains-high-lockdown-restrictions-are-eased; Tim Groot Kormelink
and Anne Klein Gunnewiek, "From 'Far Away' to 'Fatigue' to 'Back to Normal': How
Young People Experienced News During the First Wave of the COVID-19 Pandemic,"
Journalism Studies 23 (2021), https://doi.org/10.1080/1461670X.2021.1932560; Brita Ytre-
Arne and Hallvard Moe, "Doomscrolling, Monitoring, and Avoiding News: News Use
in COVID 19 Pandemic Lockdown," *Journalism Studies* 22 (2021), https://doi.org/10.1080
/1461670X.2021.1952475.

3. Both qualitative and quantitative studies find people say they feel better when they avoid
news at least occasionally or in response to stressful conditions. For interview-based studies, see Tali Aharoni, Neta Kligler-Vilenchik, and Keren Tenenboim-Weinblatt, "'Be
Less of a Slave to the News': A Texto-material Perspective on News Avoidance Among
Young Adults," *Journalism Studies* 22, no. 1 (2021): 42–59, https://doi.org/10.1080/1461670X
.2020.1852885; Louise Woodstock, "The News–Democracy Narrative and the Unexpected Benefits of Limited News Consumption: The Case of News Avoiders," *Journalism* 15, no. 7 (2021): 834–49, https://doi.org/10.1177/1464884913504260; and Wagner and
Boczkowski, "Angry, Frustrated, and Overwhelmed." For surveys that find a correlation
between occasional news avoidance and better mental health, see Kiki De Bruin, Yael
de Haan, Rens Vliegenthart, Sanne Kruikemeier, and Mark Boukes, "News Avoidance
During the COVID-19 Crisis: Understanding Information Overload," *Digital Journalism* 9, no. 9 (2021): 1286–302. Other studies find that consuming news that people perceive as negative makes them feel worse, especially when they perceive the news as
particularly relevant to them or are already in a state of emotional burnout. See Natascha
de Hoogand and Peter Verboon, "Is the News Making Us Unhappy? The Influence of
Daily News Exposure on Affective States," *British Journal of Psychology* 111, no. 2 (2019):
157–73, https://bpspsychub.onlinelibrary.wiley.com/doi/full/10.1111/bjop.12389; Yurri
Havrylets, Sergii Tukaiev, Volodymyr Rizun, and Maksym Khylko, "State Anxiety,
Mood, and Emotional Effects of Negative TV News Depend on Burnout," *PsyArXiv*,
online publication, November 27, 2018, https://doi.org/10.31234/osf.io/m3xv2. Other studies
find that partisans get angry when they read political news. See Ariel Hasell and Brian E.
Weeks, "Partisan Provocation: The Role of Partisan News Use and Emotional Responses
in Political Information Sharing in Social Media," *Human Communication Research*
42, no. 4 (2016): 641–61, https://doi.org/10.1111/hcre.12092.

4. Ruth Palmer, Benjamin Toff, and Rasmus Kleis Nielsen, "Examining Assumptions
Around How News Avoidance Gets Defined: The Importance of Overall News Con-
sumption, Intention, and Structural Inequalities," *Journalism Studies*, online publication,
March 4, 2023, https://doi.org/10.1080/1461670X.2023.2183058.

5. For arguments about how much current events knowledge is enough for citizens to be
sufficiently informed and democracy to function well, see Michael Schudson, *The Good
Citizen: A History of American Civic Life* (New York: Martin Kessler, 1998); John Zaller,
"A New Standard of News Quality: Burglar Alarms for the Monitorial Citizen,"

Political Communication 20, no. 2 (2003): 109–30; and Lance W. Bennett, "The Burglar Alarm That Just Keeps Ringing: A Response to Zaller," *Political Communication* 20, no. 2 (2003): 131–38.

6. For a discussion of different ways news avoidance is operationalized, see the supplementary online appendixes to this book as well as Morten Skovsgaard and Kim Andersen, "News Avoidance," in *The SAGE Encyclopedia of Journalism*, ed. Gregory A. Borchard (Thousand Oaks, CA: Sage, 2022), https://dx.doi.org/10.4135/9781544391199.n274.

7. Newman et al., *Digital News Report 2022*. "3 percent" refers to the percentage of individuals "screened out" from the Reuters Institute *DNR*s for 2018–2020. Respondents were screened out if they said they accessed news "less often than once a month" or "never."

8. The best data on increases in news avoidance over time come from Newman et al., *Digital News Report 2022*. But see also Arild Blekesaune, Eiri Elvestad, and Toril Aalberg, "Tuning Out the World of News and Current Affairs—an Empirical Study of Europe's Disconnected Citizens," *European Sociological Review* 28, no. 1 (2012): 110–26, https://doi.org/10.1093/esr/jcq051; Lea C. Gorski and Fabian Thomas, "Staying Tuned or Tuning Out? A Longitudinal Analysis of News Avoiders on the Micro and Macro-level," *Communication Research* 49, no. 7 (2022): 942–65, https://doi.org/10.1177/00936502211025907; Jesper Strömbäck, Monika Djerf-Pierre, and Adam Shehata, "The Dynamics of Political Interest and News Media Consumption: A Longitudinal Perspective," *International Journal of Public Opinion Research* 25, no. 4 (2013): 414–35, https://doi.org/10.1093/ijpor/eds018.

9. The percentage who said they made an ongoing payment (subscription or membership) to any digital news service was 4 percent in the United Kingdom and Spain and 6 percent for all markets worldwide included in Nic Newman, Richard Fletcher, Anne Schulz, Simge Andi, Craig T. Robertson, and Rasmus Kleis Nielsen, *Digital News Report 2021* (Oxford: Reuters Institute for the Study of Journalism, 2021), https://reutersinstitute .politics.ox.ac.uk/digital-news-report/2021.

10. According to Newman et al., *Digital News Report 2022*, the percentage of Americans who read *The Atlantic*, *The Guardian*, or *The New Yorker* online in the previous week was 5, 6, and 4 percent, respectively.

11. Other scholars have recently made a similar argument that audience attitudes toward news are not determined solely by their response to news but rather are shaped by their own identities and the structures that shape their exposure to news. Some of these arguments build on James G. Webster's concept of "structuration," as we discuss later in the chapter. See Jacob L. Nelson, *Imagined Audiences: How Journalists Perceive and Pursue the Public* (Oxford: Oxford University Press, 2021); Jacob L. Nelson and Seth Lewis, "Only 'Sheep' Trust Journalists? How Citizens' Self-Perceptions Shape Their Approach to News," *New Media & Society*, online publication, June 28, 2021, 1, https://doi.org/10.1177 /14614448211018160; James G. Webster, "The Duality of Media: A Structurational Theory of Public Attention," *Communication Theory* 21, no. 1 (2011): 43–66, https://doi.org/10 .1111/j.1468-2885.2010.01375.x; James G. Webster and Jacob L. Nelson, "The Evolution of News Consumption: A Structurational Interpretation," in *News Across Media:*

Production, Distribution, and Consumption, ed. Jakob L. Jensen, Mette Mortensen, and Jacob Ørmen (New York: Routledge, 2016), 84–101.

12. This metaphor works only in times and places where people do not grow up eating oysters all the time. The metaphor could be adapted easily by using a different food about which many local people have ideas that may not stem from firsthand experience. One reason oysters work particularly well is that although there was a time when they were cheap street food in some places, such as New York, today oysters are expensive, and acquiring a taste for them requires access to resources that are not available to everyone—they are a food that is less accessible to lower socioeconomic classes. Enjoying them is therefore both a product and a symbol of class distinction in the Bourdieusian sense. As we explain later in the book, news consumption is the same as food consumption to a certain extent. See Pierre Bourdieu, *Distinction: A Social Critique of the Judgment of Taste*, trans. Richard Nice (Cambridge, MA: Harvard University Press, 1984); and Johan Lindell, "Distinction Recapped: Digital News Repertoires in the Class Structure," *New Media & Society* 20, no. 8 (2018): 3029–49, https://doi.org/10.1177/1461444817739622.

13. Nick Couldry makes the case that in the current "media manifold" there is great value in studying why people choose not to use certain media—that "selecting out" is a part of media practice. See Nick Couldry, "Life with the Media Manifold: Between Freedom and Subjection," in *Politics, Civil Society, and Participation: Media and Communications in a Transforming Environment*, ed. Leif Kramp, Nico Carpentier, Andreas Hepp, Richard Kilborn, Risto Kunelius, Hannu Nieminen, Tobias Olsson, et al. (Bremen, Germany: Édition lumière, 2016), 25–39.

14. The intellectual effort to understand news users better has been called an "audience turn" in journalism and journalism studies, the latter of which has otherwise tended to focus primarily on the norms and practices of reporters, editors, and publishers rather than on the public's role in receiving and engaging with what these groups produce. See Irene Costera Meijer, "Understanding the Audience Turn in Journalism: From Quality Discourse to Innovation Discourse as Anchoring Practices, 1995–2020," *Journalism Studies* 21, no. 16 (2020): 2326–42, https://doi.org/10.1080/1461670X.2020.1847681. Well before the most recent "audience turn" in journalism studies scholarship, audiences loomed large, at least at a theoretical level, in subdisciplines such as media studies and political communication.

15. See, for example, Jennifer Allen, Baird Howland, Markus Mobius, David Rothschild, and Duncan J. Watts, "Evaluating the Fake News Problem at the Scale of the Information Ecosystem," *Science Advances* 6, no. 14 (2020), https://doi.org/10.1126/sciadv.aay3539; Matthew Hindman, *The Internet Trap: How the Digital Economy Builds Monopolies and Undermines Democracy* (Princeton, NJ: Princeton University Press, 2018); Duncan J. Watts, David M. Rothschild, and Markus Mobius, "Measuring the News and Its Impact on Democracy," *Proceedings of the National Academy of Sciences* 118, no. 15 (2021), https://doi.org/10.1073/pnas.1912443118.

16. Markus Prior, *Post-broadcast Democracy: How Media Choice Increases Inequality in Political Involvement and Polarizes Elections* (Cambridge: Cambridge University Press, 2007).

17. Hindman, *The Internet Trap*, 148.

18. Newman et al., *Digital News Report 2022.*

19. Nic Newman, "Journalism, Media, and Technology Trends and Predictions 2023," Reuters Institute for the Study of Journalism, 2023, https://reutersinstitute.politics.ox.ac .uk/journalism-media-and-technology-trends-and-predictions-2023.

20. Lukas Nelson & Promise of the Real, *Turn Off the News (Build a Garden)* (Fantasy Records, 2019).

21. For arguments that too much bad or low-quality news is harmful to mental health and wellness, see, for example, Peter Laufer, *Slow News: A Manifesto for the Critical News Consumer* (Corvallis: Oregon State University Press, 2014); and Jennifer Rauch, *Slow Media: Why "Slow" Is Satisfying, Sustainable, and Smart* (New York: Oxford University Press, 2018). For studies that examine arguments in favor of "resisting" mainstream news because it is distorted by commercial pressures or drains energy that could be used for political engagement, see Jennifer Rauch, *Resisting the News: Engaged Audiences, Alternative Media, and Popular Critique of Journalism* (London: Routledge, 2021); and Woodstock, "The News–Democracy Narrative."

22. See, for example, Candis Callison and Mary Lynn Young, *Reckoning: Journalism's Limits and Possibilities* (Oxford: Oxford University Press, 2020); Lindell, "Distinction Recapped"; and Nikki Usher, *News for the Rich, White, and Blue: How Place and Power Distort American Journalism* (New York: Columbia University Press, 2021).

23. Stephanie Edgerly, Emily K. Vraga, Leticia Bode, Kjerstin Thorson, and Esther Thorson, "New Media, New Relationship to Participation? A Closer Look at Youth News Repertoires and Political Participation," *Journalism & Mass Communication Quarterly* 95, no. 1 (2018): 192–212; Pippa Norris, *A Virtuous Circle: Political Communications in Postindustrial Societies* (Cambridge: Cambridge University Press, 2000); Jesper Strömbäck and Adam Shehata, "Media Malaise or a Virtuous Circle? Exploring the Causal Relationships Between News Media Exposure, Political News Attention, and Political Interest," *European Journal of Political Research* 49, no. 5 (2010): 575–97. Some recent studies do, however, find that the relationship between news media consumption and political knowledge may be more complicated. They find that whereas news consumption is positively associated with political knowledge of uncontested matters, exposure to news does not necessarily lead to more accurate knowledge and may have the opposite effect when it comes to knowledge about controversial issues that people interpret through their personal identities and values. See Alyt Damstra, Rens Vliegenthart, Hajo Boomgaarden, Kathrin Glüer, Elina Lindgren, Jesper Strömbäck, and Yariv Tsfati, "Knowledge and the News: An Investigation of the Relation Between News Use, News Avoidance, and the Presence of (Mis)beliefs," *International Journal of Press/Politics* 28, no. 1 (2023): 29–48, https://doi.org/10.1177/19401612211031457; and D. J. Flynn, Brendan Nyhan, and Jason Reifler, "The Nature and Origins of Misperceptions: Understanding False and Unsupported Beliefs About Politics," *Political Psychology* 38, no. 1 (2017): 127–50, https://doi.org /10.1111/pops.12394.

24. There is a small but growing literature in political science on biases in legislators' responsiveness to the public, focused mostly on the U.S. context. See, for instance, David

Broockman and Christopher Skovron, "Bias in Perceptions of Public Opinion Among Political Elites," *American Political Science Review* 112, no. 3 (2018): 542–63; Martin Gilens and Benjamin I. Page, "Testing Theories of American Politics: Elites, Interest Groups, and Average Citizens," *Perspectives on Politics* 12, no. 3 (2014): 564–81; Alexander Hertel-Fernandez, Matto Mildenberger, and Leah C. Stokes, "Legislative Staff and Representation in Congress," *American Political Science Review* 113, no. 1 (2019): 1–18.

25. James G. Webster, *The Marketplace of Attention: How Audiences Take Shape in a Digital Age* (Cambridge, MA: MIT Press, 2014).

26. Richard Fletcher, Craig T. Robertson, and Rasmus Kleis Nielsen, "How Many People Live in Politically Partisan Online News Echo Chambers in Different Countries?," *Journal of Quantitative Description: Digital Media* 1 (2021): 1–56, https://doi.org/10.51685/jqd.2021.020; Andrew Guess, "Almost Everything in Moderation: New Evidence on Americans' Online Media Diets," *American Journal of Political Science* 65, no. 4 (2021): 1007–22, https://doi.org/10.1111/ajps.12589.

27. Benjamin Toff and Antonis Kalogeropoulos, "All the News That's Fit to Ignore: How the Information Environment Does and Does Not Shape News Avoidance," *Public Opinion Quarterly* 84 (2020): 366–90, https://doi.org/10.1093/poq/nfaa016.

28. Benjamin Toff and Rasmus Kleis Nielsen, "'I Just Google It': Folk Theories of Distributed Discovery," *Journal of Communication* 68, no. 3 (2018): 636–57, https://doi.org/10.1093/joc/jqy009.

29. Stephanie Edgerly, "Seeking Out and Avoiding the News Media: Young Adults' Proposed Strategies for Obtaining Current Events Information," *Mass Information and Society* 20, no. 3 (2017): 358–77; Stephanie Edgerly, "The Head and Heart of News Avoidance: How Attitudes About the News Media Relate to Levels of News Consumption," *Journalism* 23, no. 9 (2022): 1828–45; Judith Moeller and Claes de Vreese, "Spiral of Political Learning: The Reciprocal Relationship of News Media Use and Political Knowledge Among Adolescents," *Communication Research* 46, no. 8 (2015): 1078–94, https://doi.org/10.1177/0093650215605148.

30. See, for example, Toril Aalberg and James Curran, *How Media Inform Democracy: A Comparative Approach*, vol. 1 (London: Routledge, 2012); Erik Albæk, Arjen Van Dalen, Nael Jebril, and Claes H. De Vreese, *Political Journalism in Comparative Perspective* (Cambridge: Cambridge University Press, 2014); and Sacha Altay, Rasmus Kleis Nielsen, and Richard Fletcher, "News Can Help! The Impact of News Media and Digital Platforms on Awareness of and Belief in Misinformation," *International Journal of Press/Politics*, online publication, February 6, 2023, https://doi.org/10.1177/19401612221148981.

31. Rasmus Kleis Nielsen, "The One Thing Journalism Just Might Do for Democracy: Counterfactual Idealism, Liberal Optimism, Democratic Realism," *Journalism Studies* 18 (2017): 1–12, https://doi.org/10.1080/1461670X.2017.1338152.

32. David Ryfe gives an excellent overview of this concept and its various iterations in "The Role of Self-Reports in the Study of News Production," *Journalism* 21, no. 3 (2020): 349–64. On vocabularies of motive, see C. Wright Mills, "Situated Actions and

Vocabularies of Motive," *American Sociological Review* 5, no. 6 (1940): 904–13, https://doi .org/10.2307/2084524. On repertoires of justification, see Michele Lamont and Laurent Thévenot, *Rethinking Comparative Cultural Sociology: Repertoires of Evaluation in France and the United States* (Cambridge: Cambridge University Press, 2000). Unlike lines of thinking focused on how culture (in, for example, the work of the anthropologist Clifford Geertz) or more or less abstract discourses (sometimes also termed "epistêmês," including the fancy accents in, for example, the work of the social theorist Michel Foucault) make us who we are, our inspirations here are more focused on *what we do with culture* and less focused on *what culture does to us*. We draw here in particular on the work of the sociologist Ann Swidler, where she suggests a shift from seeing culture as more or less determining action to instead seeing culture as a set of tools that we put into action. According to Swidler, we see culture not as one or more grand schemes that define who we are and how we live our everyday lives but as a more-or-less shared "bag of tricks" from which we all put together a narrower range of "strategies for action" that we then actively deploy to navigate everyday life. These strategies of action in turn are likely to lead to different forms of practical engagement with journalism. This is a crucial reason to focus on folk theories and media choice narratives: their explanatory power when it comes to, for example, people's engagement with journalism lies not in defining the ends of actions but in providing tools to construct strategies for action. See Ann Swidler, "Culture in Action: Symbols and Strategies," *American Sociological Review* 51, no. 2 (1986): 273–86, https://doi.org/10.2307/2095521; and Ann Swidler, *Talk of Love: How Culture Matters* (Chicago: University of Chicago Press, 2001).

33. Media scholars have used a variety of terms to capture the concept of nonscientific beliefs about how media work and what they are good for. We use *folk theories* because we find it the most intuitive term for what we mean and because it has taken hold recently in studies of journalism audiences. For an introduction to folk theories of journalism, see Rasmus Kleis Nielsen, "Folk Theories of Journalism: The Many Faces of a Local Newspaper," *Journalism Studies* 17, no. 7 (2016): 840–48, https://doi.org/10.1080/1461670X.2016 .1165140. That said, in their studies of news audiences, Jennifer Rauch uses the term *lay theories*, whereas Christian Schwarzenegger opts for the phrase "personal epistemologies of the media." See Rauch, *Resisting the News*; and Christian Schwarzenegger, "Personal Epistemologies of the Media: Selective Criticality, Pragmatic Trust, and Competence-Confidence in Navigating Media Repertoires in the Digital Age," *New Media & Society* 22, no. 2 (2020): 361–77, https://doi.org/10.1177/1461444819856919. Scholars have also used the term *media ideologies* to describe folk beliefs about what media technologies and social media networks are good and bad for. See Pablo Boczkowski, Mora Matassi, and Eugenia Mitchelstein, "How Young Users Deal with Multiple Platforms: The Role of Meaning-Making in Social Media Repertoires," *Journal of Computer-Mediated Communication* 23 (2018): 245–59, https://doi.org/10.1093/jcmc/zmy012; Ilana Gershon, "Breaking Up Is Hard to Do: Media Switching and Media Ideologies," *Linguistic Anthropology* 20, no. 2 (2010): 389–405, https://doi.org/10.1111/j.1548-1395.2010.01076.x.

34. Rasmus Kleis Nielsen and Lucas Graves, "News You Don't Believe: Audience Perspectives on Fake News," Reuters Institute for the Study of Journalism, 2017, https://reutersinstitute.politics.ox.ac.uk/our-research/news-you-dont-believe-audience-perspectives-fake-news; Emily Van Duyn and Jessica Collier, "Priming and Fake News: The Effects of Elite Discourse on Evaluations of News Media," *Mass Communication and Society* 22, no. 1 (2019): 29–48.

35. Jonathan Gray, *Dislike-Minded: Media Audiences and the Dynamics of Taste* (New York: New York University Press, 2021); Jonathan Gray and Sarah Murray, "Hidden: Studying Media Dislike," *International Journal of Cultural Studies* 19, no. 4 (2016): 357–72.

36. Robert LaRose, "The Problem of Media Habits," *Communication Theory* 20, no. 2 (2010): 194–222.

37. Nina Eliasoph, *Avoiding Politics: How Americans Produce Apathy in Everyday Life* (Cambridge: Cambridge University Press, 1998).

38. Markus Prior, "The Immensely Inflated News Audience: Assessing Bias in Self-Reported News Exposure," *Public Opinion Quarterly* 73, no. 11 (2009): 130–43, https://doi.org/10.1093/poq/nfp002.

39. In Spanish: "Normalmente, ¿con qué frecuencia consulta las noticias? Por noticias nos referimos a la información nacional, internacional, regional/local y otros acontecimientos de actualidad consultados en cualquier plataforma (radio, televisión, periódicos o internet)."

40. Elizabeth S. Bird, "News We Can Use: An Audience Perspective on the Tabloidization of News in the United States," *Javnost*, no. 3 (1998): 33–50; Elizabeth S. Bird, *The Audience in Everyday Life: Living in a Media World* (New York: Routledge, 2003). For a more recent study, see Stephanie Edgerly and Emily K. Vraga, "News, Entertainment, or Both? Exploring Audience Perceptions of Media Genre in a Hybrid Media Environment," *Journalism* 20, no. 6 (2019): 807–26, https://doi.org/10.1177/1464884917730709.

41. On the merits of this approach, see Irene Costera Meijer and Tim Groot Kormelink, *Changing News Use: Unchanged News Experiences?* (London: Routledge, 2021). As these authors argue, "The value of asking open questions about what people are doing with news and how they categorize this themselves lies in avoiding scholarly preconceptions about what counts as 'news' and what counts as 'doing'" (17).

42. Tim Groot Kormelink, "Seeing, Thinking, Feeling: A Critical Reflection on Interview-Based Methods for Studying News Use," *Journalism Studies* 21, no. 7 (2020): 863–78, https://doi.org/10.1080/1461670X.2020.1716829; Meijer and Kormelink, *Changing News Use*; Ytre-Arne and Moe, "Doomscrolling, Monitoring, and Avoiding News."

43. Morten Skovsgaard and Kim Andersen, "Conceptualizing News Avoidance: Towards a Shared Understanding of Different Causes and Potential Solutions," *Journalism Studies* 21, no. 4 (2020): 459–76.

44. Kjerstin Thorson, "Attracting the News: Algorithms, Platforms, and Reframing Incidental Exposure," *Journalism* 21, no. 8 (2020): 1067–82, https://doi.org/10.1177/1464884920915352; Kjerstin Thorson, Kelley Cotter, Mel Medeiros, and Chankyung Pak, "Algorithmic Inference, Political Interest, and Exposure to News and Politics on

Facebook," *Information Communication, and Society* 24, no. 2 (2019): 183–200, https://doi
.org/10.1080/1369118X.2019.1642934; Kjerstin Thorson, Yu Xu, and Stephanie Edgerly,
"Political Inequalities Start at Home: Parents, Children, and the Socialization of Civic
Infrastructure Online," *Political Communication* 35, no. 2 (2018): 178–95.

45. We elaborate on this argument in Ruth Palmer, Benjamin Toff, and Rasmus Kleis
Nielsen, "Examining Assumptions Around How News Avoidance Gets Defined: The
Importance of Overall News Consumption, Intention, and Structural Inequalities,"
Journalism Studies, online publication, March 4, 2023, https://doi.org/10.1080/1461670X
.2023.2183058.

46. Morten Skovsgaard and Kim Andersen make the theoretical case that news avoidance
can be situational in their article "Conceptualizing News Avoidance: Towards a Shared
Understanding of Different Causes and Potential Solutions," *Journalism Studies* 21, no. 4
(2020): 459–76. This case is also shown empirically in Ytre-Arne and Moe, "Doomscrolling, Monitoring, and Avoiding News," as well as in Mikko Villi, Tali Aharoni, Keren
Tenenboim-Weinblatt, Pablo J. Boczkowski, Kaori Hayashi, Eugenia Mitchelstein,
Akira Tanaka, et al., "Taking a Break from News: A Five-Nation Study of News Avoidance in the Digital Era," *Digital Journalism* 10, no. 1 (2022): 148–64.

47. Habits in general and media habits in particular are difficult to change, but scholars have
found that they are more likely to change during or following disruptive life events, such
as the COVID pandemic or the birth of a child. See Marcel Broersma and Joelle Swart,
"Do Novel Routines Stick After the Pandemic? The Formation of News Habits During
COVID-19," *Journalism Studies* 23, nos. 5–6 (2022): 551–68, https://doi.org/10.1080
/1461670X.2021.1932561; and Brita Ytre-Arne, "Media Use in Changing Everyday Life:
How Biographical Disruption Could Destabilize Media Repertoires and Public Connection," *European Journal of Communication* 34, no. 5 (2019): 488–502, https://doi.org/10
.1177/0267323119869112.

48. De Bruin et al., "News Avoidance During the COVID-19 Crisis"; Groot Kormelink and
Klein Gunnewiek, "From 'Far Away' to 'Fatigue' to 'Back to Normal'"; Antonis Kalogeropoulos, Richard Fletcher, and Rasmus Kleis Nielsen, "Initial Surge in News Use
Around Coronavirus in the UK Has Been Followed by Significant Increase in News
Avoidance," Reuters Institute for the Study of Journalism, 2020, https://reutersinstitute
.politics.ox.ac.uk/initial-surge-news-use-around-coronavirus-uk-has-been-followed
-significant-increase-news-avoidance; Ytre-Arne and Moe, "Doomscrolling, Monitoring, and Avoiding News."

49. We build here on an extensive sociological literature on identity in terms of both the
internalization of social positions and their meanings as part of the self-structure (e.g.,
Mead) and the impact of cultural meanings and social situations on actors' identities
(e.g., Goffman) rather than on theories that focus on collective identities (e.g., Dur-
kheim, Marx). For a recent review of this literature, see Timothy J. Owens, Dawn
T. Robinson, and Lynn Smith-Lovin, "Three Faces of Identity," *Annual Review of Sociology* 36, no. 1 (2010): 477–99, https://doi.org/10.1146/annurev.soc.34.040507.134725.

50. Nelson and Lewis, "Only 'Sheep' Trust Journalists?"

51. Edgerly, "The Head and Heart of News Avoidance"; Sabine Geers, "News Consumption Across Media Platforms and Content: A Typology of Young News Users," *Public Opinion Quarterly* 84 (2020): 332–54, https://doi.org/10.1093/poq/nfaa010; Su Jung Kim, "A Repertoire Approach to Cross-Platform Media Use," *New Media & Society* 18, no. 3 (2016): 353–72, https://doi.org/10.1177/1461444814543162; Thomas B. Ksiazek, Edward C. Malthouse, and James G. Webster, "News-Seekers and Avoiders: Exploring Patterns of Total News Consumptions Across Media and the Relationship to Civic Participation," *Journal of Broadcasting & Entertainment Media* 54, no. 4 (2010): 551–68.

52. See also Benjamin Toff and Ruth Palmer, "Explaining the Gender Gap in News Avoidance: 'News-Is-for-Men' Perceptions and the Burdens of Caretaking," *Journalism Studies* 20, no. 11 (2019): 1563–79, https://doi.org/10.1080/1461670X.2018.1528882.

53. Many studies have found that seeing news use modeled at home (even presumably less visible digital news use) and hearing it discussed by parents can influence news habits later in life. See Stephanie Edgerly, Kjerstin Thorson, Esther Thorson, Emily K. Vraga, and Leticia Bode, "Do Parents Still Model News Consumption? Socializing News Use Among Adolescents in a Digital World," *New Media & Society* 4 (2017): 1263–81, https://doi.org/10.1177/1461444816688451; Adam Shehata, "News Habits Among Adolescents: The Influence of Family Communication on Adolescents' News Media Use—Evidence from a Three-Wave Panel Study," *Mass Communication and Society* 19 (2016): 758–81, https://doi.org/10.1080/15205436.2016.1199705; and Chance York and Rosanne M. Scholl, "Youth Antecedents to News Media Consumption: Parent and Youth Newspaper Use, News Discussion, and Long-Term News Behavior," *Journalism & Mass Communication Quarterly* 92, no. 3 (2015): 681–99, https://doi.org/10.1177/1077699015588191.

54. Like infrastructure and identity, ideology is the subject of a rich and varied theoretical literature. We use the term *ideology* here separate from *folk theories* because of the former's explicit connections with politics (whether partisan sympathies or an explicit professed dislike for or alienation from politics) and because we are inspired by the work of Stuart Hall (while leaving aside his focus on class), who highlighted that the most important aspect of ideology is often "not what is false about it but what about it is true"—that is, not in terms of a universal truth or a coherent, comprehensive intellectual framework but rather in terms of what "makes good sense" to those who engage with ideology and make use of it in their lives. See Stuart Hall, "The Toad in the Garden: Thatcherism Among the Theorists," in *Marxism and the Interpretation of Culture*, ed. Cary Nelson and Lawrence Grossberg (New York: Macmillan Education, 1988), 35–57, quote on 46.

55. Edgerly, "The Head and Heart of News Avoidance"; Shehata, "News Habits Among Adolescents"; Yanna Krupnikov and John Barry Ryan, *The Other Divide: Polarization and Disengagement in American Politics* (Cambridge: Cambridge University Press, 2022); Jesper Strömbäck, "News Seekers, News Avoiders, and the Mobilizing Effects of Election Campaigns: Comparing Election Campaigns for the National and European Parliaments," *International Journal of Communication* 11 (2017): 237–58, https://ijoc.org/index.php/ijoc/article/view/5919/0.

56. Past studies of disconnected citizens would lead us to expect that news avoiders would feel alienated from politics. See, for example, Blekesaune, Elvestad, and Aalberg, "Tuning Out the World of News"; and Nick Couldry, Sonia Livingstone, and Tim Markham, *Media Consumption and Public Engagement: Beyond the Presumption of Attention* (London: Palgrave Macmillan, 2007).

57. Benjamin Page and Robert Shapiro, *The Rational Public: Fifty Years of Trends in Americans' Policy Preferences* (Chicago: University of Chicago Press, 1992); Samuel L. Popkin, *The Reasoning Voter: Communication and Persuasion in Presidential Campaigns* (Chicago: University of Chicago Press, 1991).

58. Scholars have argued that attitudes toward a variety of media can be a way to express personal beliefs, values, and identity. For studies focused on news, see Nelson and Lewis, "Only 'Sheep' Trust Journalists?," 1; and Rauch, *Resisting the News*. On entertainment, see Gray and Murray, "Hidden." On social media, see Laura Portwood-Stacer, "Media Refusal and Conspicuous Non-consumption: The Performative and Political Dimensions of Facebook Abstention," *New Media & Society* 15, no. 7 (2013): 1041–57.

59. For examples of such scholarship, see Nelson, *Imagined Audiences*; Webster, "The Duality of Media"; and Webster and Nelson, "The Evolution of News Consumption."

60. Building on recent scholarship on the "platformization of infrastructure" and an "infrastructuralization of platforms," we consider here a broad range of features of platforms— their robustness and the degree to which they are widely shared, widely accessible, essential, and often near invisible and taken for granted—that arguably apply not only to search engines and social media but also to news media more broadly as things we learn to rely on "as part of membership" in our communities and societies. See Jean-Christophe Plantin, Carl Lagoze, Paul N. Edwards, and Christian Sandvig, "Infrastructure Studies Meet Platform Studies in the Age of Google and Facebook," *New Media & Society* 20, no. 1 (2018): 293–310, https://doi.org/10.1177/1461444816661553; and Geoffrey C. Bowker and Susan Leigh Star, *Sorting Things Out: Classification and Its Consequences* (Cambridge, MA: MIT Press, 1999).

61. Prior, *Post-broadcast Democracy*.

62. Platform infrastructures also come into play here. Social media algorithms push news toward some people and away from others, depending on whether they and their friends have indicated an interest in it by, for example, liking, sharing, or commenting on news stories. See Thorson, "Attracting the News"; Thorson et al., "Algorithmic Inference"; Thorson, Xu, and Edgerly, "Political Inequalities Start at Home."

2. WHO *ARE* CONSISTENT NEWS AVOIDERS?

Parts of this chapter are adapted from Ruth Palmer, Benjamin Toff, and Rasmus Kleis Nielsen, "Examining Assumptions Around How News Avoidance Gets Defined: The Importance of Overall News Consumption, Intention, and Structural Inequalities,"

Journalism Studies, online publication, March 4, 2023, https://doi.org/10.1080/1461670X.2023.2183058.

1. Yanna Krupnikov and John Barry Ryan, *The Other Divide: Polarization and Disengagement in American Politics* (Cambridge: Cambridge University Press, 2022).

2. See, for example, Shakuntala Banaji and Bart Cammaerts, "Citizens of Nowhere Land: Youth and News Consumption in Europe," *Journalism Studies* 16, no. 1 (2015): 115–32; Kristoffer Holt, Adam Shehata, Jesper Strömbäck, and Elisabet Ljungberg, "Age and the Effects of News Media Attention and Social Media Use on Political Interest and Participation: Do Social Media Function as Leveller?," *European Journal of Communication* 28, no. 1 (2013): 19–34. See also Markus Prior, *Hooked: How Politics Captures People's Interest* (Cambridge: Cambridge University Press, 2019).

3. The Netherlands is the one country where rates of consistent news avoidance were higher among those older than thirty-five, although the differences by age in that country were negligible. See Nic Newman, Richard Fletcher, Craig T. Robertson, Kirsten Eddy, and Rasmus Kleis Nielsen, *Digital News Report 2022* (Oxford: Reuters Institute for the Study of Journalism, 2022), https://reutersinstitute.politics.ox.ac.uk/digital-news-report/2022.

4. See Chance York and Rosanne M. Scholl, "Youth Antecedents to News Media Consumption: Parent and Youth Newspaper Use, News Discussion, and Long-Term News Behavior," *Journalism & Mass Communication Quarterly* 92, no. 3 (2015): 681–99, https://doi.org/10.1177/1077699015588191.

5. Tali Aharoni, Neta Kligler-Vilenchik, and Keren Tenenboim-Weinblatt, "'Be Less of a Slave to the News': A Texto-material Perspective on News Avoidance among Young Adults," *Journalism Studies* 22, no. 1 (2021): 42–59; Pablo J. Boczkowski, Eugenia Mitchelstein, and Facundo Suenzo, "The Smells, Sights, and Pleasures of Ink on Paper: The Consumption of Print Newspapers During a Period Marked by Their Crisis," *Journalism Studies* 21, no. 5 (2020): 565–81.

6. Homero Gil de Zúñiga, Brian Weeks, and Alberto Ardèvol-Abreu, "Effects of the News-Finds-Me Perception in Communication: Social Media Use Implications for News Seeking and Learning About Politics," *Journal of Computer-Mediated Communication* 22, no. 3 (2017): 105–23; Benjamin Toff and Rasmus Kleis Nielsen, "'I Just Google It': Folk Theories of Distributed Discovery," *Journal of Communication* 68, no. 3 (2018): 636–57.

7. Across the forty-six global markets in the *DNR 2022*, 36 percent of adults younger than thirty-five say their main source of news is social media compared to 12 percent of adults fifty-five and older. See Newman et al., *Digital News Report 2022*.

8. Markus Prior, *Post-broadcast Democracy: How Media Choice Increases Inequality in Political Involvement and Polarizes Elections* (Cambridge: Cambridge University Press, 2007).

9. Kjerstin Thorson, Yu Xu, and Stephanie Edgerly, "Political Inequalities Start at Home: Parents, Children, and the Socialization of Civic Infrastructure Online," *Political Communication* 35, no. 2 (2018): 178–95, https://doi.org/10.1080/10584609.2017.1333550; Kjerstin Thorson, "Attracting the News: Algorithms, Platforms, and Reframing Incidental Exposure," *Journalism* 21, no. 8 (2020): 1067–82, https://doi.org/10.1177/1464884920915352.

10. See also Benjamin Toff and Ruth A. Palmer, "Explaining the Gender Gap in News Avoidance: 'News-Is-for-Men' Perceptions and the Burdens of Caretaking," *Journalism Studies* 20, no. 11 (2019): 1563–79.

11. In our U.S. survey data, 55 percent of women said they agreed somewhat or strongly that "news tends to upset or depress me" compared to 41 percent of men.

12. Our measure of unemployment is broader than others, encompassing people who are not working and looking for a job as well as people who are on a temporary layoff from a job or not working for other reasons. People enrolled full-time in school were not included in this measure, nor were people who said they were not working because they were retired or disabled.

13. Shelley Boulianne, "Does Internet Use Affect Engagement? A Meta-analysis of Research," *Political Communication* 26, no. 2 (2009): 193–211; Annika Bergström, Jesper Strömbäck, and Sofia Arkhede, "Towards Rising Inequalities in Newspaper and Television News Consumption? A Longitudinal Analysis, 2000–2016," *European Journal of Communication* 34, no. 2 (2019): 175–89.

14. Johan Lindell, "Distinction Recapped: Digital News Repertoires in the Class Structure," *New Media & Society* 20, no. 8 (2018): 3029–49; Jonas Ohlsson, Johan Lindell, and Sofia Arkhede, "A Matter of Cultural Distinction: News Consumption in the Online Media Landscape," *European Journal of Communication* 32, no. 2 (2017): 116–30.

15. In addition to differences in terms of political ideology, we also know that the United States contrasts with many other countries in terms of how religious its citizens tend to be. According to Pew Research Center data that compare the United States to other wealthy, Western democracies, Americans are significantly more likely to say they pray more often, attend religious services, and attach personal importance to their faith. See Dalia Fahmy, "Americans Are Far More Religious Than Adults in Other Wealthy Nations," Pew Research Center, July 31, 2018, https://www.pewresearch.org/fact-tank /2018/07/31/americans-are-far-more-religious-than-adults-in-other-wealthy-nations/. These tendencies were often evident in our in-depth interviews in Iowa, where religion was invoked as an important lens through which both news avoiders and news lovers viewed the world. In contrast, religion was rarely mentioned at all in either Spain or the United Kingdom. That said, our examination of differences between news avoiders and news lovers in our U.S. survey data shows that religion was not closely related to news-consumption patterns.

16. See also Benjamin Toff and Antonis Kalogeropoulos, "All the News That's Fit to Ignore: How the Information Environment Does and Does Not Shape News Avoidance," *Public Opinion Quarterly* 84 (2020): 366–90, https://doi.org/10.1093/poq/nfaa016.

17. About a fifth of respondents in each of the forty-six markets responded "don't know" when asked to place themselves on a left–right ideological scale. This percentage varied from a low of 6 percent in South Korea to a high of 41 percent in Argentina.

18. This question was taken from the long-running American National Election Studies. Earlier research has shown that this single measure does a very good job of capturing various forms of interest in politics. See Prior, *Hooked*.

19. Political interest is such a predictive variable in classifying people as news avoiders that when we estimated statistical models that control for multiple overlapping characteristics that might explain differences in rates of news use, factors such as gender and class become insignificant explanatory variables (see the online appendixes for the full model output). This is not because these variables do not matter but because both gender and class are also closely correlated with political interest—an attitude that is intertwined with people's overlapping identities.

20. See Pippa Norris, *A Virtuous Circle: Political Communications in Postindustrial Societies* (Cambridge: Cambridge University Press, 2000). Some research suggests that too much exposure to news media—or exposure primarily to particular forms of news—can reduce interest in political affairs, a phenomenon sometimes called "media malaise." See, for example, James Curran, Sharon Coen, Stuart Soroka, Toril Aalberg, Kaori Hayashi, Zira Hichy, Shanto Iyengar, et al., "Reconsidering 'Virtuous Circle' and 'Media Malaise' Theories of the Media: An 11-Nation Study," *Journalism* 15, no. 7 (2014): 815–33.

21. Judith Moeller and Claes de Vreese, "Spiral of Political Learning: The Reciprocal Relationship of News Media Use and Political Knowledge Among Adolescents," *Communication Research* 46, no. 8 (2019): 1079. See also Jennifer Jerit, Jason Barabas, and Toby Bolsen, "Citizens, Knowledge, and the Information Environment," *American Journal of Political Science* 50, no. 2 (2006): 266–82.

22. Prior, *Post-broadcast Democracy*; Jesper Strömbäck, Monika Djerf-Pierre, and Adam Shehata, "The Dynamics of Political Interest and News Media Consumption: A Longitudinal Perspective," *International Journal of Public Opinion Research* 25, no. 4 (2013): 414–35.

23. Angus Campbell, Gerald Gurin, and Warren E. Miller, *The Voter Decides* (New York: Row, Peterson, 1954), 187.

24. In our U.S. survey data, news avoiders do tend to be somewhat lower on the political efficacy scale than more frequent news users, but the differences are small.

25. George I. Balch, "Multiple Indicators in Survey Research: The Concept 'Sense of Political Efficacy,'" *Political Methodology* 1, no. 2 (1974): 1–43; Stephen C. Craig, "Efficacy, Trust, and Political Behavior: An Attempt to Resolve a Lingering Conceptual Dilemma," *American Politics Quarterly* 7, no. 2 (1979): 225–39; Stephen C. Craig, Richard G. Niemi, and Glenn E. Silver, "Political Efficacy and Trust: A Report on the NES Pilot Study Items," *Political Behavior* 12, no. 3 (1990): 289–314.

26. Elizabeth Beaumont, "Promoting Political Agency, Addressing Political Inequality: A Multilevel Model of Internal Political Efficacy," *Journal of Politics* 73, no. 1 (2011): 216–31; Richard G. Niemi, Stephen C. Craig, and Franco Mattei, "Measuring Internal Political Efficacy in the 1988 National Election Study," *American Political Science Review* 85, no. 4 (1991): 1407–13.

3. WHY NEWS AVOIDERS SAY THEY DON'T USE NEWS

1. Antonis Kalogeropoulos, "News Avoidance," in *Digital News Report 2017* (Oxford: Reuters Institute for the Study of Journalism, 2017), https://www.digitalnewsreport.org

/survey/2017/news-avoidance-2017/; Nic Newman, Richard Fletcher, Craig T. Robertson, Kirsten Eddy, and Rasmus Kleis Nielsen, *Digital News Report 2022* (Oxford: Reuters Institute for the Study of Journalism, 2022), https://reutersinstitute.politics.ox.ac.uk/digital-news-report/2022.

2. Kalogeropoulos, "News Avoidance"; Newman et al., *Digital News Report 2022*.

3. These findings are consistent with what one of us has found in past research on ordinary people who "make" the news: when they have positive experiences, they often perceive them as exceptions to the general rule that journalists are untrustworthy, whereas more negative experiences just serve to confirm that belief. See Ruth Palmer, *Becoming the News: How Ordinary People Respond to the Media Spotlight* (New York: Columbia University Press, 2018).

4. See, for example, Candis Callison and Mary Lynn Young, *Reckoning: Journalism's Limits and Possibilities* (Oxford: Oxford University Press, 2020); Sue Robinson, *Networked News, Racial Divides: How Power and Privilege Shape Public Discourse in Progressive Communities* (Cambridge: Cambridge University Press, 2017); Nikki Usher, *News for the Rich, White, and Blue: How Place and Power Distort American Journalism* (New York: Columbia University Press, 2021); Andrea Wenzel, *Community-Centered Journalism: Engaging People, Exploring Solutions, and Building Trust* (Urbana: University of Illinois Press, 2020).

5. As part of our survey of American news audiences, we included a battery of questions designed to capture differences along the "Big Five" personality dimensions (adapted from Beatrice Rammstedt and Oliver P. John, "Measuring Personality in One Minute or Less: A 10-Item Short Version of the Big Five Inventory in English and German," *Journal of Research in Personality* 41, no. 1 [2007]: 203–12; and Adam M. Dynes, Hans J. G. Hassell, Matthew R. Miles, and Jessica Robinson Preece, "Personality and Gendered Selection Processes in the Political Pipeline," *Politics & Gender* 17, no. 1 [2021]: 53–73). We did find significant differences between news avoiders and others along three dimensions: news avoiders were higher in neuroticism and lower in openness and conscientiousness (see figure G.3 in the supplementary online appendixes). However, these differences were substantively small, and given challenges associated with measuring personality traits consistently with a small number of survey items, these results must be interpreted cautiously. Nonetheless, the striking differences we found in how news avoiders and news lovers described their own personalities lead us to believe this area is ripe for further research.

6. Markus Prior, *Post-broadcast Democracy: How Media Choice Increases Inequality in Political Involvement and Polarizes Elections* (Cambridge: Cambridge University Press, 2007).

7. For more on the worthwhileness and relevance of news, see Kim C. Schrøder, "News Media Old and New: Fluctuating Audiences, News Repertoires, and Locations of Consumption," *Journalism Studies* 16, no. 1 (2015): 1–19; Joelle Swart, Chris Peters, and Marcel Broersma, "Repositioning News and Public Connection in Everyday Life," *Media, Culture, and Society* 39, no. 6 (2017): 902–18.

8. Swart, Peters, and Broersma, "Repositioning News and Public Connection in Everyday Life."

9. In her book about people who avoid politics, Nina Eliasoph finds a similar tendency: they prefer to focus their energy on issues "close to home." See Nina Eliasoph, *Avoiding Politics: How Americans Produce Apathy in Everyday Life* (Cambridge: Cambridge University Press, 1998). Louise Woodstock finds a similar trend among news resisters in her article "The News–Democracy Narrative and the Unexpected Benefits of Limited News Consumption: The Case of News Avoiders," *Journalism* 15, no. 7 (2013): 834–49.

10. For studies on the relationship between news avoidance and mental health, see chapter 1, note 3.

11. The equivalent in Spain is "Ojos que no ven, corazón que no siente," which translates literally as "What the eyes don't see, the heart doesn't feel" or less literally as "Out of sight, out of mind."

4. IDENTITIES: HOW OUR RELATIONSHIPS TO COMMUNITIES SHAPE NEWS AVOIDANCE

1. Henri Tajfel and John C. Turner, "The Social Identity Theory of Intergroup Behavior," in *Political Psychology*, ed. John T. Jost and Jim Sidanius (New York: Psychology Press, 2004), 276–93.

2. Stephanie Edgerly, Kjerstin Thorson, Esther Thorson, Emily K. Vraga, and Leticia Bode, "Do Parents Still Model News Consumption? Socializing News Use Among Adolescents in a Multi-device World," *New Media & Society* 20, no. 4 (2018): 1263–81, https://doi.org/10.1177/1461444816688451; Paula M. Poindexter, *Millennials, News, and Social Media* (New York: Peter Lang, 2012); Adam Shehata, "News Habits Among Adolescents: The Influence of Family Communication on Adolescents' News Media Use—Evidence from a Three-Wave Panel Study," *Mass Communication and Society* 19, no. 6 (2016): 758–81, https://doi.org/10.1080/15205436.2016.1199705; Chance York and Rosanne M. Scholl, "Youth Antecedents to News Media Consumption: Parent and Youth Newspaper Use, News Discussion, and Long-Term News Behavior," *Journalism & Mass Communication Quarterly* 92, no. 3 (2015): 681–99, https://doi.org/10.1177/1077699015588191.

3. Albert Bandura, "Social Cognitive Theory: An Agentic Perspective," *Annual Review of Psychology* 52, no. 1 (2001): 1–26.

4. Edgerly et al., "Do Parents Still Model News Consumption?"; Poindexter, *Millennials, News, and Social Media*; Shehata, "News Habits Among Adolescents"; York and Scholl, "Youth Antecedents to News Media Consumption."

5. Edgerly et al., "Do Parents Still Model News Consumption?"

6. Stephanie Edgerly and Kjerstin Thorson, "Developing Media Preferences in a Post-broadcast Democracy," in *Political Socialization in a Media Saturated World*, ed. Esther Thorson, Mitchell S. McKinney, and Dhavan V. Shah (New York: Peter Lang, 2016), 375–91; Adam Maksl, Stephanie Craft, Seth Ashley, and Dean Miller, "The Usefulness of a News Media Literacy Measure in Evaluating a News Literacy Curriculum," *Journalism & Mass Communication Educator* 72, no. 2 (2016): 228–41.

7. Weiyue Chenand and Esther Thorson, "Perceived Individual and Societal Values of News and Paying for Subscriptions," *Journalism* 22, no. 6 (2021): 1296–316, https://doi.org/10.1177/1464884919847792; Uwe Hasebrink and Andreas Hepp, "How to Research Cross-Media Practices? Investigating Media Repertoires and Media Ensembles," *Convergence* 23, no. 4 (2017): 362–77, https://doi.org/10.1177/1354856517700384.

8. Emily K. Vraga, Melissa Tully, Adam Maksl, Stephanie Craft, and Seth Ashley, "Theorizing News Literacy Behaviors," *Communication Theory* 31, no. 1 (2020): 1–21, https://doi.org/10.1093/ct/qtaa005; John Marshall, "Signaling Sophistication: How Social Expectations Can Increase Political Information Acquisition," *Journal of Politics* 81, no. 1 (2018): 167–86; Sue Robinson, "The Active Citizen's Information Media Repertoire: An Exploration of Community News Habits during the Digital Age," *Mass Communication and Society* 17, no. 4 (2014): 509–30, https://doi.org/10.1080/15205436.2013.816745. See also Nick Couldry, Sonia Livingstone, and Tim Markham, *Media Consumption and Public Engagement: Beyond the Presumption of Attention* (Basingstoke, U.K.: Palgrave Macmillan, 2007).

9. Self-reported responses are admittedly flawed. They require individuals both to recognize and to recall such conversations, which people tend to do poorly. We suspect many fall back on impressions of their experiences that they derive from their sense of their own interests—just as research has shown educated people tend to overestimate how often they access news. However, without the ability to directly observe people talking with each other, we are reliant on these measures.

10. To get a clearer picture of what people's discussion networks looked like, we asked a separate set of questions adapted from previous studies examining political implications of people's social networks. For earlier studies, see Robert R. Huckfeldt and John Sprague, *Citizens, Politics, and Social Communication: Information and Influence in an Election Campaign* (Cambridge: Cambridge University Press, 1995); and Scott D. McClurg, "The Electoral Relevance of Political Talk: Examining Disagreement and Expertise Effects in Social Networks on Political Participation," *American Journal of Political Science* 50, no. 3 (2006): 737–54. Survey respondents were asked to name up to five people with whom they discussed "important matters"—separate from anything explicitly having to do with news. For each of those discussion partners, respondents were then asked (*a*) how "interested in news" they thought that person to be and (*b*) how often they discussed the news with that individual. For respondents who named one or more person, we averaged across named individuals to generate scores for that respondent's social circle of close confidants. This method necessitated excluding several hundred respondents who did not name any individuals at all. Given that news avoiders tended to name fewer news conversation partners generally, we suspect this means our results are conservative estimates of the true effects of news communities on news habits. These scores are not a perfect measure of what people's "news communities" look like, but, absent alternatives, we think they are a decent proxy.

11. James W. Carey, *Communication as Culture: Essays on Media and Society* (New York: Routledge, 2008).

12. Our survey data show these workplace differences are systematic. Although it was rare for any American to agree that keeping up with the news is "important for their career," news avoiders were especially unlikely to agree (see figure H.2 in the supplementary online appendixes).

13. See also Johan Lindell, "Distinction Recapped: Digital News Repertoires in the Class Structure," *New Media & Society* 20, no. 8 (2018): 3029–49, https://doi.org/10.1177 /1461444817739622; and Johan Lindell and Else Mikkelsen Båge, "Disconnecting from Digital News: News Avoidance and the Ignored Role of Social Class," *Journalism*, online publication, April 17, 2022, https://doi.org/10.1177/14648849221085389.

14. Other scholars have also found that a sense of civic duty is a strong incentive to keep up with news, sometimes compensating for negative feelings associated with news consumption, and that news avoiders tend to have less of this sense of civic duty. See Damian Trilling and Klaus Schoenbach, "Skipping Current Affairs: The Non-users of Online and Offline News," *European Journal of Communication* 28, no. 1 (2013): 35–51, https://doi .org/10.1177/0267323112453671; and Maria Wagner and Pablo Boczkowski, "Angry, Frustrated, and Overwhelmed: The Emotional Experience of Consuming News About Trump," *Journalism* 22, no. 7 (2021): 1577–93, https://doi.org/10.1177/1464884919878545.

15. Pierre Bourdieu, *Distinction: A Social Critique on the Judgment of Taste*, trans. Richard Nice (Cambridge, MA: Harvard University Press, 1984). See also Lindell, "Distinction Recapped"; and Lindell and Mikkelsen Båge, "Disconnecting from Digital News."

5. IDEOLOGIES: HOW BELIEFS ABOUT POLITICS SHAPE NEWS AVOIDANCE

Parts of this chapter are adapted from Ruth Palmer, Benjamin Toff, and Rasmus Kleis Nielsen, "'The Media Covers Up a Lot of Things': Watchdog Ideals Meet Folk Theories of Journalism," *Journalism Studies* 21, no. 14 (2020): 1973–89, https://doi.org/10.1080 /1461670X.2020.1808516.

1. Iowa's status as "first in the nation" was revoked, at least by the Democratic Party, following the 2020 election cycle.

2. On legislators' responsiveness to the public, see David E. Broockman and Christopher Skovron, "Bias in Perceptions of Public Opinion Among Political Elites," *American Political Science Review* 112, no. 3 (2018): 542–63. On the media industry's responsiveness to more attentive segments of the public, see James G. Webster, *The Marketplace of Attention: How Audiences Take Shape in a Digital Age* (Cambridge, MA: MIT Press, 2014).

3. Eitan Hersh, *Politics Is for Power: How to Move Beyond Political Hobbyism, Take Action, and Make Real Change* (New York: Simon and Schuster, 2020).

4. See, for example, Angus Campbell, Phillip E. Converse, Warren E. Miller, and Donald E. Stokes, *The American Voter* (New York: Wiley, 1960); Brian F. Schaffner and Matthew J. Streb, "The Partisan Heuristic in Low-Information Elections," *Public Opinion Quarterly* 66, no. 4 (2002): 559–81.

5. In our U.S. survey data, we find that 30 percent of news avoiders say they identify "strongly" with either the Democratic Party or the Republican Party, compared to 59 percent of news lovers. Likewise, only 41 percent of news avoiders identified at all with either political party, compared to 86 percent of news lovers.

6. Richard Fletcher, "Trust Will Get Worse Before It Gets Better," in *Journalism, Media, and Technology Trends and Predictions 2020* (Oxford: Reuters Institute for the Study of Journalism, 2020), 30–33, https://www.digitalnewsreport.org/publications/2020/jour nalism-media-and-technology-trends-and-predictions-2020/; Tom W. G. Van der Meer, "Political Trust and the 'Crisis of Democracy,'" in *Oxford Research Encyclopedia of Politics*, ed. W. R. Thompson (Oxford: Oxford University Press, 2017), https://doi.org/10.1093 /acrefore/9780190228637.013.77.

7. George I. Balch, "Multiple Indicators in Survey Research: The Concept 'Sense of Political Efficacy,'" *Political Methodology* 1, no. 2 (1974): 1–43; Stephen C. Craig, "Efficacy, Trust, and Political Behavior: An Attempt to Resolve a Lingering Conceptual Dilemma," *American Politics Quarterly* 7, no. 2 (1979): 225–39; Stephen C. Craig, Richard G. Niemi, and Glenn E. Silver, "Political Efficacy and Trust: A Report on the NES Pilot Study Items," *Political Behavior* 12, no. 3 (1990): 289–314.

8. Elizabeth Beaumont, "Promoting Political Agency, Addressing Political Inequality: A Multilevel Model of Internal Political Efficacy," *Journal of Politics* 73, no. 1 (2011): 216–31; Richard G. Niemi, Stephen C. Craig, and Franco Mattei, "Measuring Internal Political Efficacy in the 1988 National Election Study," *American Political Science Review* 85, no. 4 (1991): 1407–13.

9. Richard Wike and Shannon Schumacher, "Democratic Rights Popular Globally but Commitment to Them Not Always Strong," Pew Research Center, February 27, 2020, https://www.pewresearch.org/global/2020/02/27/democratic-rights-popular-globally -but-commitment-to-them-not-always-strong/.

10. Ruth Palmer, Benjamin Toff, and Rasmus Kleis Nielsen, "'The Media Covers Up a Lot of Things': Watchdog Ideals Meet Folk Theories of Journalism," *Journalism Studies* 21, no. 14 (2020): 1973–89.

11. See, for example, Mark Jurkowitz and Amy Mitchell, "Most Say Journalists Should Be Watchdogs, but Views of How Well They Fill This Role Vary by Party, Media Diet," Journalism Project, Pew Research Center, 2020; Nic Newman, Richard Fletcher, Antonis Kalogeropoulos, and Rasmus Kleis Nielsen, *Digital News Report 2019* (Oxford: Reuters Institute for the Study of Journalism, 2019).

12. Michael Brüggemann, Sven Engesser, Florin Büchel, Edda Humprecht, and Laia Castro, "Hallin and Mancini Revisited: Four Empirical Types of Western Media Systems," *Journal of Communication* 64, no. 6 (2014): 1037–65, https://doi.org/10.1111/jcom.12127; Daniel C. Hallin and Paolo Mancini, *Comparing Media Systems: Three Models of Media and Politics* (Cambridge: Cambridge University Press, 2004); Maria Luisa Humanes and Isabel Fernández Alonso, "News Pluralism and Public Media in Spain: Televisión Española's Regression Following a Change of Government (2012–2013)," *Revista latina de comunicación social* (English ed.) 70 (2015): 270–87, https://doi.org/10.4185/RLCS-2015

-1046en; Maria Luisa Humanes, "Political Journalism in Spain: Practices, Roles, and Attitudes," *Estudios sobre el mensaje periodístico* 19, no. 2 (2013): 715–31, http://dx.doi.org /10.5209/rev_ESMP.2013.v19.n2.43467.

13. Interviews were conducted in Madrid, not in Catalonia, where responses probably would have been very different on this point.

14. These dynamics are similar to those Nina Eliasoph finds in her book on political apathy. See Nina Eliasoph, *Avoiding Politics: How Americans Produce Apathy in Everyday Life* (Cambridge: Cambridge University Press, 1998).

15. Among these more partisan news avoiders, we saw clear evidence of what is known as the "hostile media effect"—the tendency to see news that does not align with one's own political views as biased, a tendency that is stronger the more extreme the views one holds. See Richard M. Perloff, "A Three-Decade Retrospective on the Hostile Media Effect," *Mass Communication and Society* 18, no. 6 (2015): 701–29.

16. The influence of "fake news" labels on political discourse is a small but growing subset of the literature on misinformation. See, for example, Jana Laura Egelhofer and Sophie Lecheler, "Fake News as a Two-Dimensional Phenomenon: A Framework and Research Agenda," *Annals of the International Communication Association* 43, no. 2 (2019): 97–116; and Emily Van Duyn and Jessica Collier, "Priming and Fake News: The Effects of Elite Discourse on Evaluations of News Media," *Mass Communication and Society* 22, no. 1 (2019): 29–48. In our interviews, this kind of rhetoric cut both ways. Bethany, for example, who claimed she did not know much about politics but knew she was not conservative, said that occasionally she will "get on CNN.com since that's considered fake news to the whole Republican Party, which is, I feel, way more factual than a lot of other stuff out here, because I'm almost thirty-six, and as far as I know, CNN's been the truth." In Bethany's case, right-wing accusations of bias were a badge of credibility, and her declaration that she finds CNN trustworthy was intertwined with her own partisan identity.

17. Broockman and Skovron, "Bias in Perceptions of Public Opinion Among Political Elites"; Martin Gilens and Benjamin I. Page, "Testing Theories of American Politics: Elites, Interest Groups, and Average Citizens," *Perspectives on Politics* 12, no. 3 (2014): 564–81; Alexander Hertel-Fernandez, Matto Mildenberger, and Leah C. Stokes, "Legislative Staff and Representation in Congress," *American Political Science Review* 113, no. 1 (2019): 1–18; Webster, *The Marketplace of Attention*.

6. INFRASTRUCTURES: HOW MEDIA PLATFORMS AND PATHWAYS SHAPE NEWS AVOIDANCE

Portions of this chapter are adapted from two separate academic publications: Ruth A. Palmer and Benjamin Toff, "Neither Absent nor Ambient: Incidental News Exposure from the Perspective of News Avoiders in the UK, United States, and Spain," *International Journal of Press/Politics*, online publication, June 9, 2022, https://doi.org

/10.1177/19401612221103144; and Benjamin Toff and Rasmus Kleis Nielsen, "'I Just Google It': Folk Theories of Distributed Discovery," *Journal of Communication* 68, no. 3 (2018): 636–57.

1. Other researchers have documented similar kinds of positive outcomes among those who develop similar strategies. See, for example, Peter Laufer, *Slow News: A Manifesto for the Critical News Consumer* (Corvallis: Oregon State University Press, 2014); Jennifer Rauch, *Resisting the News: Engaged Audiences, Alternative Media, and Popular Critique of Journalism* (New York: Routledge, 2021); Jennifer Rauch, *Slow Media: Why "Slow" Is Satisfying, Sustainable, and Smart* (Oxford: Oxford University Press, 2018); Trine Syvertsen, *Media Resistance: Protest, Dislike, Abstention* (London: Palgrave MacMillan, 2017); and Louise Woodstock, "Media Resistance: Opportunities for Practice Theory and New Media Research," *International Journal of Communication* 8, no. 1 (2014), https://ijoc.org/index.php/ijoc/article/view/2415.

2. Other scholarship has also identified versions of this first folk theory, referring to it as "news finds me" perceptions. See Homero Gil de Zúñiga and Trevor Diehl, "News Finds Me Perception and Democracy: Effects on Political Knowledge, Political Interest, and Voting," *New Media & Society* 21, no. 6 (2019): 1253–71. Furthermore, an extensive literature has developed on the subject of incidental exposure to news and information in the digital age, which the work in this chapter builds on and engages with, albeit without always explicitly doing so in the text. See, for example, Leticia Bode, "Political News in the News Feed: Learning Politics from Social Media," *Mass Communication and Society* 19 (2016): 24–48; Richard Fletcher and Rasmus Kleis Nielsen, "Are People Incidentally Exposed to News on Social Media? A Comparative Analysis," *New Media & Society* 20, no. 7 (2018): 2450–68; and Johannes Kaiser, Tobias R. Keller, and Katharina Kleinen-von Königlsöw, "Incidental News Exposure on Facebook as a Social Experience: The Influence of Recommender and Media Cues on News Selection," *Communication Research* 48, no. 1 (2021): 77–99.

3. On the idea that news is "ambient" in the current media environment, see Alfred Hermida, "Twittering the News: The Emergence of Ambient Journalism," *Journalism Practice* 4, no. 3 (2010): 297–308.

4. See, for example, Homero Gil de Zúñiga, Brian Weeks, and Alberto Ardèvol-Abreu, "Effects of the News-Finds-Me Perception in Communication: Social Media Use Implications for News Seeking and Learning About Politics," *Journal of Computer-Mediated Communication* 22, no. 3 (2017): 105–23; Gil de Zúñiga and Diehl, "News Finds Me Perception and Democracy"; and Sangwon Lee, "Probing the Mechanisms Through Which Social Media Erodes Political Knowledge: The Role of the News-Finds-Me Perception," *Mass Communication and Society* 23, no. 6 (2020): 810–32.

5. Anna Sophie Kümpel, "Matthew Effect in Social Media News Use: Assessing Inequalities in News Exposure and News Engagement on Social Network Sites," *Journalism* 21, no. 8 (2020): 1083–98; Kjerstin Thorson, "Attracting the News: Algorithms, Platforms, and Reframing Incidental Exposure," *Journalism* 21, no. 8 (2020): 1067–82; Kjerstin

Thorson, Kelley Cotter, Mel Medeiros, and Chankyung Pak, "Algorithmic Inference, Political Interest, and Exposure to News and Politics on Facebook," *Information, Communication, and Society* 24, no. 2 (2019): 183–200; Kristin Van Damme, Marijn Martens, Sarah Van Leuven, Mariek Vanden Abeele, and Lieven De Marez, "Mapping the Mobile DNA of News: Understanding Incidental and Serendipitous Mobile News Consumption," *Digital Journalism* 8, no. 1 (2020): 49–68; Mikko Villi, Tali Aharoni, Keren Tenenboim-Weinblatt, Pablo J. Boczkowski, Kaori Hayashi, Eugenia Mitchelstein, Akira Tanaka, et al., "Taking a Break from News: A Five-Nation Study of News Avoidance in the Digital Era," *Digital Journalism* 10, no. 1 (2022): 148–64.

6. Gil de Zúñiga and Diehl, "News Finds Me Perception and Democracy."

7. Incidental exposure to news on TV got a fair amount of scholarly attention from the late 1960s through the 1980s, when research showed that people could "passively learn" from news they were exposed to while waiting for news programs to come on or while flipping channels. See Jay G. Blumler and Denis McQuail, *Television in Politics: Its Uses and Influence* (London: Faber and Faber, 1968); and W. Russell Neuman, Marion R. Just, and Anne N. Crigler, *Common Knowledge: News and the Construction of Political Meaning* (Chicago: University of Chicago Press, 1992).

8. Elihu Katz and Paul F. Lazarsfeld, *Personal Influence: The Part Played by People in the Flow of Mass Communications* (New York: Free Press, 1955).

9. As Jacob Nelson and Seth Lewis point out in a study of the way American news audiences engaged with news about the COVID-19 pandemic, people often like to think of themselves as sophisticated and savvy news consumers who are too smart to be taken for a fool by media organizations vying to mislead and provoke. See Jacob L. Nelson and Seth C. Lewis, "Only 'Sheep' Trust Journalists? How Citizens' Self-Perceptions Shape Their Approach to News," *New Media & Society*, online publication, June 28, 2021, https://doi.org/10.1177/14614448211018160.

10. Richard Fletcher and Rasmus Kleis Nielsen, "Generalised Scepticism: How People Navigate News on Social Media," *Information, Communication, & Society* 22, no. 12 (2019): 1751–69.

11. Reggie admitted that the number of times he had gone so far as to do his own reporting was small, but he did provide an example where "a rumor" was going around about a local sports team's "horrible management," which prompted him to go out and interview people about what was really going on. "I talked to a lot of the players, I talked to some of the former players, a lot of the managers, and it was true. It was poor management." Despite almost universally avoiding news, Reggie had approached the subject much like a journalist might. When this irony was pointed out to him, he agreed and said he would have enjoyed being a reporter in another life: "Yeah. I would like to be. That would be fun."

12. Previous research has shown that news avoiders tend to be among the least trusting toward news. See Manuel Goyanes, Alberto Ardèvol-Abreu, and Homero Gil de Zúñiga, "Antecedents of News Avoidance: Competing Effects of Political Interest,

News Overload, Trust in News Media, and 'News Finds Me' Perception," *Digital Journalism* 11, no. 1 (2023): 1–18; Antonis Kalogeropoulos, Benjamin Toff, and Richard Fletcher, "The Watchdog Press in the Doghouse: A Comparative Study of Attitudes About Accountability Journalism, Trust in News, and News Avoidance," *International Journal of Press/Politics*, online publication, July 14, 2022, https://doi.org/10.1177/19401612221112572; and Benjamin Toff and Antonis Kalogeropoulos, "All the News That's Fit to Ignore: How the Information Environment Does and Does Not Shape News Avoidance," *Public Opinion Quarterly* 84 (2020): 366–90, https://doi.org/10.1093/poq/nfaa016.

13. Walter Lippmann, *The Phantom Public* (1925; reprint, Piscataway, NJ: Transaction, 1993), 55.

14. Alina Selyukh, "After Brexit Vote, Britain Asks Google: 'What is the EU?,'" NPR, June 24, 2016, https://www.npr.org/sections/alltechconsidered/2016/06/24/480949383/britains-google-searches-for-what-is-the-eu-spike-after-brexit-vote.

15. Previous research has shown that algorithms do prioritize showing news to those most interested in seeing it and that those less interested in news and politics are also less likely to encounter it incidentally. See Thorson et al., "Algorithmic Inference, Political Interest, and Exposure to News and Politics on Facebook."

16. It is worth noting that folk theories are sometimes backed up with evidence, in Facebook's case by recent investigative reporting. See, for example, Keach Hagey and Jeff Horwitz, "Facebook Tried to Make Its Platform a Healthier Place. It Got Angrier Instead," *Wall Street Journal*, September 15, 2021, https://www.wsj.com/articles/facebook-algorithm-change-zuckerberg-11631654215.

17. See, for example, Bernard Berelson, "What 'Missing the Newspaper' Means," in *Communications Research 1948–1949*, ed. Paul F. Lazarsfeld and Frank N. Stanton (New York: Harper & Brothers, 1949), 111–29; Marcel Broersma and Joelle Swart, "Do Novel Routines Stick After the Pandemic? The Formation of News Habits During COVID-19," *Journalism Studies* 23, nos. 5–6 (2022): 551–68, https://doi.org/10.1080/1461670X.2021.1932561; James W. Carey, *Communication as Culture, Revised Edition: Essays on Media and Society* (New York: Routledge, 2008); Tim Groot Kormelink, "How People Integrate News Into Their Everyday Routines: A Context-Centered Approach to News Habits," *Digital Journalism* 11, no. 1 (2023): 19–38, https://doi.org/10.1080/21670811.2022.2112519; Robert LaRose, "The Problem of Media Habits," *Communication Theory* 20 (2010): 194–222; and Anna Schnauber-Stockmann and Teresa Naab, "The Process of Forming a Mobile Media Habit: Results of a Longitudinal Study in a Real-World Setting," *Media Psychology* 22, no. 5 (2019): 714–42.

18. Some scholars focused on smartphone use have referred to these news habits or patterns as "checking cycles." See Irene Costera Meijer and Tim Groot Kormelink, "Checking, Sharing, Clicking, and Linking: Changing Patterns of News Use Between 2004 and 2014," *Digital Journalism* 3, no. 5 (2015): 664–79; and Brita Ytre-Arne, Trine Syvertsen, Hallvard Moe, and Faltin Karlsen, "Temporal Ambivalences in Smartphone Use:

Conflicting Flows, Conflicting Responsibilities," *New Media & Society* 22, no. 9 (2020): 1715–32.

19. Camila Mont'Alverne, Sumitra Badrinathan, Amy Ross Arguedas, Benjamin Toff, Richard Fletcher, and Rasmus Kleis Nielsen, "The Trust Gap: How and Why News on Digital Platforms Is Viewed More Sceptically Versus News in General," Reuters Institute for the Study of Journalism, 2022, https://reutersinstitute.politics.ox.ac.uk/trust-gap -how-and-why-news-digital-platforms-viewed-more-sceptically-versus-news-general.

20. Nayla Fawzi, Nina Steindl, Magdalena Obermaier, Fabian Prochazka, Dorothee Arlt, Bernd Blöbaum, Marco Dohle, et al., "Concepts, Causes, and Consequences of Trust in News Media—a Literature Review and Framework," *Annals of the International Communication Association* 45, no. 2 (2021): 154–74; Brian Hilligoss and Soo Young Rieh, "Developing a Unifying Framework of Credibility Assessment: Construct, Heuristics, and Interaction in Context," *Information Processing & Management* 44, no. 4 (2008): 1467–84; Miriam J. Metzger, Andrew J. Flanagin, and Ryan B. Medders, "Social and Heuristic Approaches to Credibility Evaluation Online," *Journal of Communication* 60, no. 3 (2010): 413–39; Hyunjin Kang, Keunmin Bae, Shaoke Zhang, and S. Shyam Sundar, "Source Cues in Online News: Is the Proximate Source More Powerful Than Distal Sources?," *Journalism & Mass Communication Quarterly* 88, no. 4 (2011): 719–36; David Sterrett, Dan Malato, Jennifer Benz, Liz Kantor, Trevor Tompson, Tom Rosenstiel, Jeff Sonderman, et al., "Who Shared It? Deciding What News to Trust on Social Media," *Digital Journalism* 7, no. 6 (2019): 783–801.

21. Amy Ross Arguedas, Sumitra Badrinathan, Camila Mont'Alverne, Benjamin Toff, Richard Fletcher, and Rasmus Kleis Nielsen, "Snap Judgements: How Audiences Who Lack Trust in News Navigate Information on Digital Platforms," Reuters Institute for the Study of Journalism, 2022, https://reutersinstitute.politics.ox.ac.uk/snap-judgements -how-audiences-who-lack-trust-news-navigate-information-digital-platforms.

22. Antonis Kalogeropoulos, Richard Fletcher, and Rasmus Kleis Nielsen, "News Brand Attribution in Distributed Environments: Do People Know Where They Get Their News?," *New Media & Society* 21, no. 3 (2019): 583–601.

23. Benjamin Toff, Sumitra Badrinathan, Camila Mont'Alverne, Amy Ross Arguedas, Richard Fletcher, and Rasmus Kleis Nielsen, "Overcoming Indifference: What Attitudes Towards News Tell Us About Building Trust," Reuters Institute for the Study of Journalism, 2021, https://reutersinstitute.politics.ox.ac.uk/overcoming-indifference-what -attitudes-towards-news-tell-us-about-building-trust.

24. Justin Ellis, "How the Skimm's Passionate Readership Helped Its Newsletter Grow to 1.5 Million Subscribers," Nieman Journalism Lab, August 18, 2015, https://www .niemanlab.org/2015/08/how-the-skimms-passionate-readership-helped-its-newsletter -grow-to-1-5-million-subscribers/.

25. Berelson, "What 'Missing the Newspaper' Means."

26. Nikki Usher, *News for the Rich, White, and Blue: How Place and Power Distort American Journalism* (New York: Columbia University Press, 2021).

27. Anne Schulz, "Local News Unbundled: Where Audience Value Still Lies," Reuters Institute for the Study of Journalism, 2021, https://reutersinstitute.politics.ox.ac.uk/digital-news-report/2021/local-news-unbundled-where-audience-value-still-lies.

7. NEWS FOR ALL THE PEOPLE?

1. Juan González and Joseph Torres, *News for All the People: The Epic Story of Race and the American Media* (London: Verso, 2011), 376.

2. Arild Blekesaune, Eiri Elvestad, and Toril Aalberg, "Tuning Out the World of News and Current Affairs—an Empirical Study of Europe's Disconnected Citizens," *European Sociological Review* 28, no. 1 (2012): 110–26, https://doi.org/10.1093/esr/jcq051; Lea C. Gorski and Fabian Thomas, "Staying Tuned or Tuning Out? A Longitudinal Analysis of News Avoiders on the Micro and Macro-level," *Communication Research* 49, no. 7 (2022): 942–65, https://doi.org/10.1177/00936502211025907; Nic Newman, Richard Fletcher, Antonis Kalogeropoulos, and Rasmus Kleis Nielsen, *Digital News Report 2019* (Oxford: Reuters Institute on the Study of Journalism, 2019), https://reutersinstitute.politics.ox.ac.uk/sites/default/files/2019-06/DNR_2019_FINAL_0.pdf; Markus Prior, *Post-broadcast Democracy: How Media Choice Increases Inequality in Political Involvement and Polarizes Elections* (Cambridge: Cambridge University Press, 2007); Jesper Strömbäck, Monika Djerf-Pierre, and Adam Shehata, "The Dynamics of Political Interest and News Media Consumption: A Longitudinal Perspective," *International Journal of Public Opinion Research* 25, no. 4 (2013): 414–35, https://doi.org/10.1093/ijpor/edso18.

3. Stephanie Edgerly, Emily K. Vraga, Leticia Bode, Kjerstin Thorson, and Esther Thorson, "New Media, New Relationship to Participation? A Closer Look at Youth News Repertoires and Political Participation," *Journalism & Mass Communication Quarterly* 95, no. 1 (2018): 192–212; William P. Eveland and Dietram A. Scheufele, "Connecting News Media Use with Gaps in Knowledge and Participation," *Political Communication* 17 (2000): 215–37; Jack McLeod, Dietram Scheufele, and Patricia Moy, "Community, Communication, and Participation: The Role of Mass Media and Interpersonal Discussion in Local Political Participation," *Political Communication* 16 (1999): 315–36; Judith Moeller and Claes de Vreese, "Spiral of Political Learning: The Reciprocal Relationship of News Media Use and Political Knowledge Among Adolescents," *Communication Research* 46, no. 8 (2019): 1078–94. See also chapter 1, note 23.

4. See Ann Swidler, "Culture in Action: Symbols and Strategies," *American Sociological Review* 51, no. 2 (1986): 273–86, https://doi.org/10.2307/2095521; and Ann Swidler, *Talk of Love: How Culture Matters* (Chicago: University of Chicago Press, 2001).

5. Nic Newman, Richard Fletcher, Craig T. Robertson, Kirsten Eddy, and Rasmus Kleis Nielsen, *Digital News Report 2022* (Oxford: Reuters Institute for the Study of Journalism, 2022), https://reutersinstitute.politics.ox.ac.uk/digital-news-report/2022.

6. John Hartley, *Popular Reality: Journalism and Popular Culture* (New York: Hodder Education, 1996), 33, emphasis in original, quoted in, among many other publications, the introductory chapter of *The Handbook of Journalism Studies*, ed. Karin Wahl-Jorgensen and Thomas Hanitzsch, International Communication Association Handbook series (New York: Routledge, 2009), 3.

7. Nick Couldry, Sonia M. Livingstone, and Tim Markham, *Media Consumption and Public Engagement: Beyond the Presumption of Attention* (Basingstoke, U.K.: Palgrave Macmillan, 2010).

8. Pierre Bourdieu, *Distinction: A Social Critique of the Judgement of Taste*, trans. Richard Nice (Cambridge, MA: Harvard University Press, 1984), 444.

9. A study by the Pew Research Center examining two decades of survey data found that only about one in four Americans paid "very close" attention to the dominant news stories of the day at any given time. See Michael J. Robinson, "Two Decades of American News Preferences," Pew Research Center, 2007, https://assets.pewresearch.org/wp-content/uploads/sites/12/old-assets/pdf/NewsInterest1986-2007.pdf; and John Zaller, "A New Standard of News Quality: Burglar Alarms for the Monitorial Citizen," *Political Communication* 20, no. 2 (2003): 109–30.

10. Newman et al., *Digital News Report 2022*.

11. Camila Mont'Alverne, Sumitra Badrinathan, Amy Ross Arguedas, Benjamin Toff, Richard Fletcher, and Rasmus Kleis Nielsen "The Trust Gap: How and Why News on Digital Platforms Is Viewed More Sceptically Versus News in General," Reuters Institute for the Study of Journalism, 2022, https://reutersinstitute.politics.ox.ac.uk/trust-gap-how-and-why-news-digital-platforms-viewed-more-sceptically-versus-news-general; Newman et al., *Digital News Report 2022*.

12. This would not be an entirely fanciful and self-serving belief. Research suggests that at least investigative journalism can serve the public interest irrespective of how much the public pays attention it. See, for example, James Hamilton, *Democracy's Detectives: The Economics of Investigative Journalism* (Cambridge, MA: Harvard University Press, 2016).

13. González and Torres, *News for All the People*, 376.

14. It is clear, though, that navigating the infrastructural side of consistent news avoidance is likely to grow more challenging because some big platforms (e.g., Facebook) are actively reducing the amount of news they distribute and others (e.g., Instagram, TikTok, YouTube) are used relatively less to access news and produce less incidental exposure to news than were older social media platforms. On this trend, see, for example, Rasmus Kleis Nielsen and Sarah Anne Ganter, *The Power of Platforms: Shaping Media and Society* (Oxford: Oxford University Press, 2022).

15. See, for example, Thomas Poell, David B. Nieborg, and Brooke Erin Duffy, *Platforms and Cultural Production* (Cambridge: Polity Press, 2022); Efrat Nechushtai, "Could Digital Platforms Capture the Media Through Infrastructure?," *Journalism* 19, no. 8 (2017): 1043–58, https://doi.org/10.1177/1464884917725163; and Nielsen and Ganter, *The Power of Platforms*.

16. For public journalism, see Jay Rosen, *What Are Journalists For?* (New Haven, CT: Yale University Press, 1999). Various companion ideas include "participatory journalism," "engaged journalism," and "reciprocal journalism."

17. See, for example, Andrea Wenzel, *Community-Centered Journalism: Engaging People, Exploring Solutions, and Building Trust* (Urbana: University of Illinois Press, 2021).

18. On analytics and their use, see, for example, Angele Christin, *Metrics at Work: Journalism and the Contested Meaning of Algorithms* (Princeton, NJ: Princeton University Press, 2020); and Caitlin Petre, *All the News That's Fit to Click: How Metrics Are Transforming the Work of Journalists* (Princeton, NJ: Princeton University Press, 2021). For the "user needs" model developed by the former BBC World Service executive Dmitry Shiskin, see, for example, Dmitry Shishkin, "Five Lessons I Learned While Digitally Changing BBC World Service," LinkedIn, July 3, 2017, https://www.linkedin.com/pulse/five -lessons-i-learned-while-digitally-changing-bbc-world-shishkin/.

19. See, for example, Peter Bro, "Constructive Journalism: Proponents, Precedents, and Principles," *Journalism* 20, no. 4 (2019): 504–19, https://doi.org/10.1177/1464884918770523; and Karen McIntyre, "Solutions Journalism," *Journalism Practice* 13, no. 1 (2019): 16–34, https:// doi.org/10.1080/17512786.2017.1409647.

20. Janice A. Radway, *Reading the Romance: Women, Patriarchy, and Popular Literature* (Chapel Hill: University of North Carolina Press, 1984); Henry Jenkins, *Convergence Culture: Where Old and New Media Collide* (New York: New York University Press, 2006); Christopher Ruggles, Greg Wadley, and Martin R. Gibbs, "Online Community Building Techniques Used by Video Game Developers," in *Entertainment Computing—ICEC 2005*, ed. Fumio Kishino, Yoshifumi Kitamura, Hirokazu Kato, and Noriko Nagata (Berlin: Springer, 2005), 114–25, https://doi.org/10.1007/11558651_12.

21. Stuart Cunningham and David Craig, *Creator Culture: An Introduction to Global Social Media Entertainment* (New York: New York University Press, 2021).

22. National Center for Education Statistics, *U.S. State and County Estimates Resources* (Washington, DC: National Center for Education Statistics, 2022), https://nces.ed.gov /surveys/piaac/state-county-estimates.asp#4.

23. Adam Shehata, "News Habits Among Adolescents: The Influence of Family Communication on Adolescents' News Media Use—Evidence from a Three-Wave Panel Study," *Mass Communication and Society* 19 (2016):758–81, https://doi.org/10.1080/15205436.2016 .1199705. The Finnish model may be a good one to follow. See Jon Henley, "How Finland Starts Its Fight Against Fake News in Primary Schools," *The Guardian*, January 29, 2020, https://www.theguardian.com/world/2020/jan/28/fact-from-fiction-finlands-new -lessons-in-combating-fake-news.

24. W. James Potter, *Media Literacy* (Thousand Oaks, CA: Sage, 2013); Melissa Tully and Emily K. Vraga, "A Mixed Methods Approach to Examining the Relationship Between News Media Literacy and Political Efficacy," *International Journal of Communication* 12 (2018): 766–87.

25. danah boyd, "Did Media Literacy Backfire?," *Medium*, March 16, 2018, https://points .datasociety.net/did-media-literacy-backfire-7418c084d88d.

26. C. Wright Mills, "Situated Actions and Vocabularies of Motive," *American Sociological Review* 5, no. 6 (1940): 904–13, https://doi.org/10.2307/2084524.

27. Quoted in Bobby Burack, "Tucker Carlson Goes One-on-One with Outkick," Outkick, July 8, 2021, https://www.outkick.com/tucker-carlson-fox-news/.

28. "Daily Mail Comment: Red Ed Has Zero Clue How Business Works," *Daily Mail*, April 2, 2015, https://www.dailymail.co.uk/debate/article-3022408/DAILY-MAIL -COMMENT-Red-Ed-zero-clue-business-works.html.

29. "Our Podcast: Alan Rusbridger Discusses His New Book and How to Rebuild Trust in News," podcast, Reuters Institute for the Study of Journalism, December 5, 2020, https:// reutersinstitute.politics.ox.ac.uk/news/our-podcast-alan-rusbridger-discusses-his-new -book-and-how-rebuild-trust-news.

APPENDIX A: STUDYING NEWS AVOIDANCE USING INTERPRETIVE METHODS

1. Nic Newman, Richard Fletcher, David A. L. Levy, and Rasmus Kleis Nielsen, *Digital News Report 2016* (Oxford: Reuters Institute for the Study of Journalism, 2016), https:// www.digitalnewsreport.org/survey/2016/.

2. Stephanie Edgerly, "The Head and Heart of News Avoidance: How Attitudes About the News Media Relate to Levels of News Consumption," *Journalism* 23, no. 9 (2021): 1828–45; Sabine Geers, "News Consumption Across Media Platforms and Content: A Typology of Young News Users," *Public Opinion Quarterly* 84 (2020): 332–54, https://doi .org/10.1093/poq/nfaa010; Su Jung Kim, "A Repertoire Approach to Cross-Platform Media Use," *New Media & Society* 18, no. 3 (2016): 353–72, https://doi.org/10.1177 /1461444814543162; Thomas B. Ksiazek, Edward C. Malthouse, and James G. Webster, "News-seekers and Avoiders: Exploring Patterns of Total News Consumption Across Media and the Relationship to Civic Participation," *Journal of Broadcasting & Electronic Media* 54, no. 4 (2010): 551–68.

3. Newman et al., *Digital News Report 2016*.

4. Michael Brüggemann, Sven Engesser, Florin Büchel, Edda Humprecht, and Laia Castro, "Hallin and Mancini Revisited: Four Empirical Types of Western Media Systems," *Journal of Communication* 64, no. 6 (2014): 1037–65, https://doi.org/10.1111/jcom.12127.

5. According to Michael Brüggemann and colleagues' classification of media systems, an updated and empirically validated version of Daniel Hallin and Paolo Mancini's influential original three-systems model, the United Kingdom falls under the "Central" type. See Brüggemann et al., "Hallin and Mancini Revisited"; and Daniel C. Hallin and Paolo Mancini, *Comparing Media Systems: Three Models of Media and Politics* (Cambridge: Cambridge University Press, 2004).

6. Frank Esser and Thomas Hanitzsch, "On the Why and How of Comparative Inquiry in Communication Studies," in *The Handbook of Comparative Communication Research*, ed. Frank Esser and Thomas Hanitzsch (New York: Routledge, 2012), 322, https://doi

.org/10.4324/9780203149102-8. On the importance of balancing similarity and difference, see Giovanni Sartori, "Comparing and Miscomparing," *Journal of Theoretical Politics* 3, no. 3 (1991): 243–57, https://doi.org/10.1177/0951692891003003001.

7. According to Brüggemann and colleagues' typology, Spain's media system is classified as a "Southern" type, and the United States as "Western" (Brüggemann et al., "Hallin and Mancini Revisited").

8. Maria Luisa Humanes and Isabel Fernández Alonso, "News Pluralism and Public Media in Spain: Televisión Española's Regression Following a Change of Government (2012–2013)," *Revista latina de comunicación social* (English ed.) 70 (2015): 270–87, https://doi.org /10.4185/RLCS-2015-1046en; Maria Luisa Humanes, "Political Journalism in Spain: Practices, Roles, and Attitudes," *Estudios sobre el mensaje periodístico* 19, no. 2 (2013): 715–31, http://dx.doi.org/10.5209/rev_ESMP.2013.v19.n2.43467.

9. Brüggemann et al., "Hallin and Mancini Revisited."

10. Partisan divides in the United Kingdom have been particularly apparent in the wake of Brexit. See Shannon Schumacher, "Brexit Divides the UK, but Partisanship and Ideology Are Still Key Factors," Pew Research Center, 2019, https://www.pewresearch.org /fact-tank/2019/10/28/brexit-divides-the-uk-but-partisanship-and-ideology-are-still -key-factors/. The idea that Spain is ideologically divided into "two Spains," one conservative and one progressive, dates back to before the Spanish Civil War (1936–1939), which pitted the two factions against one another and still profoundly shapes Spanish political culture. See Nicholas Manganas, *Las dos Españas: Terror and Crisis in Contemporary Spain* (Brighton, U.K.: Sussex Academic Press, 2016).

11. There were some additional minor differences in screening among the three countries, especially the criteria the research firms used for determining socioeconomic status. Based on the countries' own ways of operating and experience in recruiting different populations, participants' occupations were used in the United Kingdom, the occupation of the participant's head of household was used in Spain, and a combination of household income and education was applied in the United States. The firms also had strong recommendations for the amount to compensate each participant for their time. In the United Kingdom, that was £40, and in the United States roughly the equivalent, $50, but in Spain participants received €80 (approximately $90 at the time).

12. In Spain, we also worked with Kantar for recruitment. The screener question in Spanish was: "Normalmente, ¿con qué frecuencia consulta las noticias? Por noticias nos referimos a la información nacional, internacional, regional/local y otros acontecimientos de actualidad consultados en cualquier plataforma (radio, televisión, periódicos o internet)."

13. The long-planned (though illegal, according to Spain's constitutional court) referendum on Catalan secession had just taken place on October 1, 2017. Over the next several months, right when the interviews were being conducted, a messy power struggle ensued between the national and regional governments. The president of the Catalan government declared independence, then fled the country when the Spanish national government seized control in the region, jailed independence leaders, and called snap

elections—which the pro-independence parties won once more. Today the question of Catalan independence remains a deeply divisive issue throughout the country.

14. In all three countries, the recruitment firms at times found it difficult to find people who fit the eligibility requirements for the study. Because none of us lived in Iowa, we could afford to stay there for only limited periods, so when the recruiting firm there struggled to find enough willing participants who met the study parameters, we allowed it to soften the eligibility requirement to include a small number of people ($N = 7$) who accessed news less than once a week. We cannot say for sure why the Iowa firm was having so much trouble finding people who consumed news less than once a month, but we suspect it was due to a combination of factors, including the higher than national average education levels in Iowa, the context of the presidential campaign, and the fact that the research firm we were using specialized in public opinion about public policy (although it was recruiting beyond its usual lists of respondents).

15. In the United States, we worked with the firm Essman Research, a division of the State Public Policy Group, which offers nonpartisan market research services for public, private, and nonprofit clients and is focused largely on public-policy issues.

16. In the spring of 2020, concerned that the pandemic might have fundamentally changed people's media habits, we sent a short follow-up survey to all fifty of the news lovers and news avoiders with whom we had conducted interviews in Iowa, asking them a few questions about whether they found their news consumption had changed in response to the mounting COVID crisis and, if so, why. More news lovers than news avoiders responded, and we found few patterns, so little of what we found from that survey made it into the main chapters of the book.

17. For this same reason, we did not use an age restriction as a requirement for screening news avoiders in the United States, although most were younger than forty-five.

18. A small number of interviews were conducted in public locales, such as coffee shops, at interviewees' request or by phone when we first expanded fieldwork beyond Oxford.

19. Harry Wolcott quoted in S. Elizabeth Bird, *The Audience in Everyday Life: Living in a Media World* (New York: Routledge, 2003), 8.

20. Irene Costera Meijer and Tim Groot Kormelink, *Changing News Use: Unchanged News Experiences?* (London: Routledge, 2021); Tim Groot Kormelink, "Seeing, Thinking, Feeling: A Critical Reflection on Interview-Based Methods for Studying News Use," *Journalism Studies* 21, no. 7 (2020): 863–78, https://doi.org/10.1080/1461670X.2020.1716829; Ruth Palmer, "A 'Deep Story' About American Journalism: Using 'Episodes' to Explore Folk Theories of Journalism," *Journalism Studies* 20, no. 3 (2019): 327–44, https://doi.org/10.1080/1461670X.2017.1375390.

21. Maria Del Rio Carral, "Focusing on 'a Day in the Life': An Activity-Based Method for the Qualitative Analysis of Psychological Phenomena," *Qualitative Research in Psychology* 11, no. 3 (2014): 298–315, https://doi.org/10.1080/14780887.2014.902525.

22. For a discussion of the pros and cons of this method, see Groot Kormelink, "Seeing, Thinking, Feeling."

23. Ithiel de Sola Pool, "A Critique of the Twentieth Anniversary Issue," *Public Opinion Quarterly* 21 (1957): 193, quoted in James A. Holstein and Jaber F. Gubrium, *The Active Interview* (London: Sage, 2003), 73.

24. Kathy Charmaz, *Constructing Grounded Theory* (London: Sage, 2014).

APPENDIX C: INTERVIEW PROTOCOLS FOR IN-DEPTH INTERVIEWING

The Spanish-language interview guide is provided in the supplementary online appendixes (https://osf.io/ru5a4/).

INDEX

Printed and bound by CPI Group (UK) Ltd, Croydon, CR0 4YY

07/12/2023

08203602-0001